Vegetables Please

Vegetables Please

CAROLYN HUMPHRIES

LONDON, NEW YORK, MELBOURNE, MUNICH, AND DELHI

Senior Editor Bob Bridle
Project Art Editor Katherine Raj
Cookery Editor Diana Vowles
US Senior Editor Rebecca Warren
US Editor Nichole Altorfer
US Consultant Kate Curnes Ramos
Managing Editor Dawn Henderson
Managing Art Editor Christine Keilty
Senior Jacket Creative Nicola Powling
Jacket Design Assistant Rosie Levine
Producer, Pre-Production Sarah Isle
Senior Producer Jen Scothern
Art Director Peter Luff
Publisher Peggy Vance

DK INDIA
Project Editor Manasvi Vohra
Senior Editor Dorothy Kikon
Senior Art Editor Balwant Singh
Assistant Art Editor Nikita Sodhi
Managing Editor Glenda Fernandes
Managing Art Editor Navidita Thapa
CTS/DTP Manager Sunil Sharma
DTP Designer Rajdeep Singh

Photography William Reavell

First American Edition, 2013

Published in the United States by
DK Publishing
375 Hudson Street
New York, NY 10014

13 14 15 16 17 10 9 8 7 6 5 4 3 2 1
186071—April 2013

A catalog record for this book is available from the
Library of Congress

ISBN 978-1-4654-0202-8

DK books are available at special discounts when purchased
in bulk for sales promotions, premiums, fundraising, or
educational use. For details, contact: DK Publishing Special
Markets, 375 Hudson Street, New York, New York 10014 or
SpecialSales@dk.com.

Color reproduction by Opus Multimedia Services

Printed and bound by South China (DK)

Discover more at
www.dk.com

Contents

Foreword   6

Pantry essentials   **10**

Introduction   12
Cabbages and leafy greens   14
Vegetable flowers   16
Shoots and stems   17
Salad leaves   18
The onion family   20
Roots and tubers   22
Squashes and cucumbers   24
Beans and pods   25
Vegetable fruits   26
Mushrooms   28
Legumes   30
Nuts, seeds, and oils   32
Herbs   34
Spices   36

The recipes   **38**

Soups and salads   40
  Four ways with mushrooms   62

Pasta, noodles, and rice   78
  Four ways with asparagus   96

Pan-fries and fritters   112
  Four ways with potatoes   128

Curries, stews, and casseroles   142
  Four ways with avocados   162

Pizzas, wraps, and quesadillas   178
  Four ways with tomatoes   200

Tortillas, frittatas, and omelets   210
  Four ways with zucchini   218

Tarts, pies, and turnovers   230
  Four ways with bell peppers   246

Grills and bakes   260
  Four ways with eggplants   280

Pestos, pickles, salsas, and dips   294
  Four ways with onions   302

Techniques   **314**

Index   340
Acknowledgments   352

Foreword

We all know that vegetables form a crucial part of our five-a-day—and whether you shop in a farmer's market, an independent green grocer, or a large supermarket, there is certainly no shortage of produce available.

With an abundance of roots, tubers, stems, flowers, vegetable fruits, and leaves available, there is every reason for vegetarians and non-vegetarians alike to make vegetables a central part of their diet. *Vegetables Please* is packed with mouth-watering vegetarian recipes full of enough glorious produce to tempt even the most ardent meat-eater. For those who still feel, however, that a meal is not complete without meat or fish, there is the option of adding a little to the recipes in the book. Dishes are carefully balanced to provide vegetarians with all the nutrients for a healthy diet, while the optional meat or fish variations are a way to encourage committed carnivores to reduce their meat intake and enjoy more vegetables.

Eating the seasons

I grew up in the country, where my father had a large vegetable garden. My brother and I always enjoyed helping him dig the potatoes, pull the lettuces, string the onions, and pick the beans. We were used to eating fresh, seasonal vegetables every day and what we didn't grow ourselves had been produced locally. I now have just a small garden and can only grow fresh herbs and the occasional tomato, bean, or zucchini, but it doesn't stop me from continuing to enjoy fresh vegetables every day. In fact, today you can buy just about any vegetable from around the world thanks to—or rather, because of

—international transport and refrigeration. It is worth remembering, though, that vegetables have proper seasons when they mature, still attached to their plants, taking nutrients from the soil and ripening in the sun. Many are plucked before they are ripe to be transported half way around the world, and never achieve their optimum flavor or texture. Large-scale global movement of produce also has a negative impact on the environment, with the fuel used drastically increasing the amount of carbon dioxide released into the atmosphere.

Brave new world

Thanks to new growing techniques, many vegetables that are native to tropical climates are grown in controlled conditions in cooler countries, giving us all a much wider choice. There is an argument that the hoophouses used for growing these vegetables spoil the look of the countryside and that fuel is sometimes needed to heat them to the required temperature—but we can't have it both ways. When progress provides work for local people and allows us to enjoy great, locally grown food, it should, I believe, be embraced.

When selecting fresh produce, remember to consider what season it is, decide whether the vegetables are likely to have been homegrown, and check their source before you buy. When shopping in farmer's markets you can be confident that the food has been produced in the local area, but nowadays supermarkets also tell you where their produce has come from so you can make informed decisions about the food you buy. Not only will this boost the local economy but it will also ensure that you are getting the tastiest and most nutritious vegetables available.

Making the right choice

When homegrown food isn't available, it's worth considering ethical trading. The Fairtrade Foundation is an independent body offering disadvantaged producers in the developing world a better deal for their produce. Many of the goods—not just vegetables—sold through the foundation may not be available to you at home and, therefore, make excellent additions to the shopping basket. By actively seeking them out, even if it means paying a little more, you will be making a much-needed difference to people who really need the help.

Fresh food at your fingertips

If you're not lucky enough to have a vegetable garden or allotment, try growing herbs on a windowsill, lettuces in a window box, or mushrooms from a kit in the airing cupboard instead. Visit local pick-your-own farms where freshness is guaranteed and produce can be cheaper than in the shops. Another option is to go foraging. Mushrooms are the obvious choice but—and it cannot be stressed enough—only pick fungi if you know exactly what to look for. Other delicious wild plants include garlic, sorrel, and nettles. (Remember never to pull up roots or take too much, though, as wild plants must be allowed to propagate and continue to flourish in an area.)

Fresh isn't always best

It's worth highlighting that legumes—dried peas, beans, and lentils—are vital to many dishes for their protein and carbohydrate content. Also, for the record, frozen vegetables are just as nutritious as fresh and have an important role to play in a busy cook's life, so don't be afraid to keep plenty in the freezer for those meals in a hurry.

A word to the wise

While most cheeses are now suitable for vegetarians, a few of the ones called for in this book, such as Parmesan and Gorgonzola, contain animal rennet. In place of Parmesan, try using a hard Italian cheese called Vegetalia, or hard sheep milk cheese. A blue cheese such as Dolcelatte is made with vegetable rennet and can be used instead of Gorgonzola. Also note that Worcestershire sauce contains anchovies, but vegetarian options, such as The Wizard's Worcestershire Sauce, are available as well.

More veg, please!

This book has been great fun to put together and I hope I have created some inspiring dishes to get your taste buds tingling. Use the ideas here as a starting point for your own repertoire and keep in mind that it is important to be bold when cooking vegetarian food. Experiment with new flavors, use lots of herbs and spices, and don't be afraid to mix and match—when leaves meet roots or tubers tangle with stems, the colors, textures, and tastes can be simply stunning!

Carolyn Humphries

Pantry essentials

Discover how to select, store, use, and combine a wide range of fresh, seasonal vegetables—and find out about the many different herbs, spices, legumes, nuts, seeds, and oils that can help bring out the best in your recipes.

In this chapter are the vegetables featured in the book, as well as information about seasonal availability, what to look for when selecting, and preparation guidelines.

It's important to store vegetables properly, too. Most should be kept in the crisper at the bottom of the refrigerator and used within a week. The exceptions are whole, uncut onions, roots, tubers, and winter squashes, which should be stored in a cool, dark, frost-free place. On these pages you'll also find the herbs, spices, legumes, nuts, seeds, and oils that can enhance the flavor of vegetables. There's information on perfect flavor pairings, too, so you can make the most of every ingredient in your pantry.

Variety is the key to a healthy, balanced diet. Aim to eat at least five portions of vegetables and fruit every day to get the essential vitamins, minerals, and fiber needed for good health and wellbeing. This includes frozen, dried, and canned (preferably in natural juice or water) fruit and vegetables, as well as pure juices. Cereals, grains, and potatoes are also important as they contain the complex carbohydrates needed for energy and warmth.

Beans, nuts, seeds, soy beans and products such as tofu, and quinoa, a grain-like grass, make an ideal base for many vegetarian dishes and are a good source of protein (for body growth and repair), complex carbohydrates, and fiber. Eat a mixture of these to get the right balance of essential proteins, as

"Calcium is found in dried figs and apricots, green leafy vegetables such as spinach, kale, and escarole, and in whole grains, nuts, and seeds."

"Eat foods rich in omega 3 and 6—the essential fatty acids needed for warmth, nerve function, and healthy nails, hair, and skin."

they do not all contain complete, or whole, proteins. Nuts, seeds—especially flaxseed—and their oils, olive oil, leafy green vegetables, grains, and eggs are also an important source of the essential fatty acids omega 3 and 6 (for warmth, nerve function, and healthy nails, hair, and skin).

Dairy products are a good source of calcium (for healthy teeth and bones) and protein. They contain saturated fats, though, so choose reduced-fat options if possible. (Coconut milk is also high in saturated fat, so look for a reduced-fat option unless you want a particularly rich and creamy result.)

Leafy green vegetables, beans, and bread contain iron (for the production of red blood cells). These foods should be accompanied by produce rich in vitamin C, which aids iron absorption, so be sure to include plenty of red and yellow vegetables, fruit, and pure fruit juice in your diet. Avoid tea and coffee at mealtimes, however, as they impair iron absorption.

Fortified breakfast cereals and bread are a source of vitamin B12 (to help prevent anaemia and keep the brain and nervous system working well). This is the only vitamin not readily available in vegetables. Yeast extract is another good source of B12.

Everything you need for a healthy, balanced diet is contained in this book, and keeping a well-stocked pantry will mean that you can create any of the recipes whenever the mood takes you.

Cabbages and leafy greens

Always choose firm cabbages and fresh-looking leafy greens.

« SAVOY CABBAGE
This crinkly-leaved variety has a sweet heart and tender leaves that are best shredded then lightly steamed, boiled, or stir-fried. The outer leaves are good stuffed. Best in winter.

WHITE CABBAGE «
Popular as coleslaw or fermented as sauerkraut; also good steamed or stir-fried. Try with caraway or fennel seeds, and dried fruit. Best in winter and spring.

« CAVOLO NERO
Also called Tuscan black kale, has dark, coarse, leaves that should be crisp and straight. Goes well with tomatoes, garlic, and olives. Available autumn and winter.

« POINTED CABBAGE
Has an excellent, sweet flavor and even the outer leaves can be shredded and cooked. Particularly good stir-fried or lightly steamed. Best in spring.

BRUSSELS SPROUTS »
Steam, briefly boil, or shred in salads, soups, and stir-fries. Good with chestnuts and white beans. Small, firm ones are sweetest. Leafy Brussels tops can be cooked as greens. Best in winter.

SORREL «
Use these lemony-flavored spear-shaped leaves like spinach; best used fresh. Baby ones are delicious raw in salads. Available spring to autumn.

KALE »
The tight, curly, dark-green leaves have an intense flavor. Cut out any tough fibrous stalks first. Use fresh as it can turn bitter if stored too long. Best in autumn and winter.

GREEN CABBAGE ⌃
Numerous varieties are available and they are great all-rounders. Particularly good with nuts and celery or shredded in soups and stews. Available most of the year.

SWISS CHARD ⌃
Chop and cook in soups, stews, casseroles, and stir-fries, or separate leaves and stalks: wilt the leaves, steam the stalks. Available summer and autumn.

ESCAROLE ⌃
Shred in soups, stews, stir-fries, and casseroles, or very finely shred and deep-fry for a few seconds as crispy "seaweed." Best in spring.

BABY SPINACH ⌃
Great wilted as a vegetable or added to stir-fries, soups, and stews; baby leaves are delicious in salad. Particularly good flavored with nutmeg. Different varieties are grown throughout the year.

RED CABBAGE ⌃
Use finely shredded and braised, pickled, or marinated as a salad. It turns a lovely bright red when used with vinegar, lemon juice or wine. Best in winter and spring.

BOK CHOY (PAK CHOY) »
Asian mustard greens with fleshy stalks and soft leaves. Steam baby ones whole; chop or shred larger ones and stir-fry, or use raw in salads. Best summer to winter.

Pantry essentials
Vegetable flowers

These beautiful vegetables make for sumptuous eating.

BROCCOLI »
Select firm, dark-green heads. Avoid if yellowing, even slightly, or if pliable. Separate into florets and eat raw, steamed, or stir-fried. Best in summer and autumn.

« WHITE CAULIFLOWER
Choose tight curds; avoid if bolting. Steam whole; florets are delicious as crudités, coated in cheese sauce, in soups, stir-fries, and braises. Good all year.

GLOBE ARTICHOKE »
Choose firm, tight, heavy heads that have a short stalk. Avoid those that are dry or opening. Steam and eat the leaves then heart, or prepare the heart only. Best in summer and autumn.

⌃ BROCCOLI RABE
Avoid thick, woody stalks or if tiny yellow flowers are appearing on the heads. Steam, boil briefly, or stir-fry. Best in late winter and spring.

⌃ PURPLE CAULIFLOWER
Will keep its color if cut in florets and lightly steamed. Has a particularly sweet, mild flavor. Use in place of white cauliflower for any recipe.

Shoots and stems

Succulent vegetables that all grow above ground.

« WHITE ASPARAGUS
Grown without light to prevent it from turning green, white asparagus is highly prized for its delicate flavor and creamy texture. Often served cold. Best in spring and summer.

⋀ GREEN ASPARAGUS
The most common variety. Look out for sprue, the cheaper, slim "thinnings" of the crop. Steam, grill, roast, or use in soup. Best in spring and early summer.

FLORENCE FENNEL ⋀
Has an anise flavor. Shred raw in salads, or quarter and braise or roast. Don't confuse with the herb, wild fennel, which does not form a bulb. Best in summer and autumn.

⋀ PURPLE ASPARAGUS
Often less fibrous than green varieties and slightly sweeter, so there is no need to peel even thicker stalks. Cook and serve as per green asparagus.

GREEN CELERY ⋀
Has a pronounced flavor that is excellent with cheese, fruit, and nuts. Chop the outer leaves for flavoring soups and stews; use the hearts raw or braised. Best in autumn and winter.

WHITE CELERY »
More delicately flavored than green, white celery can be either "self-blanching" or green celery that is earthed up while still growing. Use like green celery.

⋀ KOHLRABI
Tastes like a cross between white cabbage and a mild-flavored turnip. Eat raw if very fresh, or stew, braise, or add to soups. Best in summer and autumn.

Pantry essentials
Salad leaves

There is a huge variety of tasty leaves available, some grown all year.

⌃ WATERCRESS
Sprigs of round, peppery tasting leaves. Trim off thick feathery stalks before use in salads or as a garnish, or chopped to flavor sauces, soups, and egg dishes. Available all year.

⌃ ROUND (BUTTERHEAD) LETTUCE
The large, outer leaves make perfect wraps instead of bread or are good cooked in soup; the heart leaves are excellent dressed (at the last minute) for a salad. Available all year.

« LAMB'S LETTUCE
Clusters of small, soft leaves with a sweet, nutty flavor, also known as corn salad. Delicious in a mix of leaves for a salad and makes a pretty garnish. Best in summer and autumn.

⌃ BELGIAN ENDIVE
Also available red, has a bitter core that should be cut out before separating into leaves, or chopping, for salads. Fill whole spears with soft cheese, dips, or salsas. Good braised whole. Available autumn to spring.

« NAPA CABBAGE
Pale-green, creamy-yellow leaves with thick, fleshy, white stalks, a crunchy texture, and a juicy, sweet flavor. Excellent steamed, used in stir-fries, or eaten raw. Best in autumn.

ROMAINE ⌃
Crisp, tall leaves with a sweet flavor. Torn in pieces, the classic leaf for Caesar salad; even the outer leaves can be used in salad. Best summer and autumn.

ICEBERG ⌃
Crisp and juicy, with a firm, tight head. Carefully peel off the outer leaves (discard if wilted) to use as a receptacle for cold or hot food; shred or tear up the inner leaves. Best in summer and autumn.

LITTLE GEM »
A small, tight lettuce with juicy round leaves. Use sautéed in halves or quarters, or enjoy raw. The whole leaves make good receptacles for pastes and salsas. Best from spring to autumn.

ARUGULA ⌃
Has a pronounced peppery flavor. Usually served raw but can be wilted on pizzas and in tarts; great for pesto. Keeps best if bought unwashed. Available all year.

⌃ MIZUNA
When young, the dark green serrated leaves with thin, white stalks have a mild, slightly spicy, mustardy taste, similar to arugula. Cook large leaves like bok choy. Best in winter.

« PEA SHOOTS
The tender young tops and tendrils of pea plants, these have a sweet, pea flavor. Perfect for salads and sandwiches (handle carefully as they are delicate). Available late spring and summer.

The onion family

When cooked, alliums take on an irresistible, creamy sweetness.

⌃ ROUND SHALLOTS
With sweet, mild, purple-tinged flesh, use finely chopped in any dish needing a delicate onion flavor. Good for pickling and in dressings, too. Best from autumn to spring.

YELLOW ONIONS ⌃
Excellent all-rounders with gold to brown skins and a fairly strong flavor. Baby ones are used for pickling or cooking whole. Best in late summer and autumn.

« BANANA SHALLOTS
These torpedo-shaped shallots are highly prized by cooks for their sweet, delicate flavor. Use like round shallots. Best from autumn to spring.

⌃ RED ONION
With a sweet and mild flavor, use thinly sliced in salads; also great roasted but a good all-rounder. Best in late summer and autumn.

WHITE ONION »
With white flesh and a sweet, mild flavor, doesn't have to be fried before adding to a dish. Best in late summer.

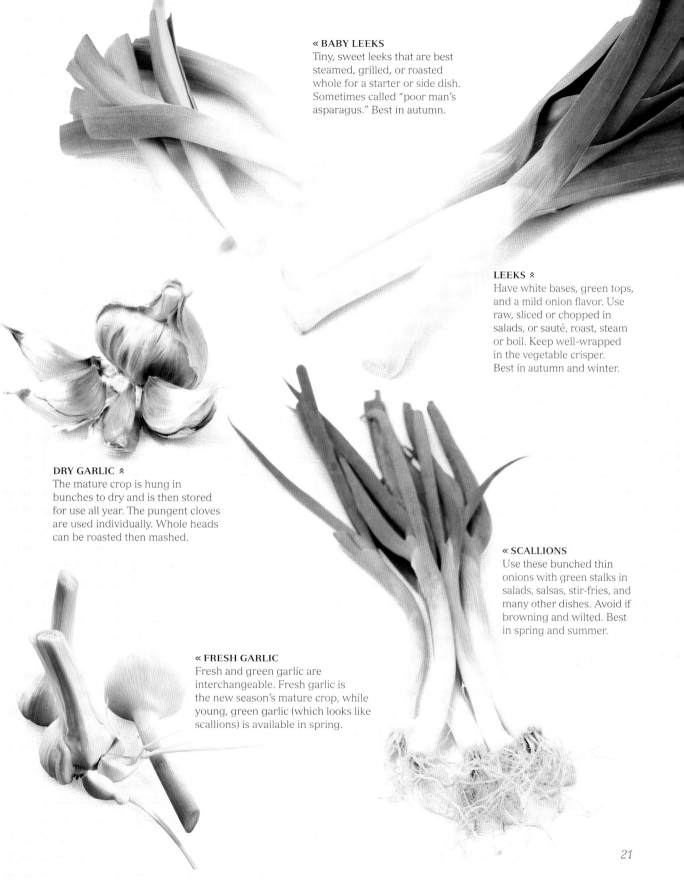

« BABY LEEKS
Tiny, sweet leeks that are best steamed, grilled, or roasted whole for a starter or side dish. Sometimes called "poor man's asparagus." Best in autumn.

LEEKS ⌃
Have white bases, green tops, and a mild onion flavor. Use raw, sliced or chopped in salads, or sauté, roast, steam or boil. Keep well-wrapped in the vegetable crisper. Best in autumn and winter.

DRY GARLIC ⌃
The mature crop is hung in bunches to dry and is then stored for use all year. The pungent cloves are used individually. Whole heads can be roasted then mashed.

« SCALLIONS
Use these bunched thin onions with green stalks in salads, salsas, stir-fries, and many other dishes. Avoid if browning and wilted. Best in spring and summer.

« FRESH GARLIC
Fresh and green garlic are interchangeable. Fresh garlic is the new season's mature crop, while young, green garlic (which looks like scallions) is available in spring.

Roots and tubers

These staples of the vegetable world are full of nutrients and flavor.

TURNIPS »
Baby turnips are mild; larger ones have a mustard-like kick. Peel thinly and grate raw or dice, boil, or steam. Baby ones (use whole) are available in summer, larger ones all year.

NEW POTATOES »
Small, earthy-tasting new potatoes like these are harvested in summer. They have thin skins that should scrape or scrub off easily. Steam or boil.

« RED POTATOES
This Dutch variety is a good all-rounder (much like baby new potatoes). With fairly firm flesh they are neither too floury nor too waxy. Great for fries.

« FINGERLING POTATOES
Small, waxy, round varieties like these are good steamed or boiled, whole or halved, and served warm or cold with salad. Best in summer and autumn.

SWEET POTATOES »
Not actually related to the potato, these tubers have sweet creamy-yellow or orange flesh. Can be cooked just like potatoes, with or without skins. Available all year.

KING EDWARD POTATOES ⌃
Similar to a Russet potato, this floury variety has a dry texture, which becomes "fluffy" when cooked. Good for roasting, mashing, baking, and for fries.

DAIKON ⌄
Also known as mooli or white radish. Originally from Japan, it has a strong taste similar to turnip or a hot radish and can be used in the same way as either. Best in summer and autumn.

⌃ YUKON GOLD POTATOES
This waxy variety has a firm, yellow flesh with a buttery flavor. Best boiled, steamed, baked, or for potato wedges.

BEETS »
These round roots have firm skin and red, golden, or pink and white-striped flesh. They have a rich, sweet, earthy flavor. Serve raw or cooked, grated, sliced, or diced. Best from summer to winter.

BUNCHED CARROTS »
These sweet, fragrant summer carrots can be scrubbed and grated raw, or lightly cooked. The greens should be fresh and bright, but remove before storing or the carrots will go limp.

« PARSNIPS
The sweetness and creaminess of parsnips are most intense in winter. Look out for baby ones to cook whole. Steam, boil, roast, or grate raw.

« JERUSALEM ARTICHOKES
These tubers have a sweet, smoky flavor. Scrub or peel before use and choose ones with fewest knobs. Delicious in soup; also roast, steam, boil, or purée. Best from autumn to spring.

« RADISHES
Small, red, pink or purple spheres, with a hot, peppery taste, or milder, longer-bodied breakfast varieties. Use raw or cook in place of turnips. Best in spring and autumn.

⌃ MAINCROP CARROTS
These are mature carrots that, once harvested, are stored for use during winter. Purple and yellow or white varieties are also available. Don't buy if over-chilled and damp.

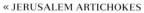

RUTABAGA »
A large vegetable with thick outer skin and sweet orangey-gold flesh. Delicious roasted or mashed, and in soups, stews, and casseroles. Best during winter.

⌃ CELERY ROOT
Creamy textured with a strong, sweet, celery-like aroma and flavor. Peel thickly then grate raw, or boil, steam, mash, or roast. Great for low-carb fries. Best in autumn and winter.

CHANTENAY CARROTS »
Originating in France, these very sweet cone-shaped carrots can be just trimmed and cooked whole; larger ones can be quartered lengthways. Best in summer.

Squashes and cucumbers

Winter squashes need cooking, while summer ones can be eaten raw.

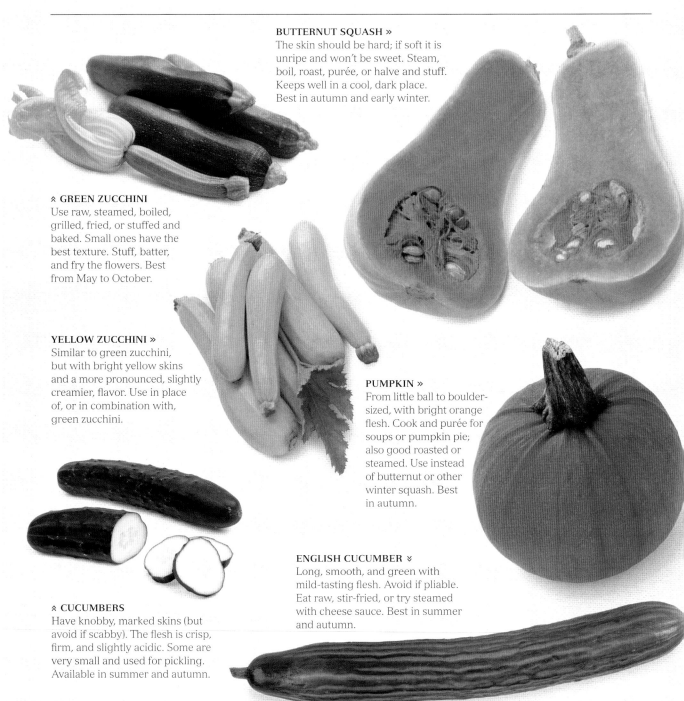

BUTTERNUT SQUASH »
The skin should be hard; if soft it is unripe and won't be sweet. Steam, boil, roast, purée, or halve and stuff. Keeps well in a cool, dark place. Best in autumn and early winter.

⌃ GREEN ZUCCHINI
Use raw, steamed, boiled, grilled, fried, or stuffed and baked. Small ones have the best texture. Stuff, batter, and fry the flowers. Best from May to October.

YELLOW ZUCCHINI »
Similar to green zucchini, but with bright yellow skins and a more pronounced, slightly creamier, flavor. Use in place of, or in combination with, green zucchini.

PUMPKIN »
From little ball to boulder-sized, with bright orange flesh. Cook and purée for soups or pumpkin pie; also good roasted or steamed. Use instead of butternut or other winter squash. Best in autumn.

ENGLISH CUCUMBER ⌄
Long, smooth, and green with mild-tasting flesh. Avoid if pliable. Eat raw, stir-fried, or try steamed with cheese sauce. Best in summer and autumn.

⌃ CUCUMBERS
Have knobby, marked skins (but avoid if scabby). The flesh is crisp, firm, and slightly acidic. Some are very small and used for pickling. Available in summer and autumn.

Beans and pods

Some are eaten pods and all; others are shelled before use.

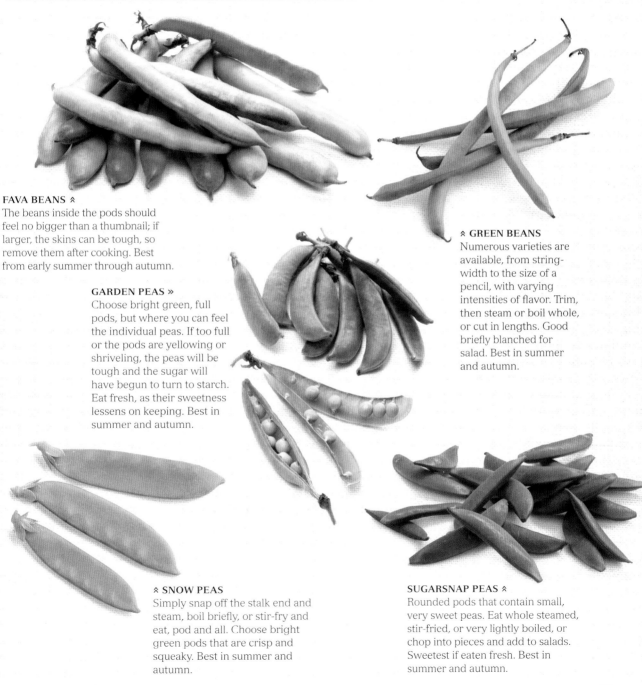

FAVA BEANS ⌃
The beans inside the pods should feel no bigger than a thumbnail; if larger, the skins can be tough, so remove them after cooking. Best from early summer through autumn.

GARDEN PEAS »
Choose bright green, full pods, but where you can feel the individual peas. If too full or the pods are yellowing or shriveling, the peas will be tough and the sugar will have begun to turn to starch. Eat fresh, as their sweetness lessens on keeping. Best in summer and autumn.

⌃ GREEN BEANS
Numerous varieties are available, from string-width to the size of a pencil, with varying intensities of flavor. Trim, then steam or boil whole, or cut in lengths. Good briefly blanched for salad. Best in summer and autumn.

⌃ SNOW PEAS
Simply snap off the stalk end and steam, boil briefly, or stir-fry and eat, pod and all. Choose bright green pods that are crisp and squeaky. Best in summer and autumn.

SUGARSNAP PEAS ⌃
Rounded pods that contain small, very sweet peas. Eat whole steamed, stir-fried, or very lightly boiled, or chop into pieces and add to salads. Sweetest if eaten fresh. Best in summer and autumn.

Vegetable fruits

Although classed as fruits, the following are all eaten as vegetables.

FUERTE AVOCADOS »
Larger than Hass with smooth, shiny-green skins. They have a mild flavor and pale yellow flesh that slices well. Use like Hass. Ideal for salads and salsas. Best from winter to early summer.

⌃ HASS AVOCADOS
The rough skin turns black when ripe. Halve and fill the cavity, purée, mash, slice, or dice. Can be baked. A good choice for dips and spreads. Best from spring to autumn.

« EGGPLANT
Baby ones, stripy pink and white, white, or tiny pea varieties are also available. All have a slightly smoky-sweet flavor. Roast, grill, fry, or purée. Best in summer and autumn.

BABY CORN »
A specialist vegetable, deliberately grown to be harvested before the kernels develop. Eat whole or chopped in pieces, raw, steamed, boiled, or in stir-fries. Best in late summer and early autumn.

CORN »
Cobs are harvested when the kernels are just ripening. Pick pale-looking corn and eat fresh; golden, riper corn is not as sweet. Best in late summer and early autumn.

⌃ RED BELL PEPPER
A member of the *Capsicum* genus, the plant also produces green, yellow, and orange fruits according to ripeness (and even purple or white ones). Use in any recipe calling for sweet peppers. Best in summer and autumn.

SCOTCH BONNETS »
Said to resemble a "Tam o' Shanter" hat, these crinkly, rounded chiles are available in a variety of colors. They are popular in Caribbean cooking and are similar to habanero chiles. Extremely hot.

⌃ BIRD'S EYE CHILES
Also known as Thai chiles, these are thin and tapering (approx. 1¼–3in long/3–7.5cm). As a rule, long, thin chiles such as these are hotter than long, fat ones such as jalapeños. Often used in Thai and Indian cooking. Hot.

⌃ JALAPEÑO CHILES
Shiny green or red, large, and cone-shaped. Also available pickled. Can be stuffed and are particularly good in Mexican cooking. Moderately hot.

BEEFSTEAK TOMATOES ⌄
Large, fat tomatoes that can weigh up to 1lb (450g) each. Excellent stuffed and baked, or sliced for salad and sandwiches. Best in summer and autumn.

ROMANO PEPPERS »
Spear shaped and longer and flatter than bell peppers, these are very sweet. Usually available as red or yellow fruits, they are good stuffed whole, or split first then broiled or roasted. Best in summer and autumn.

« BABY PLUM TOMATOES
A tiny, plum-shaped variety with a very sweet flavor. Particularly good halved or whole tossed in pasta, rice, or other grain-based dishes (add near the end of cooking). Best in summer and autumn.

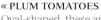

⌃ CHERRY TOMATOES
Baby versions of standard tomatoes. Best bought on the vine to eat whole or halved in salads, or thrown into dishes toward the end of cooking so they hold their shape. Best in summer and autumn.

« PLUM TOMATOES
Oval-shaped, these are excellent for cooking as they have more pulp and less juice than other varieties. Very good for tomato sauce and widely used for canning. Best in summer and autumn.

⌃ STANDARD TOMATOES
The classic round tomato. An excellent all-rounder for grilling, frying, slicing, or for salads. Buy on the vine for the most flavor. Best in summer and autumn.

27

Mushrooms

Only forage for wild mushrooms if you know exactly what to look for.

⌃ BUTTON MUSHROOMS

These cultivated white mushrooms are picked at various stages of growth (from tiny button ones, through closed-cup, to large open-cup or flat mushrooms). The flavor develops as they grow. Eat raw or cooked, whole, sliced, or chopped. Also available dried.

⌃ FIELD MUSHROOMS

These wild white mushrooms have gills varying from pink to almost black. They are found in meadows where horses, sheep, or cows graze. Very good flavor. Large, flat ones may be peeled before use. Grow wild in autumn.

« MOREL MUSHROOM

Highly prized and sought after, the morel is found in woodlands (particularly ash and elm). It has a honeycomb hood and a rich flavor. Often sold dried. Grows wild in spring and early summer.

« NAMEKO MUSHROOMS

A cultivated mushroom very popular in Japan. Has an earthy flavor and a silky, almost gelatinous texture when cooked in stir-fries and soups. Trim off the base and separate the mushrooms before use.

« PORCINI MUSHROOM

Found in woodland clearings, particularly beech, this mushroom is also known as porcini in Italian cuisine. It is meaty and delicious with smooth, creamy flesh. Available dried. Grows wild in autumn and early winter.

⌃ OYSTER MUSHROOMS

Delicately flavored, pale grey (or sometimes in pastel shades of brown, yellow, or pink), silky mushrooms favored in Asian cooking. Cut up or cook whole. Often cultivated, they grow wild in autumn and early winter.

ENOKI MUSHROOMS »

Originally from Asia, these cultivated pale clumps have a crisp texture and a mild mushroom flavor. Trim and separate the mushrooms into smaller groupings before use in stir-fries, salads, wraps, and sandwiches.

⌃ PORTOBELLO MUSHROOMS

These cultivated brown mushrooms have a meaty texture and a good flavor. As with white cultivated mushrooms, these are picked at various stages of growth, from crimini (button), through chestnut (cup), to portobello (large and flat). Use like field or white mushrooms.

⌃ CHANTERELLE MUSHROOMS

Have a yellow or orange trumpet shape, a frilly top, and gills running down the stem. Found in many woodlands but also cultivated and available dried. Have a slight smell of apricots and a delicious flavor. Grow wild from summer to winter.

⌃ SHIITAKE MUSHROOMS

Cultivated mushrooms originally from Asia with a brown cap and white gills. Have an excellent, meaty flavor that is particularly good in Chinese- and Japanese-style dishes. The stalks are often tough, so remove and use for stock. Also available dried.

Legumes

Dried peas, beans, and lentils are rich in proteins, carbs, and fiber.

ADZUKI BEANS ⌃
Richly-colored with a good, sweet, nutty flavor. Excellent all-rounders as a substitute for meat, holding their shape well. Great in casseroles, soups, and stews. Also good for burgers.

PINTO BEANS ⌃
Big, brown, rich, meaty, and with a lovely creamy texture, these beans are excellent in pasta dishes, stews, soups, and casseroles, as they hold their shape even when cooked for a long time.

« BUTTER BEANS
Large, soft, and floury with a slightly dry texture when cooked, these beans have a distinctive, rich flavor. They are great for soups, stews, dips, and pâtés.

CANNELLINI BEANS »
A member of the navy bean family, these classic Tuscan white beans can be mashed to a smooth paste. They have a creamy, slightly nutty flavor.

BROWN LENTILS ⌃
There are several varieties of brown (and green) lentils, which are interchangeable. All have a nutty flavor and a soft, almost meaty texture, making them a great substitute for ground meat in many dishes.

PUY LENTILS ⌃

These small, green lentils from France are often considered an upmarket ingredient. Particularly good braised with vegetables. They have an earthy, rich flavor and hold their shape even after cooking so are also good in salads.

FLAGELOT BEANS ⌃

These pretty green beans have an excellent, creamy texture and a mild, sweet flavor. They are particularly good in salads but also take on flavors such as garlic and herbs extremely well.

RED KIDNEY BEANS ⌃

Robust, floury-textured beans with a sweet, full-bodied flavor. They taste particularly good with chile peppers and strong spices.

SOY BEANS ⌃

Highly nutritious, these silky-textured beans have a mild flavor, which makes them a good base for complex flavor combinations. Also used for making other soy products such as tofu.

CHICKPEAS ⌃

These coarse beans have a distinctive, nutty flavor and a buttery texture. They hold their shape even after long cooking. Also use puréed for dips (particularly hummus) and sauces.

« NAVY BEANS

Popular small, white beans, famous for their role in cassoulet, and as baked beans in tomato sauce. Excellent all-rounders for soups, stews, and casseroles with a mild flavor and a soft, creamy, yet slightly floury texture.

YELLOW SPLIT LENTILS »

Unlike yellow split peas, lentils hold their shape when cooked (although, for chana dhal you can substitute split peas; the result is just more pulpy). They have a distinctive, nutty flavor.

RED LENTILS ⌃

Small, split lentils that cook quickly to a pulp. They are ideal for soups and sauces as they thicken the liquid naturally. Also essential for spicy dhals.

Nuts, seeds, and oils

These add nutrients, and delicious flavors and textures to many dishes.

PECANS »
Native to North America, these nuts, which have a smooth, ovoid shell, can be used in place of walnuts but have a milder, sweeter, more buttery flavor.

WALNUTS ⌃
The dry, brown, ripe kernels are good with blue cheeses, celery, cabbages, parsnips, sweet potatoes, and leeks. The bright green, unripe fruits, which have soft, milky nuts inside, are picked whole and pickled.

« ALMONDS
Sweet almonds add a delicate yet distinctive flavor. Use them whole, sliced, chopped, or ground in a variety of dishes, including curries, stir-fries, and rice and other grain dishes.

PEANUTS ⌃
Technically legumes (they grow underground). Use them raw, roasted, or ground in peanut butter in spicy sauces, rice and noodle dishes, stir-fries, and soup.

« CASHEWS
The creamy texture and sweet flavor of raw or roasted cashews go well with corn, root vegetables, and smoked paprika. Also use in Asian curries, stir-fries, rice, and noodle dishes.

« HAZELNUTS
These small, round nuts have a wonderful, distinctive flavor. Use them whole, chopped, or ground. They are good in stuffings, rice and other grain dishes, and with mushrooms.

CHESTNUTS »
Sweet, floury, and perfect for puréeing for soups and pâtés. Roast them in their skins, or shell them, then boil or bake. Also available pre-cooked in cans or vacuum-packs.

PINE NUTS ⌃
Soft, with an oily texture and subtle flavor. Often toasted, use in stuffings, rice and other grain dishes, and as an essential ingredient for pesto and pistou. Also great with spinach.

COCONUT »
Coconut flesh (grated fresh or dried), flakes, cream, and milk all add an amazing flavor to many recipes, particularly curries, soups, rice, and noodle dishes.

BLACK ONION SEEDS »
Also known as Nigella seeds, they have a nutty, earthy flavor and are good with beans, rice, root and green vegetables. Also add to breads.

FENNEL SEEDS ⌃
Light brownish-green in color, with pale, stripy ridges, these have a strong licorice flavor. They work well with beets, cucumber, cabbage, lentils, rice, potatoes, and beans.

SESAME SEEDS ⌃
Gold, black, or, most commonly, creamy-white, these benefit from being toasted before use to enhance their flavor. Good with all vegetables, beans, rice, and noodle dishes. Also used to make tahini paste.

CARAWAY SEEDS »
These anise-flavored seeds are brown with pale, stripy ridges all around. Add to breads or use with cabbages, onions, potatoes, root vegetables, tomatoes, and noodle dishes.

⌃ PUMPKIN SEEDS
Popular as a snack or garnish, these seeds have a crunchy texture and a nutty flavor that is enhanced by toasting. Good with pasta, cheese, chiles, harissa paste, and in salads.

CHILE OIL ⌃
There are many different types, but all are pungent with spicy tones. Drizzle over pasta, pizzas, and salads, or add to noodle dishes, soups, and stews for added heat.

OLIVE OIL ⌃
May be a blend of oils or from one type of olive, is an excellent all-purpose oil with a great (and variable) taste. Use as a base for marinades, for grilling, shallow-frying, in sauces, and in breads.

EXTRA VIRGIN OLIVE OIL ⌃
The best, cold-pressed olive oil has an excellent, rich flavor and an intense dark-green or green-gold color. Use for dressings and for dipping bread.

TRUFFLE OIL ⌃
An expensive oil with the distinctive flavor of woody, earthy truffles. Delicious with eggs and drizzled over pasta or salads. Use with grated fresh or bottled truffles for added effect.

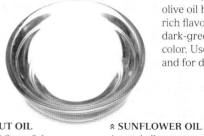

SESAME OIL ⌃
Made using toasted sesame seeds, this oil has a strong, roasted-nut aroma and flavor. Add at the end of cooking for an intense finish or with sunflower oil for stir-fries. Also delicious in dressings.

« WALNUT OIL
Rich and flavorful, with a distinctive walnut taste. Use in salad dressings, drizzled over pasta, with vegetables, and in stir-fries.

⌃ SUNFLOWER OIL
A good all-purpose oil for cooking and light dressings, has a mild, light, oily taste. Suitable for deep-frying but don't use more than three times or it will start decomposing into saturated fat.

Herbs

Imparting fragrance and flavor, herbs will lift any dish to a new level.

⌃ DILL
A delicate and feathery herb with a mild anise flavor. Seeds are used for flavoring, too. Good with beets and other roots, fava beans, zucchini, potatoes, spinach, rice, and eggs

⌃ SPEARMINT
Many varieties are available but spearmint and garden mint are the most common for flavoring. Dried mint is often used in Middle Eastern and Indian cooking. Good with potatoes, peas, lettuce, cucumber, yogurt, bulgur, rice, and lentils.

ROSEMARY ⌃
Has a flowery fragrance. Use sprigs whole then remove after cooking, or chop leaves and add. Good with peppers, eggplants, lentils, mushrooms, onions, parsnips, and tomatoes.

« OREGANO
Interchangeable with marjoram, with a strong, sweet flavor. Dried is popular in Greek and Italian cuisine. Add fresh at the end of cooking. Good with most vegetables, rice, pasta, and beans.

« CILANTRO
Sweet and pungent, loved or hated, with thin, frilly-edged leaves similar to flat-leaf parsley. Its seeds (called coriander) are dried and used as a spice (see p37). A must for curries and spicy dishes; good with avocados, cucumbers, root vegetables, and corn.

« MARJORAM
Interchangeable with oregano and similar in flavor but slightly spicier. Dried is often used in its own right in Greek and Italian cuisine. Add fresh at the end of cooking. Use with most vegetables, rice, pasta, and beans.

« CHIVES
These grass-like stalks have an aroma and flavor between onions and leeks. Snip with scissors. Add stalks and flowers as a garnish before serving. Use with avocados, zucchini, potatoes, root vegetables, cream cheese, and eggs.

« DRIED BAY LEAVES
Have a sweet fragrance reminiscent of cloves and basil. The leaves (both dried and fresh) are used to impart their flavor in a dish but are not eaten. Essential for béchamel sauce and good with tomatoes, beans, chestnuts, and rice.

⌃ SAGE
Pale, felt-like greenish-grey leaves with a stringent, spicy, sweet yet bitter taste. Use sparingly in cooking. Lovely fried for a garnish. Good with beans, cheeses, onions, and tomatoes.

« FLAT-LEAF PARSLEY
Italian flat-leaf parsley is favored by cooks. Use on its own or with other herbs. Perfect chopped, in sprigs, or deep fried as a garnish. Use with most vegetables, eggs, rice, lentils, and bulgur.

« COMMON PARSLEY
Readily available, common parsley is good for basic flavoring and as a garnish. Use a sprig tied with bay leaf and thyme for a simple bouquet garni.

« CHERVIL
Chervil's feathery leaves have an unusual sweet, spicy aroma with a hint of caraway. Don't cook. Particularly good as a garnish with asparagus, peas, beans, beets, carrots, tomatoes, cheese, and eggs.

⌃ BASIL
Has a warm, heady, slightly peppery flavor. Look out for Greek and Thai basil (*horapa*), too. Add at the end of cooking. A must for green pesto and pistou; also good with tomatoes, eggplants, beans, zucchini, eggs, and mozzarella cheese.

GARDEN THYME »
There are many varieties of thyme, but garden thyme is the most common. Has a sweet, spicy, soothing scent. The tiny leaves are stripped off the stem and added whole or chopped during cooking. Good with most vegetables.

TARRAGON »
Long, soft, thin leaves with a distinctive spicy-sweet fragrance and a pungent anise flavor. Use sparingly. Good with artichokes, asparagus, zucchini, mushrooms, potatoes, and tomatoes.

Spices

Spices add breadth and depth of flavor to vegetable-based dishes.

« CAPERS
The buds of the caper bush, pickled in vinegar or preserved in salt. Essential in tapenade and tartare sauce, but also good with artichokes and eggplants.

« CINNAMON STICKS
Have a warm, sweet scent and flavor. Used widely in Greek, Middle Eastern, and Indian cuisines. Use with almonds, tomatoes, rice, and other grains.

« DRIED FENUGREEK LEAVES
Crushed, dried leaves with a fragrant smell like sweet hay. Add to green and root vegetables, potatoes, beans, rice, and tomatoes.

⌃ CLOVES
Warm and powerful with a sweet, mouth-numbing taste. One of the Chinese five-spices. Use with cabbage, carrots, beets, onions, squashes, and sweet potatoes.

BLACK MUSTARD SEEDS »
Often used in Indian cooking, either ground in spice blends or as whole seeds. Delicious toasted and added to dressings for grated root vegetables.

SWEET PAPRIKA ⌃
Ground, dried red peppers, with a caramel fruitiness. Adds fragrance and color to tomato- and bean-based goulashes and is good with cheeses. Smoked or Spanish paprika (pimentón), on the other hand, has a rich smokiness that adds an intense meaty flavor to vegetable dishes. Use with chick peas and choose either mild or hot.

FRESH LEMONGRASS »
Refreshing, tart spice with a strong citrus flavor. Crush or finely chop for use with most vegetables. Essential in many noodle dishes and Asian curries.

⌃ GROUND TURMERIC
Has a rich, woody aroma, slightly bitter flavor, and intense yellow color. Essential in Indian curry powders and pastes. Use with lentils, rice, pasta, eggs, beans, eggplants, spinach, and potatoes.

« WHOLE DRIED CHILES
Also available as crushed flakes and powder, adds pungency and heat. Essential in curry powders and pastes, harissa, jerk seasoning, salsas, and pickles.

TAMARIND PASTE ⌃
From the soaked pods of the tamarind tree. An essential ingredient in Worcestershire sauce. Adds a fruity tartness to curries and spice dishes.

« STAR ANISE
Pretty star-shaped spice with a licorice flavor and aroma and a warm pungency. Use with leeks, squashes, root vegetables, and beans.

JUNIPER BERRIES ⌃
Bitter-sweet berries of the juniper bush, usually available dried. Use crushed in cabbage dishes (particularly sauerkraut), and with celery, peppers, and root vegetables.

GROUND CUMIN ⌃
Also available as seeds, has a strong, heavy scent and a rich, slightly earthy flavor. Use with eggplants, beans, root vegetables, potatoes, and squashes.

KAFFIR LIME LEAVES ⌃
Have a powerful fragrance between lemon and lime. Use with mushrooms, green vegetables, and with coconut milk in Thai-style curries.

FRESH CURRY LEAVES ⌃
Also available dried but fresh leaves have a better flavor. Often added toward the end of cooking. Use with most vegetables, lentils, and rice.

⌃ CORIANDER SEEDS
Also available ground, coriander has a sweet, woody fragrance and floral flavor. Particularly good with mushrooms and onions.

« GARAM MASALA
Used a lot in northern Indian cuisine, a pungent spice blend that is often added at the end of cooking to enhance the flavors in the dish.

FRESH GINGER ⌃
Essential for curries and most spicy dishes. The knobby fresh root should be peeled then sliced or grated. Ground ginger is hotter than fresh.

« SAFFRON
The yellow stigmas of the sativus crocus are the most expensive spice in the world. Rich, pungent, musky, and floral. Infuse in water or stock. Use with rice, pasta, and most vegetables.

WHOLE NUTMEG ⌃
Also available ground but best grated fresh from the whole nut. Use with spinach, parsnips, potatoes, cabbage, squashes, and sweet potatoes.

GALANGAL ⌃
Much used in Southeast Asia, has a lemony sourness, and a gingery flavor. Use in sauces, curries, soups, and stews. Good with chile, fennel, shallots, garlic, and lime.

GREEN CARDAMOM »
Use whole pods, lightly cracked, to flavor rice and curries. Also split to remove the seeds, which can then be added to beans, potatoes, sweet potatoes, and root vegetables.

The recipes

Every recipe in this book puts vegetables at the center of the plate. You'll find delicious vegetable combinations and flavor pairings, as well as exciting ways to make the most of any vegetable by using a range of herbs, spices, nuts, beans, and seeds.

Soups and salads

Gazpacho

SERVES 6–8   **PREPARATION 30 MINS**

Wonderfully refreshing, this is a perfect lunch for a hot summer day. **It's fantastically quick to make and healthy, too.** Serve with garlic-rubbed toast.

INGREDIENTS

1 red bell pepper, seeded
   and chopped
10 scallions, chopped, or 1 red
   onion, finely chopped
5 garlic cloves, chopped
1 cucumber, finely chopped
2¼lb (1kg) ripe tomatoes,
   finely chopped
1 tbsp chopped thyme,
   marjoram, parsley, mint,
   or basil
3½oz (100g) stale bread
1 chile, seeded and finely
   chopped, or ½ tsp cayenne
   pepper (optional)
2 tbsp red wine vinegar
3 tbsp olive oil, plus extra
   for drizzling
salt and freshly ground
   black pepper

OPTIONAL SHELLFISH
4oz (115g) small cooked,
   peeled shrimp (thawed
   if frozen)

1 Place a serving bowl in the refrigerator. Put the pepper, scallions or onion, garlic, cucumber, and tomatoes in a mixing bowl, then add the herbs.

2 Pulse the bread in a blender to make breadcrumbs, then add to the mixing bowl along with the chile, if using, vinegar, and oil. Gradually add ½ cup chilled water to give it a nice thick consistency; use more if preferred.

3 Transfer to the blender and, depending on your preference, either pulse briefly so that the mixture remains slightly chunky or blend the soup until smooth. Season generously with salt and pepper. Transfer to the serving bowl, add a few ice cubes, and drizzle with oil.

IF ADDING SHELLFISH, put the shrimp into the serving bowl of soup at step 3. If you like, garnish the edge of the bowl with 6–8 cooked whole shrimp, hanging them over the edge by their tails, heads outward.

Soups and salads
Endive gazpacho

SERVES 4   **PREPARATION 15 MINS, PLUS CHILLING**

A delicious variation on the cool classic, this soup has a zesty twist. Use a **romaine lettuce heart or even a bunch of watercress** instead of endive, if preferred.

1 Thinly peel the zest of half the orange. Cut in thin strips and boil in water for 1 minute. Drain, rinse with cold water, and drain again. Set aside for garnish. Finely grate the remaining zest of the orange, squeeze the juice, and set aside.

2 Cut a cone shape out of the base of each head of endive and discard. Separate the heads into spears. Reserve four of the smallest spears for the garnish. Roughly chop the remainder.

3 Soak the bread in water for 2 minutes. Squeeze out some of the moisture, then put the bread in a blender with the chopped endive, garlic, scallions, tomato, stock, oil, white balsamic vinegar, basil leaves, and the orange juice and finely grated zest. Purée the soup in a blender or food processor, then season with salt and pepper. Chill until ready to serve.

4 Ladle into 4 shallow soup plates and drizzle with a little oil. Garnish each with a tiny endive spear and a few strands of blanched orange zest. Serve cold.

IF ADDING SHELLFISH, fry the slices of baguette in a little oil until pale golden and crisp but still soft in the middle. Spread with the crab. Dust with pepper and garnish with the tiny endive spears and orange shreds, then float a slice in each bowl of soup.

INGREDIENTS

1 large orange
2 heads endive
2 slices bread,
  crusts removed
1 garlic clove,
  roughly chopped
4 scallions,
  roughly chopped
1 large beefsteak tomato,
  quartered and seeded
2 cups vegetable stock
2 tbsp olive oil, plus extra
  for drizzling
2 tbsp white balsamic vinegar
4 large basil leaves
salt and freshly ground
  black pepper

OPTIONAL SHELLFISH

4 slices baguette
a little olive oil
1½ oz (43g) can crab meat
cayenne pepper

French red onion soup with brandy and Gruyère croûtes

SERVES 4   PREPARATION **10 MINS**   TO COOK **40 MINS**

Rich and full of flavor, onion soup cannot be beaten on a cold day. Red onions add color and are sweeter and more intensely flavored than yellow onions.

INGREDIENTS

4 tbsp butter
4 large red onions, quartered
   and thinly sliced
2 tbsp light brown sugar
3½ cups vegetable stock
2 tbsp brandy
salt and freshly ground
   black pepper
8 diagonal slices of baguette
6oz (175g) Gruyère
   cheese, grated

OPTIONAL MEAT

2–4 slices ham

1 Melt the butter in a large saucepan. Add the onions and fry, stirring, for 2 minutes. Cover, reduce the heat to low, and cook gently for 10 minutes until really soft, shaking the pan occasionally.

2 Increase the heat, add the sugar, and fry for 5 minutes or until richly browned, stirring continuously. (Take care not to burn.) Add the stock, brandy, and a little salt and pepper. Bring to a boil, reduce the heat, and simmer gently for 15 minutes.

3 Meanwhile, make the croûtes. Preheat the broiler and toast the bread on both sides. When ready to serve, add the cheese to the croûtes and broil until just melted and sizzling.

4 Ladle the soup into warmed bowls and float two cheese croûtes on each. Add a grinding of pepper and serve immediately.

IF ADDING MEAT, add half a slice of ham on each toasted croûte, trimmed to fit the toast, at step 3 before adding the cheese.

Fennel soup with Parmesan thins

SERVES 4   **PREPARATION 20 MINS**   TO COOK **45 MINS**

Parmesan thins are simplicity itself to make and, along with a garnish of delicate fennel fronds, **elevate this rich, creamy soup** to dinner-party sophistication.

INGREDIENTS

1–2 tbsp olive oil
4 tbsp butter
1 onion, finely chopped
salt and freshly ground
    black pepper
1 celery stalk, finely chopped
1 carrot, finely chopped
2 garlic cloves, finely chopped
3–4 fennel bulbs, trimmed
    and finely chopped, fronds
    reserved to garnish
2½ cups hot vegetable stock
¼ cup finely grated
    Parmesan cheese
¾ cup heavy cream
pinch of grated nutmeg

OPTIONAL SHELLFISH

1lb 2oz (500g) mussels,
    scrubbed and debearded
⅔ cup dry white wine
1 tbsp chopped parsley

1 Heat 1 tbsp oil and the butter in a large pan. Add the onion and cook over low heat, stirring, for 5–6 minutes until soft. Season with salt and pepper. Add the celery and carrot and continue to cook, stirring occasionally, for 10 minutes, or until nicely golden. Add the garlic and fennel and cook over very low heat, stirring occasionally, for 5 minutes until the fennel begins to soften, adding more oil if needed. Pour over a little stock and bring to a boil. Add the remaining stock and bring to a boil again. Reduce to a simmer and cook for 20 minutes until the fennel is tender.

2 For the Parmesan thins, place 4 equal heaps of the grated Parmesan in a large, non-stick frying pan. Set the pan over low heat and flatten each heap with the back of a spoon. Cook for a few minutes until the Parmesan begins to melt and forms a crust. Once it has begun to crisp on the bottom and tiny bubbles start to appear around the edges, carefully flip each thin using a palette knife or thin metal spatula. Cook for a further minute or so, then remove the pan from the heat, leaving the thins in the pan to keep warm.

3 Transfer the soup to a food processor and blend until smooth, then return to the pan; alternatively, use a hand blender. Season well, then pour in the cream and heat gently. Serve in wide bowls, sprinkled with a pinch of nutmeg and topped with a Parmesan thin. Garnish with the reserved fennel fronds.

IF ADDING SHELLFISH, make the soup using only 2 fennel bulbs. Do not purée. Steam the mussels with the wine in a covered pan for 5 minutes, then strain through a cheesecloth-lined sieve over a bowl. Remove the mussels from their shells, discarding any closed ones. Add the mussels and their liquor to the soup, along with the parsley.

Borscht

SERVES 4   **PREPARATION 15 MINS**   **TO COOK 1 HR 30 MINS**

This thickly textured, satisfying soup is a Russian classic
that can be enjoyed at any time of year. Try it with grated
carrot piled on top and hunks of dark rye bread.

1 Melt the butter in a large saucepan over medium heat. Add the
beets, onion, carrot, and celery. Cook, stirring, for 5 minutes,
or until just softened. Add the tomatoes and garlic, if using, and cook
for 2–3 minutes, stirring frequently, then stir in the stock.

2 Tie the bay leaves and cloves in a small piece of cheesecloth or new
disposable kitchen cloth and add to the pan. Bring the soup to a
boil, then lower the heat, cover, and simmer for 1 hour 20 minutes.
Discard the cheesecloth bag, stir in the lemon juice, and season to
taste with salt and pepper. Ladle the soup into warmed bowls and add
a swirl of sour cream to each one.

IF ADDING FISH, chill the soup. Ladle into bowls and top with a dollop
of sour cream. Arrange 2–3 slices of pickled herring on top. Garnish
with dill or parsley.

INGREDIENTS

3 tbsp butter or goose fat
2 large beets, grated
1 onion, roughly grated
1 carrot, roughly grated
1 celery stalk, roughly grated
14oz (400g) can chopped
    tomatoes
1 garlic clove, crushed
    (optional)
6 cups hot vegetable stock
2 bay leaves
4 cloves
2 tbsp lemon juice
salt and freshly ground
    black pepper
7oz (200g) sour cream

OPTIONAL FISH
2 pickled herrings, sliced
1 tbsp chopped dill or parsley

Cheese, red pepper, and corn chowder

SERVES 4 **PREPARATION 15 MINS** **TO COOK 35 MINS**

When time is short, use a large can of corn with peppers instead of the corn cobs and pepper. Simmering the cobs in the stock is not essential.

INGREDIENTS

2 large corn cobs
3½ cups vegetable stock
knob of butter
1 onion, finely chopped
1 potato, peeled and
    finely diced
1 red bell pepper, seeded
    and finely chopped
1 bouquet garni
3 tbsp cornstarch
⅔ cup milk
4oz (115g) sharp Cheddar
    cheese, grated
2 tbsp chopped parsley,
    plus extra to garnish
salt and freshly ground
    black pepper

OPTIONAL MEAT

3½ cups chicken stock
1 large boneless, skinless
    chicken breast, cut into
    very small pieces

1 Remove the corn kernels from the cobs (see p321). Put the stripped cobs in a saucepan with the stock. Bring to a boil, cover, and simmer gently for 5 minutes to extract the flavor. Strain the stock into a bowl and discard the cobs.

2 In the same saucepan, melt the butter and fry the onion gently, stirring, for 2 minutes until softened but not browned. Add the reserved stock, all the prepared vegetables, and the bouquet garni. Bring to a boil, then reduce the heat, partially cover, and simmer gently for 15 minutes until the vegetables are soft. Discard the bouquet garni.

3 Blend the cornstarch with the milk and stir into the soup. Bring back to a boil and simmer, stirring, for 1 minute until slightly thickened. Stir in the cheese until melted, add the parsley, then season with salt and pepper to taste. Ladle into bowls and sprinkle with a little extra chopped parsley.

IF ADDING MEAT, omit the cheese, use chicken stock instead of vegetable stock, and add the chicken to the pan with the prepared vegetables at step 2.

Spicy watercress soup

SERVES 4–6   **PREPARATION 20 MINS**   TO COOK **25 MINS**

Peppery watercress, curry leaf oil, and caramelized pear make a **marvelous melange of flavors**. The oil can be made a few days before and kept refrigerated.

INGREDIENTS

3 tbsp curry leaves
⅔ cup olive oil,
  plus 2 tbsp for the soup
1 onion, chopped
2 potatoes, peeled `
  and chopped
3½ cups hot vegetable stock
9oz (250g) watercress
2 tbsp crème fraîche
salt and freshly ground
  black pepper

For the garnish
1 bosc pear, peeled
  and finely diced
2 tbsp confectioner's sugar
pinch of coarsely ground
  black peppercorns
1 tbsp crème fraîche

OPTIONAL FISH
6oz (175g) skinned salmon
  fillet, diced
knob of butter

1 First, make the curry leaf oil. Drop the leaves into a pan of boiling water and cook for about 30 seconds. Remove and refresh with cold water, then pat dry with paper towels and transfer to a blender. Warm the oil and gradually pour into the blender as the leaves are being processed. Blend to a smooth paste. Line a sieve with paper towels and pour the curry leaf mixture into it—the oil will slowly drip through.

2 For the soup, heat 2 tbsp oil in a large pan and add the onion and potato. Cover and fry over low heat for about 5 minutes, stirring frequently, until softened but not colored. Pour in the stock and simmer for another 10 minutes until the potatoes are cooked. Add the watercress and cook for a further minute. Season and stir in 2–3 tsp curry leaf oil off the heat. Blend with a hand blender until smooth, and sieve to remove any tough fibers.

3 For the garnish, toss the pear in confectioner's sugar seasoned with pepper. Heat a frying pan over moderate heat and fry the pear until caramelized.

4 Reheat and season the soup again and whisk in 2 tbsp crème fraîche. Ladle into bowls and top with an extra dollop of crème fraîche. Scatter the pear over and finish with an extra drizzle of curry leaf oil.

IF ADDING FISH, omit the pear garnish. Sauté the salmon fillet in butter for 1–2 minutes until just cooked but still holding its shape. Scatter over the soup instead of the pears.

Lettuce soup with peas

SERVES 4   **PREPARATION 20 MINS, PLUS CHILLING**

Round or butterhead lettuces are ideal for puréeing, as their soft leaves are not fibrous. Here, they are combined with sweet peas and mint for a fresh summer soup.

1 Bring a small amount of water to a boil in a pan, add the peas, and cook for 3 minutes. Drain (reserving the cooking water), rinse under cold running water, and refrigerate. Cut the garlic in half, removing any green at the center, and crush with a pinch of coarse salt.

2 Combine the garlic with all the other ingredients (except the peas) in a blender or food processor, adding just enough of the reserved cooking water to get the blades moving or until the desired consistency is achieved—this will vary according to the type of lettuce and the kind of machine being used, but the soup is nice if it is fairly smooth, with a bit of texture.

3 Transfer the soup to a large bowl and place in the refrigerator for 30 minutes. When ready to serve, stir in the cooked peas, leaving a few to use as a garnish.

IF ADDING MEAT, stir in the ham with the peas at step 3, keeping some for garnish. Garnish with the reserved peas and ham before serving.

INGREDIENTS

4½oz (125g) peas
   (shelled weight)
1 small garlic clove
pinch of coarse salt
2 round lettuces (approx. 1lb
   2oz /500g in total),
   torn into pieces and
   solid cores discarded
9oz (250g) plain yogurt
¾in (2cm) piece ginger,
   finely grated
handful of mint leaves
juice of ½ lemon
salt and freshly ground
   black pepper

OPTIONAL MEAT
handful of finely chopped
   cooked ham

Potato soup with broccoli, shallot, and mascarpone cheese

SERVES 4   **PREPARATION 20 MINS**   TO COOK **40 MINS**

Broccoli and shallot add color and freshness to this delicate potato and cheese soup. Try crumbled white cheddar or Monterey Jack instead of mascarpone.

INGREDIENTS

1 tbsp olive oil

½ tbsp butter

2 large banana shallots, finely chopped

12oz (350g) Russet potatoes, peeled and chopped into 1in (2.5cm) chunks

5 cups vegetable stock

1 large bay leaf

salt and freshly ground black pepper

1 large head broccoli, cut into florets

¼ cup mascarpone cheese

4 × ½in (1cm) slices baguette

1oz (30g) creamy, strong-flavored blue cheese, such as Roquefort, Fourme d'Ambert, or Gorgonzola Piccante

OPTIONAL MEAT

4oz (115g) smoked pork sausage, thinly sliced

1 Heat the oil and butter in a saucepan over medium heat. Add the shallots and potatoes and cook for 5 minutes, stirring often.

2 Add the stock and bay leaf and stir well. Season lightly with salt and pepper and bring to a simmer. Lower the heat, cover with a lid, and simmer for 10 minutes. Add the broccoli, stir, cover again, and cook for 10–15 minutes, or until the broccoli is tender. Leave to cool for several minutes.

3 Transfer the contents of the pan to a food processor and purée until smooth. Strain the soup back into the pan through a sieve, using a wooden spoon to push as much of the mixture through as possible.

4 Place the pan over medium heat and stir in the mascarpone cheese; keep stirring until it has blended in. Season well and discard the bay leaf. Toast the baguette slices until golden and spread them with the blue cheese. Ladle the soup into bowls and float a piece of the bread in the center of each one.

IF ADDING MEAT, omit the blue cheese croûtes. Dice the potatoes and chop the broccoli, discarding the thick stump. At step 2, add the pork sausage with the broccoli and simmer for 5 minutes until the broccoli is tender. Do not purée. Gently stir in the mascarpone until blended and season with salt and pepper.

Creamy spinach and rosemary soup

SERVES 6   **PREPARATION 15 MINS**   **TO COOK 25 MINS**

With this **fragrant and vividly colored soup,** the spinach is added at the last moment so that it does not overcook and lose any of its color or flavor.

1 Melt the butter in a heavy-based pan. When it starts to foam, add the onion and potato, and stir to coat well. Season well with salt and pepper, then cover the pan with a lid and sweat the vegetables over gentle heat for 10 minutes.

2 Add the stock and milk, bring to a boil, then simmer for 5 minutes or until the potato and onion are completely cooked. Add the spinach and boil the soup with the lid removed for 2–3 minutes, or until the spinach is tender. Do not overcook. Add the chopped rosemary, then, using a hand blender or food processor, purée the soup until smooth. Reheat gently.

3 Serve in warmed bowls garnished with a swirl of half-and-half and a sprig of rosemary. When in season, sprinkle a few rosemary flowers over the top for extra pizzazz. Serve with crusty bread or cheese scones.

IF ADDING MEAT, dry-fry the bacon until crisp. Drain on paper towels, then crumble or chop. Sprinkle over the swirl of half-and-half on the soup to garnish before serving.

INGREDIENTS

4 tbsp butter
1 onion, finely chopped
1 large potato, peeled
   and diced
salt and freshly ground
   black pepper
2 cups hot vegetable stock
   or water
2 cups creamy milk, made
   from 1⅓ cup whole milk
   mixed with ⅔ cup half-
   and-half
12oz (350g) spinach, stemmed,
   rinsed, and roughly chopped
1 tbsp chopped rosemary
2 tbsp half-and-half, sprig of
   rosemary, and rosemary
   flowers (optional), to garnish

OPTIONAL MEAT
4 strips bacon

Leek, barley, and root vegetable broth with basil oil

SERVES 4–6   **PREPARATION 10 MINS**   **TO COOK 45 MINS**

Barley adds substance to this delicate soup. For a more filling meal and extra protein, add a 14oz (410g) can of navy beans and an extra ¾ cup vegetable stock.

INGREDIENTS

¾ cup dry white wine
5½ cups vegetable stock
2½oz (75g) pearl barley
1 onion, chopped
2 carrots, finely diced
½ small rutabaga, finely diced
1 potato, peeled and
   finely diced
1 turnip, finely diced
1 large bay leaf
2 star anise
salt and freshly ground
   black pepper
crusty bread, to serve

For the basil oil
handful of basil leaves,
   roughly chopped
¼ cup olive oil

OPTIONAL MEAT
3½ cups lamb stock
handful of cooked lean
   lamb, diced

1 Put the white wine in a large saucepan and bring to a boil. Boil rapidly for 2–3 minutes until reduced by half.

2 Add the remaining soup ingredients. Bring to a boil, then reduce the heat, cover, and simmer gently for 40 minutes until the barley is tender. Discard the bay leaf and star anise. Taste and adjust the seasoning.

3 To make the basil oil, blend the basil with the oil in a blender or small food processor.

4 Ladle the soup into warmed bowls. Drizzle the basil oil on top of each and serve with crusty bread.

IF ADDING MEAT, use lamb stock instead of the vegetable stock and add the lamb to the mixture at step 2 before cooking.

Celery and celery root soup

SERVES 4   **PREPARATION 15 MINS**   **TO COOK 35–40 MINS**

This earthy soup combines **mildly nutty celery root and the more assertive flavor of celery** to create a fragrant, satisfying winter warmer.

INGREDIENTS

1 tbsp sunflower or peanut oil, or mild-flavored olive oil

2 tbsp butter, plus 2 tbsp chilled butter, diced

1lb 2oz (500g) celery root, peeled and chopped

1 large head celery, cored and chopped

1 Russet potato, peeled and chopped

sea salt and freshly ground black pepper

3½ cups light vegetable stock

4 slices walnut bread, lightly toasted, to serve

OPTIONAL MEAT

1 tbsp olive oil

heaped ¼ cup diced pancetta

1 Put the oil and 2 tbsp butter in a large sauté pan over medium heat. Add the celery root, celery, and potato. Stir well for 2–3 minutes, then reduce the heat a little. Add ¼ cup water and season lightly with salt and pepper. Cover the pan and leave to stew gently for 15–20 minutes until very soft. Stir the vegetables from time to time and keep the heat low.

2 Transfer the cooked vegetables to a food processor and purée. Return to the pan and add the stock. Season and stir briskly to blend. Bring to a simmer over medium heat, stirring frequently. Reduce the heat a little and leave to simmer gently for 10–15 minutes, still stirring occasionally. Taste and adjust the seasoning.

3 Just before serving, whisk in the chilled, diced butter. Serve hot with toasted walnut bread.

IF ADDING MEAT, heat the oil in a frying pan and fry the pancetta, stirring, until golden but not hard. Drain on paper towels. Ladle the soup into shallow soup bowls and add a small cluster of the pancetta to the center of each before serving.

Turnip noodle soup with cherry pepper and chile

SERVES 4–6   **PREPARATION 10 MINS**   TO COOK **35 MINS**

Turnips are often overlooked, but this **light, colorful soup with a chile kick** will not disappoint. Larger turnips have a stronger flavor and are perfect for this recipe.

1 Put the scallions, turnips, chiles, star anise, tomato paste, and stock in a saucepan and bring to a boil. Lower the heat, partially cover, and simmer gently for 30 minutes, or until the turnips are really tender. Discard the star anise.

2 Meanwhile, put the noodles in a bowl, cover with boiling water, and leave to stand for 5 minutes, stirring to loosen. Drain the noodles and stir into the soup along with the cherry pepper. Season with soy sauce and pepper, then stir in half the cilantro. Heat through for 1–2 minutes. Ladle into warmed soup bowls, top with the remaining cilantro, and serve.

IF ADDING MEAT, put the steak in a plastic bag and beat with a meat mallet or rolling pin until as thin as possible. Cut into thin strips, discarding any gristle. Add to the pan at step 1 and simmer until the turnip and beef are very tender, then continue as above.

INGREDIENTS

4 scallions, chopped
2 large turnips, diced
½ tsp dried chile flakes
1 green jalapeño chile, seeded and cut into thin rings
2 star anise
2 tsp tomato paste
3 cups hot vegetable stock
1 slab dried, thin Chinese egg noodles
1 pickled cherry pepper, drained and diced
soy sauce, to taste
freshly ground black pepper
small handful of cilantro leaves, torn

OPTIONAL MEAT
5½oz (150g) tenderized round steak

Carrot and orange soup

SERVES 4   PREPARATION **10 MINS**   TO COOK **40 MINS**

A refreshing soup with a hint of spice, this is the perfect start to a summer meal. Try adding a swirl of cream or a spoonful of low-fat plain yogurt before serving.

INGREDIENTS

2 tsp light olive oil
  or sunflower oil
1 leek, sliced
1lb 2oz (500g) carrots, sliced
1 potato (approx. 4oz/115g),
  chopped
½ tsp ground coriander
pinch of ground cumin
1¼ cups orange juice
2 cups vegetable stock
1 bay leaf
salt and freshly ground
  black pepper
2 tbsp chopped cilantro,
  to garnish

OPTIONAL MEAT

roasted duck carcass or
  1 duck leg portion
2½ cups light chicken stock
  or water
1 onion, quartered

1 Place the oil, leek, and carrots in a large saucepan and cook over low heat for 5 minutes, stirring frequently, or until the leek has softened. Add the potato, coriander, and cumin, then pour in the orange juice and stock. Add the bay leaf, season with salt and pepper, and stir occasionally.

2 Increase the heat, bring the soup to a boil, then lower the heat, cover, and simmer for 40 minutes, or until the vegetables are very tender.

3 Allow the soup to cool slightly, then transfer to a blender or food processor and process until smooth, working in batches if necessary.

4 Return to the saucepan and add a little extra stock or water if the soup is too thick. Bring back to a simmer, then transfer to warmed serving bowls and sprinkle with chopped cilantro.

IF ADDING MEAT, make a duck stock. Put the duck carcass or leg in a large pan, cover with the stock or water, and add the onion. Bring to a boil, cover, reduce the heat, and simmer for 1 hour. Strain, then pick all the meat off the bones, discarding the skin. Chop and reserve the meat. Use the stock to make the soup, then add the chopped meat after puréeing and reheat before serving, garnished as before.

Avocado, cucumber, and sorrel soup

SERVES 4–6   **PREPARATION 5–10 MINS**

This lovely, cool summer soup is just perfect when it's too hot to cook. Track sorrel down at a local farmer's market; its lemony-spinach flavor is unique.

1 Put the avocado in a blender with the sorrel, cucumber, yogurt, and garlic. Add about ½ cup water and blend until smooth. Taste and adjust the seasoning, adding more sorrel, or salt or pepper, or thinning down with a little more water as desired.

2 Divide between 4–6 serving bowls or cups and drizzle a thin thread of avocado oil on the surface. Serve at once, or at least within the next hour while it is fresh and vivid.

IF ADDING SHELLFISH, ladle the prepared soup into shallow soup bowls and arrange a few shrimp attractively in the center of each before trickling the avocado oil over.

INGREDIENTS

1 ripe, buttery avocado, halved, pitted, and peeled (see pp324–5)
generous handful of sorrel leaves (discard any tough stalks)
¼ large cucumber, roughly diced but not peeled
2½oz (75g) Greek-style yogurt
1–2 garlic cloves, chopped
salt and freshly ground black pepper
avocado oil, for drizzling

OPTIONAL SHELLFISH
8oz (225g) cooked, peeled large shrimp (thawed if frozen)

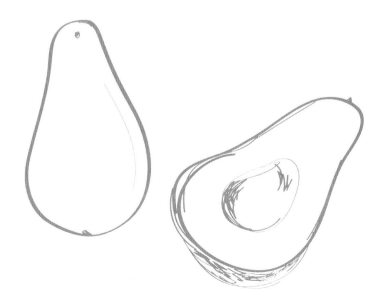

Jerusalem artichoke soup with saffron and thyme

SERVES 4–6   **PREPARATION 15 MINS**   **TO COOK 35–45 MINS**

Use whatever proportion of carrots and Jerusalem artichokes you have, making 1lb 9oz (700g) in total. Carrots enhance the color and sweetness of the soup.

INGREDIENTS

2 tbsp sunflower oil or olive oil, plus extra to garnish
2 onions, chopped
3 garlic cloves, chopped
12oz (350g) Jerusalem artichokes, scrubbed and roughly chopped
12oz (350g) carrots, scrubbed and roughly chopped
sea salt and freshly ground black pepper
4 cups hot vegetable stock
1 tbsp thyme leaves or 1½ tsp dried thyme
large pinch (about 30 strands) of saffron
juice of ½ lemon

OPTIONAL MEAT

4 cups hot chicken stock
1 small boneless, skinless chicken breast

1 Heat the oil in a large pan over medium heat. Add the onions and fry for 5 minutes, or until soft and translucent. Add the garlic and fry for 30 seconds, or until fragrant. Stir in the artichokes, carrots, and a little salt. Cover with a lid and sweat, stirring frequently, for 10–15 minutes, or until the vegetables are softened.

2 Add the stock, thyme, and saffron. Bring to a boil, then lower the heat to a simmer and cook for 20 minutes, or until the vegetables are thoroughly soft. Cool briefly, then purée until smooth in a blender. Stir in the lemon juice and season with salt and pepper. Serve in warmed bowls, with a drizzle of oil on top.

IF ADDING MEAT, use chicken stock instead of vegetable. Add the chicken breast to the pan at step 2. Remove with a slotted spoon before puréeing the soup. Finely dice the chicken and stir in before serving. Reheat if necessary to ensure the soup is piping hot.

Lentil soup

SERVES 4   **PREPARATION 20 MINS**   **TO COOK 35 MINS**

This hearty soup has just **a touch of spice and is quick and easy to prepare**. It can be puréed for a smooth finish. Serve with plenty of warm, crusty bread.

1 Heat the oil in a large pan over medium heat. Add the onions, celery, and carrots. Cook, stirring, for 5 minutes, or until the onions are soft and translucent.

2 Add the garlic and curry powder and cook, stirring, for another minute. Then add the lentils, stock, and tomato juice.

3 Bring to a boil, then lower the heat, cover, and simmer for 25 minutes, or until the vegetables are tender. Season with salt and pepper and serve hot.

IF ADDING MEAT, use ham stock instead of vegetable and at step 3 add the ham. Allow to simmer in the soup with the vegetables and lentils.

INGREDIENTS

1 tbsp olive oil
2 onions, finely chopped
2 celery stalks, finely chopped
2 carrots, finely chopped
2 garlic cloves, crushed
1–2 tsp curry powder
5½oz (150g) red lentils
5 cups vegetable stock
½ cup tomato juice
  or vegetable juice
salt and freshly ground
  black pepper

OPTIONAL MEAT

5 cups ham stock
4oz (115g) cooked ham
  pieces, trimmed of any
  fat and chopped

Four ways with
Mushrooms

Mushroom soup ▷

TAKES 55 mins **SERVES** 4

Melt 2 tbsp **butter** in a large Dutch oven, add 1 finely chopped **onion**, 2 finely chopped **celery stalks**, and 1 crushed **garlic clove**, and fry for 3–4 minutes, or until softened. Stir in 1lb (450g) roughly chopped **mixed mushrooms** and continue to fry for 5–6 minutes. Add 7oz (200g) peeled and cubed **potatoes** and 3½ cups **vegetable stock** and bring to a boil. Reduce the heat and simmer gently for 30 minutes. Use a hand blender to purée the soup until smooth, working in batches if necessary. Sprinkle in 2 tbsp finely chopped **parsley**, season with **salt** and freshly ground **black pepper**, and serve.

◁ Tofu and mushroom stroganoff

TAKES 35 mins **SERVES** 4

Heat 1 tbsp **sunflower or vegetable oil** in a pan. Stir-fry 12oz (350g) diced **tofu** over high heat until golden. Set aside. Add 1 tbsp oil, reduce the heat, and fry 1 sliced **red onion** and 2 crushed **garlic cloves** until soft. Add 1 **red** and 1 **orange bell pepper**, sliced, and 9oz (250g) **mixed mushrooms**, quartered. Stir-fry for 5 minutes. Add 2 tbsp each **tomato paste** and **smooth peanut butter** and the tofu. Stir in ⅔ cup **vegetable stock** and 2 tsp **cornstarch** mixed to a paste with water. Cook for 3 minutes. Add 7oz (200g) **crème fraîche** and **salt** and freshly ground **black pepper**. Simmer for 2 minutes, sprinkle with **chives**, and serve with **rice**.

Mushrooms come in a range of flavors, from the mild button type to full-bodied portobellos and nutty chanterelles. **All should be firm and earthy-smelling.** Always wipe them—but don't wash them—before use.

Mushrooms in garlic sauce ▶

TAKES 25 mins **SERVES** 4

Heat ¼ cup **olive oil** in a frying pan. Add 14oz (400g) **crimini mushrooms**, halved, 4 finely sliced **garlic cloves**, and 2 **red chiles**, seeded and finely sliced. Fry for 2 minutes over low heat. Add ¼ cup **dry sherry**, crumble in 1 **chicken bouillion** cube, and season with freshly ground **black pepper**. Cook over medium heat for 10 minutes, or until the mushrooms have released their juices. Cook for a further 3 minutes, or until the juices have reduced by half, and then serve with some fresh **crusty bread**.

◀ Mushroom bruschetta

TAKES 30 mins **SERVES** 12

Preheat the oven to 350°F (180°C). Brush 12 slices of **ciabatta** with **olive oil**, then bake for 10 minutes. Melt 4 tbsp **butter** in a pan, add 4 finely chopped **shallots** and 2 finely chopped **garlic cloves**, and fry gently for 5 minutes. Add 1lb (450g) sliced **wild mushrooms** and fry until wilted. Add ¼ cup **Marsala**, bring to a boil, then simmer until reduced to 1 tsp. Reduce the heat, add ½ cup **heavy cream**, and simmer for 5 minutes. Add **salt** and freshly ground **black pepper**, and stir in 2 tbsp finely chopped **parsley** and 3 tbsp grated **Parmesan cheese**. Spoon the mixture over the toasted bread.

Antipasti salad

SERVES 4   **PREPARATION 30 MINS**   **TO COOK 10 MINS**

A mix of lettuce varieties and spicy leaves such as arugula or mizuna really lifts the flavors of this salad, while the mozzarella, olives, and tomatoes add to its visual appeal.

INGREDIENTS

14oz (400g) thin green beans
salt and freshly ground
   black pepper
3 tbsp chopped parsley
2 tsp lemon thyme leaves
1 tbsp chopped fennel
2 tbsp extra virgin olive oil
4½oz (125g) mixed lettuce
   and spicy greens
14oz (400g) jar or can
   artichoke hearts, drained
   and halved
4½oz (125g) bocconcini (baby
   mozzarella cheese balls)
16 black olives, pitted
   and chopped
4½oz (125g) cherry
   tomatoes, halved
2 scallions, chopped
3 tbsp chopped chervil

For the dressing
5 tbsp extra virgin olive oil
½ garlic clove, crushed
1½ tbsp balsamic vinegar

OPTIONAL MEAT
4 slices Parma ham, cut into
   small strips

1 Bring a pan of lightly salted water to a boil. Trim the green beans and blanch in the boiling water for 5–7 minutes. Refresh in cold water and drain.

2 Place the beans in a wide, shallow salad bowl and season lightly with salt and pepper. Scatter half the parsley, lemon thyme, and fennel over the beans. Drizzle the oil over, toss, and set aside.

3 Make the dressing by pouring the oil into a measuring cup. Season with salt and pepper, then whisk in the garlic and balsamic vinegar. Next, whisk in the remaining parsley, thyme, and fennel.

4 Scatter the greens over the beans, then the artichoke hearts, bocconcini, olives, tomatoes, and scallions. Whisk the dressing and drizzle it over the salad. Toss, sprinkle over the chervil, and serve.

IF ADDING MEAT, add the Parma ham to the salad at step 4 and dress as before. Omit the bocconcini, if preferred.

Celery and apple salad with blue cheese dressing

SERVES 4   **PREPARATION 10 MINS**   TO COOK **2 MINS**

The strong tastes of celery and bitter greens more than hold their own against the **pungency of a blue cheese dressing** in this salad. Walnuts add crunch and texture.

1 In a frying pan or wok, dry fry the walnuts for a couple of minutes until they are golden and crispy. Set aside to cool.

2 In a food processor, mix together 3½oz (100g) blue cheese, vinegar, oil, and a good grinding of pepper. Purée it to a smooth, creamy dressing, which should have a thick pouring consistency. Add up to 1 tbsp cold water to thin the dressing a little if it is too thick.

3 In a large bowl, mix the celery, apples, and watercress or arugula. Coat the salad with the dressing and taste for seasoning. Top with the walnuts and the rest of the blue cheese, crumbled or diced into bite-sized pieces.

IF ADDING MEAT, omit the walnuts. Stir-fry the tenderloin in hot oil for 1 minute and set aside to cool. Add to the salad instead of the walnuts at step 3.

INGREDIENTS

2oz (60g) walnuts, chopped
10oz (300g) blue cheese, such as Gorgonzola or Dolcelatte
¼ cup cider vinegar
¼ cup hazelnut or walnut oil
salt and freshly ground black pepper
4 celery stalks, trimmed and sliced diagonally into ½in (1cm) slices
2 green apples, cored and cut into thin wedges
4 large handfuls of watercress or arugula

OPTIONAL MEAT

5½oz (150g) tenderloin, cut into very thin strips
1 tbsp olive oil

Eggplant salad

SERVES 6   **PREPARATION** **15 MINS**   TO COOK **10 MINS**

Steaming rather than frying the eggplants in this recipe enables them **to readily absorb the flavor of the walnut oil** in the dressing.

INGREDIENTS

2 eggplants, peeled and cut
  into ¾in (2cm) cubes
2oz (60g) soft goat
  cheese, crumbled
2 ripe tomatoes, seeded
  and diced
1 small red onion, finely diced
handful of flat-leaf parsley,
  finely chopped
2oz (60g) walnuts, lightly
  toasted and chopped
1 tbsp sesame seeds,
  lightly toasted
sea salt and freshly ground
  black pepper

For the dressing
1 garlic clove, crushed
4 tbsp walnut oil
juice of 1 lemon

OPTIONAL MEAT
4 lamb medallions
a little olive oil
2 tsp chopped rosemary

1 Cook the eggplant in a covered steamer basket placed over simmering water for 10 minutes. Leave to cool slightly, then gently squeeze the cubes to extract as much water as possible.

2 Combine all the ingredients in a mixing bowl and toss gently. Whisk together all the dressing ingredients and toss the dressing with the salad. Season well with salt and pepper.

IF ADDING MEAT, brush the lamb medallions with a little oil and sprinkle with rosemary and some pepper. Cook on a hot grill for 2–4 minutes on each side until cooked to your liking. Wrap the lamb in foil and leave to rest in a warm place for 5 minutes before serving with the salad.

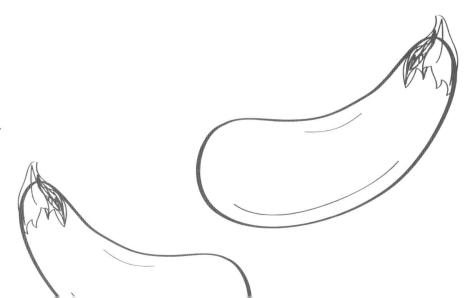

Endive salad with spinach and pears

SERVES 4   **PREPARATION 10 MINS**

The crispness of the endive and the mild, soft spinach
in this salad work well with the creamy cheese, the sweetness of the pears, and the strong mustard dressing.

1 To make the vinaigrette, place the honey, mustard, oil, and vinegar in a screw-top jar and shake well. Season well with salt and pepper. Alternatively, whisk the ingredients together in a bowl.

2 Cut a cone-shaped core out of the base of the endive to remove any bitterness, then cut the head into chunks and separate the leaves. Place the spinach, endive, sliced pears, Dolcelatte, and shallots in a salad bowl. Drizzle the vinaigrette over the salad, toss gently, and serve.

IF ADDING MEAT, brush the steaks with oil and season with salt, plenty of pepper, and a pinch of dried oregano. Cook on a hot grill for 1½–4 minutes on each side until cooked to your liking. Wrap in foil and leave to rest in a warm place for 5 minutes before serving with the salad.

INGREDIENTS

2 heads endive
7oz (200g) baby spinach leaves
2 firm, ripe pears,
    peeled and sliced
4oz (115g) Dolcelatte, cut into
    small cubes
3 shallots, finely sliced

For the vinaigrette
1 tbsp honey
½ tbsp Dijon mustard
6 tbsp extra virgin olive oil
2 tbsp red wine vinegar
salt and freshly ground
    black pepper

OPTIONAL MEAT
4 tenderloin steaks
    (approx. 4oz /115g each)
a little olive oil
pinch of dried oregano

Eggplant, zucchini, and flageolet salad with mozzarella and red pesto dressing

SERVES 4–6   **PREPARATION 10 MINS**   TO COOK **25 MINS**

Serve this colorful salad as a **light lunch for four or as a starter for six**. To prepare the onion, cut it into thin slices, discarding the ends, before peeling off the outer layer.

INGREDIENTS

2 small eggplants

2 zucchini

7 tbsp olive oil

14oz (400g) can flageolet or cannellini beans, rinsed and drained

1 garlic clove, crushed

salt and freshly ground black pepper

1–2 tbsp lime juice

4oz (115g) cherry tomatoes, halved

1 small red onion, thinly sliced

¼ cup red pesto (see pp298–9 or use store-bought)

4½oz (125g) ball fresh mozzarella cheese, torn

a few pimento-stuffed green olives, halved

crusty bread, to serve

OPTIONAL FISH

2 × 5½oz (150g) tuna steaks

1 Preheat a grill pan. Trim the eggplants and zucchini and cut lengthways into ¼in (5mm) slices. Brush with oil. Cook in batches on a hot grill pan for 3 minutes on each side, pressing down with a metal spatula, until tender and striped brown. Wrap in foil to keep warm and set aside.

2 Put the flageolet beans in a large saucepan. Drizzle with 2 tbsp oil and add the garlic, salt and pepper, and lime juice, to taste. Heat through, stirring gently, then remove from the heat. Add the tomatoes and onion slices and toss gently.

3 Thin the pesto with ¼ cup oil or enough to form a spoonable dressing. Taste and sharpen with lime juice.

4 Gently mix the eggplants and zucchini into the beans. The mixture should now be just warm.

5 Stir in the mozzarella, then spoon the salad into serving bowls. Drizzle the pesto dressing over and scatter with the olives. Serve with crusty bread.

IF ADDING FISH, brush the tuna steaks with oil and grill for just 1 minute on each side (they should still be pink in the middle). Cut into slices and add to the dish at step 4. Use only 1 eggplant and omit the mozzarella.

Thai vegetable salad with cabbage and peanuts

SERVES 4   **PREPARATION 15 MINS**

This is a simpler version of the Thai salad som tam, which has a hot, salty, sweet, and sour dressing. Add some cooled rice noodles to turn it into a main course.

INGREDIENTS

2 sweet apples
4 carrots, grated
1 small white cabbage, shredded
handful of sunflower seeds
handful of salted or dry-roasted peanuts

For the dressing

2 tbsp light soy sauce
1 green chile, seeded and finely chopped
1 garlic clove, grated
juice of 2 limes
1–2 tsp granulated sugar
handful of cilantro, finely chopped

OPTIONAL SHELLFISH

1 tbsp Thai fish sauce
handful of cooked, peeled shrimp, roughly chopped
a few whole cooked, peeled shrimp
2 scallions, chopped

1 First, make the dressing. Put all the dressing ingredients in a small bowl and mix thoroughly until the sugar has dissolved. Taste to check the flavor—if it needs sweetening, add more sugar, and if it needs saltiness, add a little more soy sauce.

2 Quarter and core the apples, then chop into bite-sized pieces. Put in a bowl with the carrot, cabbage, and sunflower seeds. Mix together thoroughly.

3 Drizzle the dressing over and toss together so that everything is well mixed. Transfer to a serving dish and scatter the peanuts over.

IF ADDING SHELLFISH, use 1 tbsp soy sauce and 1 tbsp Thai fish sauce in the dressing and add the chopped shrimp to the salad. Garnish the dish with the whole shrimp and scallions, omitting the peanuts.

Squash with cranberries and chestnuts

SERVES 4   **PREPARATION 10 MINS**   TO COOK **30 MINS**

This gently spiced, flavorful dish makes **excellent use of seasonal ingredients for a warm winter salad**. It is also good served as an accompaniment to a roast.

1 Heat the oil and butter in a large frying pan. Add the allspice, cinnamon, and squash. Season well with salt and pepper and cook over low-medium heat, stirring occasionally, for 15 minutes, or until the squash begins to soften a little. Add a little more oil, if needed.

2 Add the chestnuts and stir so that they are coated with the oil. Cook over low heat for 5–10 minutes, then add the cranberries and cook for a further 5 minutes.

3 Taste and season again, if needed, adding a little sugar if the cranberries are too tart (cook until the sugar has dissolved).

4 Pile a bed of arugula and watercress on a shallow dish and scatter the squash mixture over it. Serve warm.

IF ADDING MEAT, serve the salad with slices of cold roast turkey, or add diced cooked turkey to the mixture with the cranberries at step 2.

INGREDIENTS

1–2 tbsp extra virgin olive oil
knob of butter
pinch of ground allspice
pinch of ground cinnamon
1 butternut squash, peeled, halved, seeded, and cut into bite-sized pieces
salt and freshly ground black pepper
8½oz (240g) can cooked chestnuts
1¾oz (50g) cranberries
sugar, to taste (optional)
3½oz (100g) mixed arugula and watercress

OPTIONAL MEAT
slices of cold roast turkey, or 2 handfuls of diced cooked turkey

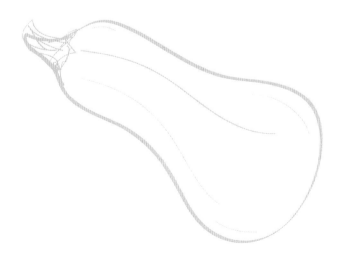
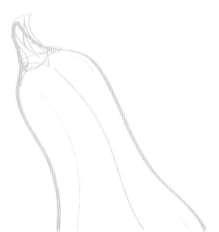

Warm pasta, kale, and duck egg salad with truffle oil

SERVES 4   **PREPARATION 20 MINS**   TO COOK **10 MINS**

If fresh wild mushrooms aren't available, use 5oz (140g) white or crimini ones, thickly sliced, and a handful of dried **morels, chanterelles, or porcini,** reconstituted.

INGREDIENTS

4 large duck eggs, scrubbed
salt and freshly ground
   black pepper
8oz (225g) conchiglie
   (medium shell) pasta
7oz (200g) finely shredded
   curly kale, thick
   stalks removed
knob of butter
2 tbsp olive oil
7oz (200g) mixed wild
   mushrooms, cut up if large
2 tbsp chopped thyme,
   plus a few thyme leaves,
   to garnish
2 scallions, chopped
¼ cup truffle oil
2 tbsp white balsamic vinegar
small black truffle, grated,
   to garnish (optional)
warm ciabatta bread, to serve

OPTIONAL MEAT

knob of butter
9oz (250g) chicken
   livers, trimmed

1 Place the duck eggs in a steamer basket or large metal colander. Fill a bowl with cold water and set near the stove top.

2 Add a generous pinch of salt to a large pan of water and bring to a boil, then add the pasta and stir. Bring back to a boil, top with the steamer containing the eggs, cover, and cook for 5 minutes. Add the kale to the steamer, cover, and cook for a further 5 minutes. Quickly take the steamer off the pan and immediately put the eggs in the bowl of cold water. Drain the pasta and rinse with cold water. Drain again and return to the pan.

3 While the kale is cooking, melt the butter and olive oil in a frying pan. Add the mushrooms and thyme and sauté, stirring, for 3 minutes. Season with salt and pepper. Add to the pasta with the kale and scallions.

4 Whisk 2 tbsp truffle oil into the juices in the mushroom pan, along with the balsamic vinegar, and a pinch of salt and a good grinding of pepper. Heat through, stirring, then pour into the pasta mixture. Toss gently.

5 Pile into dishes and drizzle with the remaining truffle oil. Carefully shell the duck eggs and place one on top of each salad. Cut open so that the yolk trickles out slightly. Add a grating of black truffle, if using, and a few thyme leaves. Serve with warm ciabatta.

IF ADDING MEAT, heat the butter in a sauté pan and sauté the chicken livers, cut into bite-sized chunks if necessary, for 3–4 minutes until brown but still pink inside. Season lightly with salt and pepper. Add to the salad with the mushrooms at step 3. Serve with or without the eggs, as preferred.

Bulgur wheat with okra

SERVES 4 **PREPARATION** **15 MINS** **TO COOK** **30 MINS**

Bulgur makes a wonderful base for a salad, served warm or cold. Try this piled on a bed of shredded crisp lettuce or spooned into whole leaves.

INGREDIENTS

7oz (200g) bulgur wheat
¼ cup olive oil, plus extra
    for drizzling
1 large onion, finely chopped
7oz (200g) okra, trimmed and
    cut into chunks
3½oz (100g) baby corn, cut
    into short lengths
8oz (225g) shelled baby fava
    beans, blanched and popped
    out of their skins
3 garlic cloves, grated or
    finely chopped
¼ cup dry white wine
handful of dill, chopped, plus
    small sprigs to garnish
salt and freshly ground
    black pepper
2 tomatoes, cut into wedges,
    to garnish

OPTIONAL SHELLFISH
12oz (350g) raw, peeled
    shrimp (thawed
    if frozen)

1 Preheat the oven to 300°F (150°C). Put the bulgur wheat in a bowl and pour in enough boiling water to cover it. Cover with a dish towel, leave for 5 minutes, then stir.

2 Meanwhile, heat the oil in a large heavy-based pan, add the onions, and cook over medium heat for 5 minutes, or until they start to soften. Add the okra, corn, and fava beans and cook for 2 minutes, then add the garlic and continue to cook, stirring frequently, for 2–3 minutes.

3 Stir in the wine and dill and cook for 2 minutes, then stir in the wheat. Transfer to an ovenproof dish, season with salt and pepper, and cover with foil. Cook in the oven for 20 minutes, stirring occasionally. Remove from the oven, fluff up with a fork, then cover again and leave until warm or completely cold. Drizzle with a little oil and serve garnished with tomato wedges and sprigs of dill.

IF ADDING SHELLFISH, omit the fava beans and add the shrimp with the garlic at step 2, then continue as before.

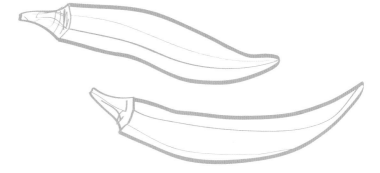

Quinoa, fava bean, and dill salad

SERVES 4   PREPARATION **15 MINS**   TO COOK **20 MINS**

If possible, **prepare this salad at least an hour in advance** so that the individual flavors have plenty of time to develop.

1 Put the quinoa in a pan, cover with water, bring to a boil, and cook according to package instructions. Drain well, rinse under cold running water, drain again, then transfer to a large serving dish.

2 Cook the fava beans in a pan of salted boiling water for 2 minutes until tender. Drain and rinse under cold water. If using fresh beans, peel the outer skin of any that are larger than your thumbnail. Add to the quinoa in the serving dish.

3 Heat the oil in a large frying pan, add the zucchini, and season well with salt and pepper. Stir in the garlic, chile flakes, and lemon zest, and cook over medium heat for 5–6 minutes until golden. Stir the zucchini into the quinoa and beans. Add the golden raisins (if using) and dill, then mix well. Add the lemon juice and the fruity olive oil. Taste and season, if necessary. Serve with some bread.

IF ADDING MEAT, halve the quantity of fava beans and add the lamb to the cooked quinoa with the fava beans at step 2. Use a small bunch of mint instead of dill and serve in individual bowls garnished with a dollop of Greek-style yogurt, an extra drizzle of olive oil, and a dusting of sweet paprika.

INGREDIENTS

7oz (200g) quinoa
9oz (250g) fava beans, fresh or
  frozen (shelled weight)
salt and freshly ground
  black pepper
1 tbsp olive oil
3 small zucchini, trimmed,
  halved lengthways,
  and chopped
2 garlic cloves, finely chopped
pinch of dried chile flakes
grated zest and juice
  of 1 lemon
handful of golden raisins
  (optional)
bunch of dill, finely chopped
1 tbsp fruity extra virgin
  olive oil
bread, to serve

OPTIONAL MEAT

6oz (175g) diced lean
  cooked lamb
small bunch of mint
2 tbsp Greek-style yogurt
1 tsp sweet paprika

Fennel and goat cheese salad

SERVES 6   **PREPARATION 10 MINS, PLUS MARINATING**

The addition of **diced goat cheese and a few slices of apple** turns this salad into a light lunch and also adds plenty of red-and-white visual appeal.

INGREDIENTS

1 fennel bulb, finely sliced
and separated into shreds
½ tbsp aged balsamic vinegar
3 tbsp extra virgin olive oil
1 garlic clove, crushed
salt and freshly ground
black pepper
5½oz (150g) mixed greens,
such as watercress, baby
spinach, arugula, or lamb's
lettuce
4oz (120g) cylinder goat
cheese, diced
1 sweet red apple, quartered,
cored, sliced, and tossed in
lemon juice

OPTIONAL MEAT
4 pigeon breasts
1 tbsp olive oil

1 In a bowl, toss the fennel with a few drops of vinegar, 1 tbsp oil, and garlic, then season with salt and pepper. Set aside to marinate for at least 1 hour before serving.

2 To serve, mix the greens, fennel, and the remaining oil and vinegar, then season with salt and pepper and divide between individual serving plates. Scatter the goat cheese and apple slices over the top.

IF ADDING MEAT, omit the goat cheese. Season the pigeon breasts and sauté them in the oil for 1½ minutes on each side until cooked but still pink in the middle. Wrap in foil and leave to rest for 5 minutes, then cut into diagonal slices and arrange over the salad.

Potato salad niçoise

SERVES 4   **PREPARATION 15 MINS**   **TO COOK 15 MINS**

This substantial salad is a twist on a classic recipe. It **also works well with baby fava beans**, cooked and popped out of their shells, instead of green beans.

1 Boil the potatoes for 15 minutes until tender. Add the beans for the last 5 minutes of cooking time and the corn for the last minute. Drain, rinse with cold water, and drain again.

2 Meanwhile, hard-boil the eggs in simmering water for 12 minutes. Drain and plunge into cold water.

3 Put the cooked vegetables in a large bowl with the onion, separated into rings, tomatoes, cucumber, lettuce, basil, and olives.

4 Whisk the dressing ingredients together until thick and smooth. Pour over the salad and toss gently.

5 Shell the hard-boiled eggs and cut each into quarters. Pile the salad into bowls and top each with 4 quarters of egg.

IF ADDING FISH, add 2 smoked mackerel fillets, skinned and broken into large flakes, to the salad. Use only 2 eggs instead of 4.

INGREDIENTS

12oz (350g) baby
  new potatoes
4oz (115g) green beans,
  trimmed and cut
  into short lengths
4oz (115g) baby corn,
  cut into short lengths
4 large eggs
1 small red onion, thinly sliced
12 cherry tomatoes, halved
¼ cucumber, cut into
  small chunks
1 head Little Gem lettuce,
  torn in pieces
handful of basil leaves,
  shredded
handful of black olives,
  pitted if liked

For the dressing
3 tbsp extra virgin olive oil
1 tbsp white wine vinegar
1 tsp Dijon mustard
½ tsp granulated sugar
salt and freshly ground
  black pepper

OPTIONAL FISH
2 smoked mackerel fillets

Pasta, noodles, and rice

Pasta with asparagus and zucchini

SERVES 4   **PREPARATION 10 MINS**   TO COOK **20 MINS**

This easy pasta dish is a simple way to turn asparagus into a substantial supper, with **lemon zest and salty capers bringing out the freshness of the ingredients.**

INGREDIENTS

1 tbsp olive oil
1 onion, finely chopped
sea salt
4 small zucchini, 2 diced
    and 2 grated
3 garlic cloves, grated or
    finely chopped
bunch of thin asparagus
    spears, trimmed, and
    each cut into 3 pieces
½ cup of white wine
1–2 tsp rinsed, dried, and
    chopped capers
grated zest of 1 lemon
12oz (350g) dried penne pasta
handful of flat-leaf parsley,
    finely chopped
Parmesan cheese, grated,
    to serve

OPTIONAL MEAT

9oz (250g) chicken livers,
    trimmed and cut into
    bite-sized pieces
2 tbsp olive oil
2 tsp chopped sage

1 Heat the oil in a large frying pan, add the onion and a pinch of salt, and cook over low heat for 5 minutes, or until soft and translucent. Add all the zucchini and cook for 10 minutes, or until they have cooked down and softened, but not browned.

2 Stir in the garlic and asparagus. Add the wine, increase the heat, and boil for 2–3 minutes. Return it to a simmer and cook for 2–3 minutes more, or until the asparagus has softened. Remove from the heat and stir in the capers and lemon zest.

3 Meanwhile, cook the pasta in a large pot of salted boiling water for 10 minutes, or until it is cooked but still has a bit of bite to it. Drain, reserving a tiny amount of the cooking water. Return the pasta to the pot, add the zucchini mixture and parsley, then toss it together. Sprinkle with the Parmesan and serve.

IF ADDING MEAT, sauté the chicken livers in the oil with the sage for 3–4 minutes until browned but still pink in the center. Season well and add to the pasta with the zucchini mixture at step 3.

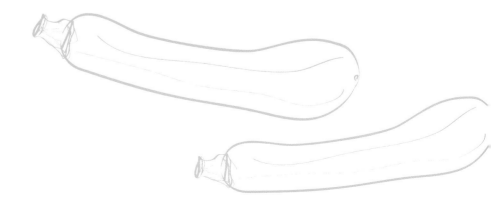

Lemon and asparagus pasta

SERVES 4   **PREPARATION 5 MINS**   **TO COOK 10–12 MINS**

Try to get the freshest new season asparagus for this simple supper dish, in which lively flavors come from just a few well-chosen ingredients.

1 Bring a small pan of salted water to a boil. Blanch the asparagus in the boiling water for 2 minutes. Drain and refresh in cold water.

2 Place a grill pan on the stove top to heat up. Drizzle the blanched asparagus with a little oil and season well with salt and pepper. Cook the asparagus on the hot grill for 5–6 minutes, turning it occasionally until heated through. Set aside.

3 Bring a large pot of salted water to a boil. Add the pasta to the pot and cook according to package instructions, giving it a stir at the beginning to prevent it from sticking together.

4 Heat the remaining oil in a large frying pan and add the garlic, lemon zest, and chile. Sauté for 30 seconds, then add the lemon juice, salt, plenty of pepper, and the nutmeg. Remove from the heat.

5 Drain the pasta and add it to the frying pan along with the asparagus and parsley. Toss well to mix. Divide between plates and serve sprinkled with Parmesan.

IF ADDING SHELLFISH, put the sea scallops in the pan at step 4 and sauté for 30–60 seconds until just opaque (but no longer or they will toughen). Continue as before.

INGREDIENTS

9oz (250g) asparagus, trimmed and halved
6 tbsp olive oil
salt and freshly ground black pepper
12oz (350g) tagliatelle
2 garlic cloves, crushed
grated zest and juice of 1 large lemon
1 red chile, seeded and finely chopped
½ tsp grated nutmeg
3 tbsp finely chopped flat-leaf parsley
Parmesan cheese, grated, to serve

OPTIONAL SHELLFISH

7oz (200g) sea scallops (thawed and dried on paper towels if frozen)

Farfalle with spinach, avocado, baby plum tomatoes, and pumpkin seeds

SERVES 4   PREPARATION **10 MINS**   TO COOK **16 MINS**

A light yet intensely flavored summer pasta dish with added crunch from pumpkin seeds. Any black olives may be used here, but briny kalamata olives work best.

INGREDIENTS

14oz (400g) dried farfalle pasta
2 tbsp olive oil
4 scallions, cut into
    short lengths
1 garlic clove, finely chopped
1 tsp dried chile flakes
12oz (350g) baby
    spinach leaves
⅔ cup vegetable stock
4 sun-dried
    tomatoes, chopped
6oz (175g) baby plum
    tomatoes, halved
1oz (30g) pitted black
    olives, sliced
1½ tbsp pickled capers
2 avocados, peeled, pitted,
    and diced
squeeze of lemon juice
salt and freshly ground
    black pepper
3 tbsp pumpkin seeds
lemon wedges and a few torn
    basil leaves, to garnish

OPTIONAL FISH

12oz (350g) skinned salmon
    fillet, cut into cubes

1 Cook the pasta according to the package directions. Drain. Heat the oil in a deep-sided sauté pan or wok. Add the scallions and garlic and fry, stirring gently, for 1 minute. Stir in the chiles.

2 Add the spinach and stock and simmer, turning over gently for about 2 minutes until beginning to wilt. Gently fold in the pasta and the remaining ingredients. Simmer for 3 minutes until most of the liquid has been absorbed.

3 Pile into warmed, shallow bowls. Garnish with lemon wedges and a few torn basil leaves.

IF ADDING FISH, omit the avocados and add the salmon fillet with the spinach at step 2.

Pasta with butternut squash, chile, and Parmesan cheese

SERVES 4   **PREPARATION 20 MINS**   TO COOK **30 MINS**

Ripening pumpkins and squashes herald the onset of autumn. Perfect for those slightly cooler days, **this dish has the comfort of cream and the warmth of red chiles**.

INGREDIENTS

3 tbsp olive oil

7oz (200g) butternut squash, peeled, halved, seeded, and diced

salt and freshly ground black pepper

1 garlic clove, crushed

½ red chile, seeded and finely chopped

8 sage leaves

⅔ cup half-and-half

scant 1oz (25g) Parmesan cheese, grated, plus extra to serve

12oz (350g) conchiglie pasta

OPTIONAL MEAT

4 good-quality mild pork sausages, cut into small chunks

1 tbsp olive oil

1 Heat 2 tbsp oil in a frying pan, add the squash, and toss in the oil. Add 3 tbsp water and some salt and pepper. Bring to a boil and reduce the heat to as low as possible. Cover and cook very gently for 10 minutes until soft, stirring occasionally. Leave to cool for a few minutes. Meanwhile, gently fry the garlic, chile, and sage in a little oil for 2–3 minutes.

2 Once the squash has cooled slightly, put it into a blender or food processor. Add the half-and-half and Parmesan, the cooked garlic, chile, and sage mixture, and a little salt and plenty of pepper. Blend it all to a fine purée, adding 1–2 tbsp water if it looks too thick.

3 Cook the pasta until al dente and drain it. Quickly reheat the sauce in the pasta pan, adding more water if it seems a little stiff. Put the pasta back into the pan and mix it well, allowing the sauce to coat the pasta. Serve with plenty of fresh Parmesan.

IF ADDING MEAT, fry the sausages in the oil, stirring, for about 3 minutes until browned and cooked through. Drain on paper towels and stir through the sauce-coated pasta at step 3.

Ricotta and squash ravioli

SERVES 4   **PREPARATION 1 HOUR, PLUS CHILLING**   **TO COOK 4–5 MINS**

You can make the ravioli a day in advance, if you wish. Dust them with cornmeal, layer in a sealable plastic container with oiled plastic wrap in between, cover, and chill.

1 Sift the flour into a bowl. Make a well in the center and add the eggs. Gradually mix together to form a dough. Knead gently on a lightly floured surface for about 5 minutes until smooth and elastic. Wrap in plastic wrap and chill for at least 30 minutes.

2 To make the ravioli filling, cook the squash as for the pasta dish on the opposite page. Cool slightly then purée until smooth in a food processor. Leave to cool. Place the ricotta, Parmesan, garlic, and nutmeg in a bowl. Stir in the squash and season with salt and pepper. Chill.

3 Roll out the pasta dough very thinly on a lightly floured surface. Cut out 76–80 rounds using a 2½in (6cm) round fluted cutter, rekneading and rolling the trimmings as necessary. Place ½ heaped tsp of filling on half the rounds. Brush the other rounds with water, place on top, dampened sides down, and pinch the edges together to seal. This will make 38–40 ravioli. Dust with cornmeal to prevent them from sticking together. Cover and chill until required.

4 Bring a large pot of salted water to a boil. Add the pasta and cook for 4–5 minutes, or until al dente. Drain and return to the pan.

5 For the sage butter, heat the oil, butter, lemon zest, and sage together, stirring until the butter melts. Season with plenty of pepper. Add to the pasta and toss well to mix. Serve in shallow bowls, sprinkled with some grated Parmesan.

IF ADDING MEAT, omit the ricotta cheese at step 2 and add the ground pork instead. Gradually mash the squash into the meat to form a paste, then continue as before.

INGREDIENTS

1½ cups tipo "00" pasta
    flour (or all-purpose flour)
3 large eggs, beaten
all-purpose flour, for dusting
cornmeal, for dusting

For the filling
1 tbsp olive oil
6oz (175g) butternut squash,
    peeled, halved, seeded,
    and diced
salt and freshly ground
    black pepper
3oz (85g) ricotta cheese
1oz (30g) Parmesan cheese,
    grated, plus extra to serve
1 garlic clove, crushed
½ tsp grated nutmeg

For the sage butter
3 tbsp olive oil
4 tbsp butter
grated zest of ½ lemon
2 tsp roughly chopped
    sage leaves

OPTIONAL MEAT
3oz (85g) ground pork

Pumpkin, spinach, and Gorgonzola lasagne

SERVES 4   **PREPARATION 25–30 MINS**   TO COOK **1–1¼ HRS**

This vegetable lasagne is **rich and satisfying, with fresh sage and nutmeg bringing the flavors alive.** If pumpkin is not available, use butternut squash or sweet potato.

INGREDIENTS

small pumpkin or butternut
  squash (approx. 1¾lb/800g)
  halved, peeled, seeded,
  and chopped into
  bite-sized pieces
1 tbsp olive oil
salt and freshly ground
  black pepper
8 sage leaves,
  roughly chopped
pinch of grated nutmeg
pinch of dried chile
  flakes (optional)
pinch of allspice
7oz (200g) spinach
10 pre-cooked lasagne sheets
4½oz (125g) Gorgonzola
  cheese, chopped
lightly dressed green salad,
  to serve

For the sauce
4 tbsp butter
¼ cup all-purpose flour
3 cups milk
1 bay leaf

OPTIONAL MEAT
8oz (225g) ground pork
1 onion, finely chopped
1 garlic clove, crushed
2 tbsp grated Parmesan cheese

1 Preheat the oven to 400°F (200°C). Place the pumpkin on a large baking sheet, add the oil and plenty of salt and pepper, and toss to coat; the baking sheet must be large or the pumpkin will steam rather than roast. Sprinkle over the sage, nutmeg, chile (if using), and allspice and stir. Roast for 20–30 minutes, stirring halfway, until golden, then remove. Stir in the spinach, which will wilt in a few minutes. Set aside. Reduce the oven temperature to 375°F (190°C).

2 For the sauce, melt the butter in a medium pan. Remove from the heat and blend in the flour. Gradually blend in the milk, stirring continuously with a wooden spoon or wire whisk. Add the bay leaf. Return to the heat and bring to a boil, stirring all the time until thickened, then cook for 2 minutes, continuing to stir as before. Add salt and pepper to taste, discard the bay leaf, and set aside.

3 Spoon half the pumpkin mixture into an 8 × 12in (20 × 30cm) ovenproof dish. Seasoning well between each layer, add half the lasagne sheets, half the sauce, and half the Gorgonzola. Repeat to use up all the ingredients. Place on a baking sheet and bake for 30–40 minutes until golden and bubbling. Serve with a green salad.

IF ADDING MEAT, stir-fry the pork, onion, and garlic in a frying pan until all the meat grains are separate and browned. Add to the cooked pumpkin mixture, made with only 14oz (400g) pumpkin, at step 1 and check the seasoning. Layer, using 3oz (85g) Gorgonzola in one layer only. Dust the top layer of sauce with the Parmesan and bake as before.

Pasta primavera

SERVES 4   **PREPARATION** **15 MINS**   **TO COOK** **30 MINS**

As the name suggests, **this light, fresh dish celebrates spring vegetables in Italy**. In cooler climates, it is more suited to serving in early summer.

INGREDIENTS

7oz (200g) green beans,
    trimmed
salt and freshly ground
    black pepper
bunch of thin asparagus,
    trimmed
12oz (350g) dried linguine
    or other pasta shapes
1 tbsp olive oil
3 zucchini, halved lengthways
    and chopped
pinch of saffron
    threads (optional)
4 tomatoes, roughly chopped
Parmesan or Pecorino cheese,
    grated, to serve

OPTIONAL FISH

2oz (50g) can anchovies,
    drained and roughly
    chopped

1 Place the beans in a pot of salted boiling water and cook for 4–5 minutes until tender but still with some bite. Remove with a slotted spoon (reserve the water in the pan), refresh in cold water, and roughly chop. Add the asparagus to the reserved boiling water and cook for 6–8 minutes until almost tender. Drain, refresh, and roughly chop.

2 Put the pasta in a large pot of salted boiling water and cook according to package instructions, stirring it at the beginning to prevent it from sticking together. Drain well, return to the pot with a little of the cooking water, and toss together to combine.

3 Meanwhile, heat the oil in a large frying pan, add the zucchini, and season with salt and pepper. Add the saffron threads (if using) and cook over low-medium heat for about 10 minutes until the zucchini turn golden.

4 Add the beans, asparagus, and tomatoes to the frying pan. Stir and cook over low heat for 5 minutes. Add the vegetables to the pasta and toss to combine. Serve with the Parmesan or Pecorino and add more pepper, if you wish.

IF ADDING FISH, cook the zucchini, seasoning with just pepper (no salt). Add the anchovies after incorporating the vegetables with the pasta at step 4 and toss them all together over low heat until thoroughly heated through.

Spicy spaghetti with broccoli

SERVES 4   **PREPARATION 5 MINS**   TO COOK **20 MINS**

Here is a quick and simple way to make the most of delicious young broccoli rabe. The **spicy chile and zesty lemon flavors** are perfect for the winter months.

1 Trim the broccoli rabe and separate any multiple florets into single heads so that all are similar in size for even cooking. Slice any thicker stems in half and others diagonally.

2 Cook the spaghetti in a large pot of salted boiling water for about 10 minutes or until al dente. Drain and return to the pan.

3 Meanwhile, heat the oil in a non-stick wok or large frying pan, then add the broccoli rabe and scallions and stir-fry over medium heat for 5–10 minutes, or until tender.

4 Add the broccoli and scallions to the pan with the spaghetti. Add the chile flakes and lemon juice, and season with salt and pepper. Toss lightly over gentle heat. Serve immediately with a sprinkling of Parmesan cheese.

IF ADDING FISH, crumble the smoked salmon trimmings over the cooked broccoli with the scallions at step 3 and cook for 1–2 minutes before adding to the spaghetti.

INGREDIENTS

7oz (200g) broccoli rabe
14oz (400g) dried spaghetti
5 tbsp olive oil, for frying
bunch of scallions, chopped
½ tsp dried chile flakes
juice of ½ lemon
sea salt and freshly ground
  black pepper
scant 1oz (25g) Parmesan
  cheese, grated

OPTIONAL FISH
6oz (175g) smoked
  salmon trimmings

Linguine with baby fava beans, cherry tomatoes, and scallions

SERVES 4   **PREPARATION 15 MINS**   TO COOK **18 MINS**

Popping the beans out of their skins can be fiddly. Although not essential, it's worth doing as the silky texture of the skinned beans enhances the dish.

INGREDIENTS

2 cups vegetable stock
9oz (250g) fresh shelled or
   frozen baby fava beans
1lb (450g) dried linguine
2 tbsp butter
bunch of scallions, chopped
5½oz (150g) cherry
   tomatoes, halved
10fl oz (300ml) crème fraîche
2 tbsp chopped parsley
2 tbsp chopped sage
salt and freshly ground
   black pepper
1oz (30g) Parmesan
   cheese, grated

OPTIONAL MEAT

3½oz (100g) chopped pancetta

1 Bring the stock to a boil in a saucepan. Add the fava beans, then bring back to a boil and cook for about 8 minutes until tender. Drain, reserving the stock. When cool enough to handle, gently squeeze the beans out of their skins and set aside.

2 Meanwhile, in a pan, cook the linguine according to the package directions. Drain and return to the pan.

3 Melt the butter in the rinsed-out bean saucepan. Add the scallions and fry, stirring, over low heat for 3 minutes until softened, but not browned. Add the reserved stock, bring to a rapid boil, and continue to boil for about 4 minutes until well reduced and syrupy. Stir in the cherry tomatoes to just heat through, but not soften too much.

4 Stir in the crème fraîche, herbs, salt and pepper, and half the Parmesan cheese. Add the fava beans and mix gently to heat through. Pour the bean mixture into the pasta and toss over gentle heat until every strand is coated. Pile into warmed bowls, sprinkle with the remaining Parmesan, and serve.

IF ADDING MEAT, at step 3, omit the butter and fry the pancetta in the saucepan, stirring, until the fat runs. Add the scallions to the pancetta and continue as before.

Vegetable chow mein with black beans

SERVES 4–6   **PREPARATION 15 MINS**   TO COOK **12 MINS**

This simple but delicious stir-fry is a **colorful melange of textures and flavors**. Use cauliflower instead of broccoli, or cucumber instead of zucchini, if you prefer.

1 Cook the noodles in boiling water according to the package directions, then drain and set aside.

2 Meanwhile, heat the oil in a wok or large frying pan. Add the garlic, ginger, scallions, pepper, and carrot and stir-fry for 2 minutes. Add the zucchini, broccoli, snowpeas, and corn and stir-fry for a further 5 minutes.

3 Add the beans, sauces, and sherry and toss for 1–2 minutes until hot. Add the noodles and toss until well combined and piping hot. Pile into warmed bowls and serve.

IF ADDING MEAT, stir-fry the chicken strips in the oil for 2 minutes before starting to cook the vegetables. Use just 1 can of black beans.

INGREDIENTS

4 nests of dried medium
   Chinese egg noodles
2 tbsp sunflower or vegetable oil
2 garlic cloves, finely chopped
1 tsp grated fresh ginger
bunch of scallions, cut into
   short diagonal lengths
1 red bell pepper, seeded
   and diced
1 carrot, cut into thin strips
1 zucchini, cut into thin strips
1 small head of broccoli
   (approx. 5oz/140g), cut
   into tiny florets
4oz (115g) snowpeas
6 baby corn, cut into
   short lengths
2 × 14oz (400g) cans black
   beans, drained and rinsed
6 tbsp black bean sauce
2 tbsp soy sauce
1 tbsp mirin or dry sherry

OPTIONAL MEAT

2 large chicken breasts,
   cut into thin strips

Mixed mushroom and bok choy stir-fry with soba noodles

SERVES 4   **PREPARATION 10 MINS**   TO COOK **8 MINS**

This dish uses cultivated mushrooms that originate from Japan. They are widely available in supermarkets, but crimini mushrooms can be substituted, if necessary.

INGREDIENTS

9oz (250g) dried soba or
  brown udon noodles
6 tbsp tamari or light
  soy sauce
1 tbsp lemon juice
2 tsp grated fresh ginger
2 garlic cloves, crushed
1 tsp chopped lemongrass
  (or lemongrass purée)
1 tbsp granulated sugar
¼–½ tsp wasabi paste
8oz (225g) fresh shelled
  or frozen edamame
3 tbsp sunflower or vegetable oil
1 bunch of scallions,
  trimmed and sliced
2 celery stalks, cut
  into matchsticks
3½oz (100g) shiitake
  mushrooms, sliced
3½oz (100g) oyster
  mushrooms, sliced
3½oz (100g) enoki
  mushrooms, trimmed
  of base and separated
2 heads bok choy (approx.
  7oz/200g), coarsely shredded
2 tbsp sesame seeds,
  to garnish

OPTIONAL MEAT
8oz (225g) pork stir-fry strips

1 Cook the noodles according to the package directions. Drain and set aside.

2 Whisk the tamari sauce, lemon juice, ginger, garlic, lemongrass, sugar, and wasabi paste in a small bowl with 2 tbsp water and set aside. Boil the edamame in water for 3 minutes. Drain and set aside.

3 Heat the oil in a large frying pan or wok. Add the scallions and celery and stir-fry for 2 minutes. Add all the mushrooms and stir-fry for 3 minutes. Add the bok choy and edamame and stir-fry for 1 minute.

4 Add the noodles and the bowl of tamari sauce. Toss until everything is heated through and coated. Spoon into bowls and sprinkle with sesame seeds before serving.

IF ADDING MEAT, omit the edamame and add the pork strips with the scallions at step 3.

Thai noodle stir-fry

SERVES 4   **PREPARATION 15 MINS**   TO COOK **20 MINS**

Perfect in stir-fries, Asian greens add color and a fresh flavor to the finished dish. The rice noodles used here are quite delicate—be careful not to overcook them.

INGREDIENTS

6oz (175g) dried thin rice
  noodles
3 tbsp sunflower or
  vegetable oil
1 onion, sliced
1 stalk of lemongrass, outer
  leaves removed, woody end
  trimmed, and finely chopped
1 tsp finely grated fresh ginger
1 red chile, seeded and
  finely chopped
1 orange bell pepper, seeded
  and sliced
4oz (115g) sugarsnap
  peas, trimmed
8oz (225g) shiitake
  mushrooms, sliced
3 heads baby bok choy,
  shredded
3 tbsp light soy sauce
1 tsp sweet chili sauce

OPTIONAL MEAT

3 boneless, skinless chicken
  breasts, cut into thin strips
1½ tbsp sunflower or
  vegetable oil

1 Soak the noodles in a bowl of boiling water until softened, or as directed on the package. Drain and set aside.

2 Heat the oil in a wok and stir-fry the onion for 2–3 minutes. Add the lemongrass, ginger, chile, pepper, sugarsnap peas, and mushrooms, and stir-fry for 2 minutes.

3 Add the bok choy and stir-fry for a further 2 minutes, then add the noodles. Pour in the soy sauce and sweet chili sauce. Toss everything together over the heat for 2–3 minutes, or until piping hot. Serve at once.

IF ADDING MEAT, season the chicken and stir-fry in oil for 2–3 minutes until lightly browned. Remove from the pan and set aside. Continue as before and add at step 3 after stir-frying the bok choy for 2 minutes.

Split pea, noodle, and vegetable pot

SERVES 4   **PREPARATION 15 MINS**   **TO COOK 1 HR**

The split peas will gradually absorb all the wonderful flavors of the spices, herbs, and coconut in this simple-to-cook noodle dish.

1 Soak the noodles in boiling water for 5 minutes, or as directed on the package, then drain and set aside.

2 Heat the oil in a large, heavy-based pan. Add the onion and cook on a low heat for 2–3 minutes. Season well with salt and pepper. Stir in the garlic, turmeric, and coriander and cook for 2 minutes.

3 Add the carrots and zucchini, turn to coat, and cook for 5 minutes. Stir in the split peas and add the coconut milk. Increase the heat and allow to bubble for 1 minute, then add the stock and bring to a boil.

4 Reduce to a simmer and cook over low heat, partially covered, for 40–50 minutes, or until the split peas begin to soften. Add hot water as needed—there should be plenty of liquid. Add the noodles for the last 5 minutes of cooking to heat through. Season well and serve garnished with the chopped cilantro.

IF ADDING FISH, before cooking the onions in step 2, fry the monkfish for 4 minutes, stirring. Remove from the pan with a slotted spoon and set aside. Return to the pan with the noodles at step 4.

INGREDIENTS

3oz (85g) dried rice noodles
1 tbsp olive oil
1 onion, finely chopped
salt and freshly ground
   black pepper
2 garlic cloves, finely chopped
1 tsp turmeric
1 tsp coriander seeds, crushed
3 carrots, diced
2 zucchini, diced
8oz (225g) yellow split
   peas, rinsed
¾ cup coconut milk
3½ cups hot vegetable stock
large handful of cilantro
   leaves, roughly chopped,
   to garnish

OPTIONAL FISH

8oz (225g) monkfish fillet,
   cut into small chunks

Four ways with
Asparagus

Crêpes with asparagus ▶

TAKES 20 mins **MAKES** 8

Mix ¾ cup **all-purpose flour** and a pinch of **salt** in a bowl. Make a well, crack 1 **large egg** in, and stir in a little of 1¼ cup **milk**. Stir in the remaining milk until mixed. Chill for 30 minutes. Cut 8–12 **asparagus spears** into thirds and boil in salted water for 4 minutes. Refresh in cold water, then mix with chopped **dill**, 9oz (250g) crumbled **feta cheese**, and freshly ground **black pepper**. Heat a little **olive oil**, swirl it around the pan, then pour it out. Stir the batter, then spoon in 2 tbsp, swirling it around the pan. Cook for 2 minutes, then turn and cook the other side for 1 minute. Slide onto a plate. Spoon filling onto half the crêpe and roll it up.

◀ Asparagus with mustard sauce

TAKES 20 mins **SERVES** 4

Take a large frying pan and add water to a depth of ½in (1½cm). Bring to a boil over high heat and add 1½lb (675g) **asparagus spears**. Reduce the heat to low, cover, and cook for 3–4 minutes. Drain the asparagus, rinse, pat dry, and chill. In a bowl, whisk together ¼ cup **olive oil** and 1 tbsp each **white wine vinegar** and **Dijon mustard**. Beat in 2 tbsp **Greek-style yogurt** and season with **salt** and freshly ground **black pepper**. Spoon the mustard sauce over the asparagus and sprinkle with some chopped **red onion** to finish.

Green and purple asparagus have a **fragrant, grassy flavor**, while white asparagus, which is grown in the dark to blanch it, is sweeter. **Choose stems with tight buds.** Trim the stalks, then peel them if they are thick.

Grilled asparagus and Gorgonzola ▶

TAKES 30 mins **SERVES** 4

Heat the barbecue or grill pan until hot. Trim 16 fresh **asparagus spears** and cook in boiling, salted water for 2–3 minutes. Drain and place on the barbecue or grill pan. Grill over medium heat for about 5 minutes, brushing the spears with a little **extra virgin olive oil** as they are cooking, and turning them as they char. To serve, divide the asparagus among 4 serving plates. Gently slice or crumble 5½oz (150g) **Gorgonzola cheese** over the asparagus. Sprinkle with freshly ground **black pepper** and drizzle with olive oil. Serve immediately.

◀ Asparagus frittata on crostini

TAKES 40 mins **SERVES** 4

Preheat the oven to 400°F (200°C). Coat 4 slices of **sourdough bread** in **olive oil**, season with **salt** and freshly ground **black pepper**, and bake for 15 minutes. Rub with 1 **garlic clove**. Blanch 8 **asparagus spears** in salted, boiling water for 3 minutes. Refresh, drain, and halve lengthways. Heat 2 tbsp olive oil and cook 2 tbsp chopped **onion** for 5 minutes. Add the spears and cook for 2 minutes. Whisk 4 **large eggs**, ½ cup **heavy cream**, and 2oz (60g) grated **Parmesan**. Season and pour over the spears. Cook until almost set, then brown under a hot broiler. Tear into 4 pieces and place on the crostini with **flat-leaf parsley**.

Spicy mixed greens and pea stir-fry with hoisin sauce and toasted sesame seeds

SERVES 4   **PREPARATION** 15 MINS   TO COOK **13 MINS**

This beautiful combination of **fresh-tasting greens with toasted sesame seeds and nuts** is simple to make. For a little heat, add a teaspoon of crushed dried chile flakes.

INGREDIENTS

2 × 10oz (300g) packs pre-cooked thick udon noodles, or a 9oz (250g) pack dried noodles
¼ cup sesame seeds
2 tbsp sunflower or vegetable oil
2 onions, halved and sliced
½ small head Napa cabbage, shredded
7oz (200g) Brussels sprouts, sliced
2 heads bok choy, shredded
4oz (115g) shiitake mushrooms, sliced
4oz (115g) frozen peas, thawed
large handful of roasted, unsalted peanuts or cashew nuts
2 tbsp soy sauce
2 tbsp hoisin sauce
⅓ cup vegetable stock
2 tbsp sesame oil, for drizzling

OPTIONAL MEAT
2 boneless, skinless duck breasts, cut into thin strips

1 If using dried noodles, cook them according to the package directions. Drain and set aside. Toast the sesame seeds in a large frying pan or wok. Pour into a bowl and set aside.

2 Heat the sunflower oil in the frying pan or wok, add the onions, and stir-fry for 3 minutes until softened and lightly golden. Add all the greens, mushrooms, and peas and stir-fry for 2 minutes until the greens are wilted, but still crunchy.

3 Add the nuts, sauces, and stock and simmer for 2 minutes. Add the noodles and half the sesame seeds and toss well.

4 Pile into bowls, drizzle with sesame oil, and sprinkle with the remaining sesame seeds. Serve hot.

IF ADDING MEAT, stir-fry the duck with the onions at step 2, then continue as before but omitting the peanuts or cashew nuts.

Stir-fried ribbon vegetables with coconut noodles

SERVES 4   **PREPARATION 15 MINS**   TO COOK **8 MINS**

The coconut noodles add a delicious base to this quick-to-cook stir-fry. They also taste great with spiced grilled eggplant and zucchini slices.

1 Cook the noodles according to the package directions, but for half the time stated. Drain and return to the pan. Add the coconut milk, salt, and half the cilantro. Bring to a boil, then cover and set aside.

2 For the ribbon vegetables, peel the zucchini, carrots, and daikon into thin strips using a potato peeler or mandolin. If using a turnip, cut any wide strips in half lengthways.

3 Heat the oils in a wok or large frying pan. Add the vegetables, chiles, ginger, and garlic and stir-fry for 1–2 minutes so they are soft but still retain some crunch. Add the soy sauce, cashew nuts, and the remaining cilantro and toss well.

4 Heat the noodles in the coconut milk until boiling again, then spoon into large bowls. Pile the vegetables on top and serve with extra soy sauce, if desired.

IF ADDING SHELLFISH, stir the shrimp into the ribbon vegetables at step 3 instead of the cashew nuts.

INGREDIENTS

9oz (250g) dried brown udon noodles
14½oz (410g) can coconut milk
salt
¼ cup chopped cilantro
2 small zucchini
4 carrots
½ small daikon, or 1 large turnip
1 tbsp sunflower or vegetable oil
1 tbsp sesame oil
2 fat red chiles, seeded and cut into thin strips
2 tsp grated fresh ginger or galangal
2 garlic cloves, crushed
2 tbsp soy sauce, plus extra to serve
handful of raw cashew nuts

OPTIONAL SHELLFISH

large handful of cooked, peeled large shrimp (thawed if frozen)

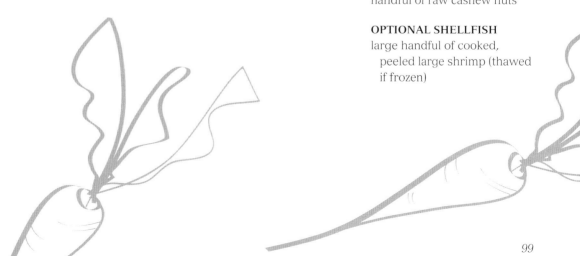

Baked vegetable and chickpea pilau

SERVES 4 **PREPARATION 10 MINS** TO COOK **25 MINS, PLUS STANDING**

This is a complete meal, but to add a little relish on the side, **serve with mint raita**—just add some dried mint to thick, plain yogurt and season to taste.

INGREDIENTS

2 tbsp sunflower or vegetable oil
1 onion, finely chopped
2 carrots, finely diced
2 zucchini, finely diced
1 red bell pepper, seeded
 and finely diced
½ tsp ground turmeric
2 garlic cloves, crushed
14oz (400g) can chickpeas,
 drained
9oz (250g) Basmati rice
2 cups hot vegetable stock
3oz (85g) fresh shelled
 or thawed frozen peas
pinch of salt
1 bay leaf
2in (5cm) piece of
 cinnamon stick
4 cardamom pods, split

OPTIONAL MEAT
2 large boneless, skinless
 chicken breasts, cut into
 small pieces

1 Preheat the oven to 425°F (220°C). Heat the oil in a Dutch oven and fry the onion, carrots, zucchini, and pepper over low heat, stirring, for 4 minutes until softened, but not browned.

2 Stir in the turmeric, garlic, chickpeas, and rice until all the grains are glistening. Add the stock, peas, salt, bay leaf, and spices. Bring to a boil, stir, cover, and cook in the oven for 20 minutes.

3 Remove from the oven but do not uncover. Leave to stand for 10 minutes, then fluff up with a fork. Remove the bay leaf and spices, if liked, before serving.

IF ADDING MEAT, fry the chicken with the onion and other vegetables at step 1 before adding the rice. Omit the chickpeas.

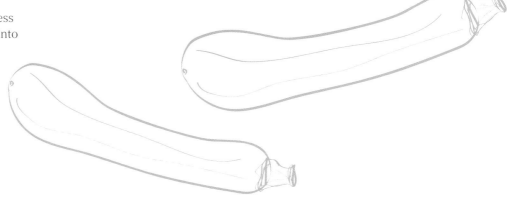

Cinnamon, almond, and raisin brown rice pilaf with grilled eggplant

SERVES 4   **PREPARATION 10 MINS**   TO COOK **45 MINS, PLUS STANDING**

There's a real **taste of the Middle East in this sweet, spiced pilaf**. Use white rice instead of brown, if you prefer—but cook it for 20 minutes only.

1 Peel the strings off the celery with a potato peeler, then chop. Heat the oil in a large saucepan. Add the celery, leek, carrots, and garlic and fry, stirring, for 3 minutes. Stir in the rice and spices and cook, stirring, until every grain is glistening.

2 Add the oregano, stock, raisins, mushrooms, almonds, and salt and pepper. Bring to a boil, stirring, then reduce the heat to low. Cover and cook for 40 minutes, then remove from the heat and leave to stand for 5 minutes.

3 While the rice is cooking, heat a grill pan. Brush the eggplant slices with oil and grill in batches for 2–3 minutes on each side until striped brown and tender, pressing down with a spatula as they cook. Set aside and keep warm.

4 Fluff up the rice, taste, and adjust the seasoning, if necessary. Gently stir in the eggplant slices and feta, pile onto warmed plates, and garnish with a few sliced olives.

IF ADDING MEAT, fry the lamb with the leeks and carrots and continue as before. Use only 2oz (60g) feta cheese and crumble it over the pilaf instead of stirring cubes into it.

INGREDIENTS

2 celery stalks
2 tbsp sunflower or vegetable oil, plus extra for brushing
1 leek, chopped
2 carrots, chopped
1 garlic clove, crushed
8oz (225g) brown Basmati rice
1 tsp ground cinnamon
1 tsp grated fresh ginger
½ tsp ground cumin
1 tsp dried oregano
2½ cups vegetable stock
¼ cup raisins
4oz (115g) crimini mushrooms, sliced
4oz (115g) whole blanched almonds
salt and freshly ground black pepper
2 eggplants, cut lengthways into ¼in (5mm) thick slices
7oz (200g) feta cheese, diced
a few sliced black and green olives, to garnish

OPTIONAL MEAT

8oz (225g) lamb loin, trimmed and cut into small cubes

Vegetable ramen noodle bowl

SERVES 4   **PREPARATION 10 MINS, PLUS SOAKING**   **TO COOK 10 MINS**

Miso paste enhances the flavor of this dish, but omit it if preferred and season with more tamari. Use dashi powder to make the vegetable stock, if it is available.

INGREDIENTS

2 × 4in (10cm) pieces
   wakame seaweed
2 heaped tbsp dried
   shiitake mushrooms
9oz (250g) dried ramen
   noodles (or brown
   rice noodles)
3½ cups vegetable stock
2 tbsp tamari or light soy sauce
2 tsp light brown sugar
3 tbsp mirin (or dry sherry)
4 scallions, chopped
1 red bell pepper, seeded
   and finely sliced
2 heads of bok choy, cut
   into thick shreds
1 zucchini, cut into
   matchsticks
4 radishes, sliced
7oz (225g) can bamboo
   shoots, drained
1 tsp dried chile flakes (optional)
1 tbsp red miso paste
9oz (250g) block firm tofu,
   cut into 8 slices
sweet chili sauce, to drizzle

OPTIONAL MEAT

3½ cups chicken stock
2 boneless, skinless chicken
   breasts, cut into thin strips

1 Soak the wakame and mushrooms in 1¼ cups warm water for 30 minutes. Lift out the wakame and cut out any thick stalk, if necessary. If the wakame is large, cut into pieces before returning to the soaking water with the mushrooms.

2 Cook the noodles according to the package directions. Drain. Put the stock in a large saucepan with the remaining ingredients, except the miso paste and tofu. Add the wakame, mushrooms, and soaking water. Bring to a boil, reduce the heat, and simmer for 3 minutes.

3 Blend a ladleful of the stock with the miso paste until smooth. Pour back into the pan and stir gently. Taste and add more tamari, if necessary. Make sure the soup is very hot but not boiling.

4 Divide the noodles between 4 large open soup bowls. Add 2 slices of tofu to each bowl and ladle the very hot soup over. Serve at once with sweet chili sauce to drizzle over, if using.

IF ADDING MEAT, omit the tofu. Use chicken stock instead of vegetable stock, if preferred. Simmer the chicken in a little of the stock for 3 minutes, then add all the remaining ingredients at step 2 and continue as before.

Fiery peanut and pepper noodles

SERVES 4   **PREPARATION 20 MINS**   TO COOK **4–5 MINS**

This is **a great meal to put together in a hurry**. If fresh noodles aren't available, use 9oz (250g) dried noodles, reconstituted according to package directions.

INGREDIENTS

1 red bell pepper
1 green bell pepper
1 tbsp sunflower or
   vegetable oil
4 scallions, chopped
1 garlic clove, finely chopped
1 zucchini, finely chopped
1–2 green jalapeño chiles,
   seeded and chopped
1 tsp grated ginger
1 tbsp chopped
   flat-leaf parsley
1 tbsp chopped cilantro, plus
   a few torn leaves, to garnish
grated zest and juice of 1 lime
¼ cup crunchy peanut butter
3 tbsp soy sauce
1 tbsp dry sherry
1lb 2oz (500g) fresh
   egg noodles
2oz (60g) roasted peanuts,
   chopped, to garnish

OPTIONAL MEAT

8oz (225g) beef tenderloin cut
   into strips
1 tbsp soy sauce
1 garlic clove, crushed
2 tbsp sunflower or
   vegetable oil

1 Grill the peppers for about 15 minutes, turning once or twice, until blackened in places. Put in a plastic bag and leave until cold. Rub off the skins and dice the flesh, discarding the stalk and seeds.

2 Heat the oil in a wok or large frying pan. Add the scallions, garlic, and zucchini and stir-fry for 1 minute. Add the peppers, chiles, ginger, herbs, lime zest and juice, peanut butter, soy sauce, sherry, and ½ cup water. Stir until the peanut butter melts. Add the noodles, then toss for 2 minutes until piping hot. Pile into warmed bowls and sprinkle with peanuts and a few torn cilantro leaves.

IF ADDING MEAT, toss the beef tenderloin strips in the soy sauce with the garlic. Stir-fry in the oil at step 2 for 2–3 minutes before adding the scallions and zucchini. Omit the peanuts in the garnish.

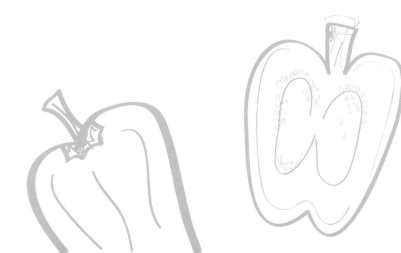

Mushroom risotto

SERVES 4   **PREPARATION 10 MINS, PLUS SOAKING**   **TO COOK 45 MINS**

Barley makes a fabulous, risotto-type dish that is easy to cook. Unlike rice, **it can produce a creamy, nutty-textured result with the liquid added all in one step**.

1 Soak the dried mushrooms in boiling water for 30 minutes until tender. Drain, chop, and set aside.

2 Soften the onion and garlic in the butter, stirring, for 2 minutes. Add the fresh mushrooms and wine. Simmer for 2 minutes. Stir in the barley and thyme. Add the stock and season with salt and pepper. Bring to a boil, then simmer for about 40 minutes, stirring twice, until the barley is tender but with a bit of bite and the liquid is almost absorbed.

3 Add the chopped mushrooms and half-and-half to the mixture and heat through, but do not boil. Garnish with thyme leaves and serve with the Parmesan cheese.

IF ADDING MEAT, dry-fry the pancetta at the beginning of step 2. Remove with a slotted spoon. Add a small knob of butter to the fat in the pan, then soften the onion as before. Return the pancetta to the pan before adding the stock and continue as before.

INGREDIENTS

1 tbsp dried mushrooms
1 onion, chopped
1 garlic clove, crushed
1 tbsp butter
8oz (225g) crimini
   mushrooms, sliced
⅔ cup dry white wine
7oz (200g) pearl barley
2 tsp chopped thyme, plus
   a few leaves, to garnish
2½ cups vegetable stock
salt and freshly ground
   black pepper
2–3 tbsp half-and-half
Parmesan cheese, grated,
   to serve

OPTIONAL MEAT
3½oz (100g) chopped pancetta

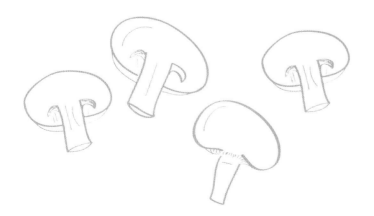

Cashew nut paella

SERVES 4   PREPARATION **10 MINS**   TO COOK **25 MINS**

Cashews are expensive nuts, but they make a delicious paella. Try substituting chopped cooked chestnuts or even toasted hazelnuts for a change.

INGREDIENTS

large pinch of saffron strands

2½ cups hot vegetable stock

2 tbsp olive oil

1 leek, chopped

1 onion, chopped

2 garlic cloves, crushed

1 red bell pepper, seeded
and chopped

1 carrot, chopped

9oz (250g) paella rice

⅔ cup dry white wine

4oz (115g) crimini
mushrooms, sliced

4oz (115g) roasted, unsalted
cashew nuts

salt and freshly ground
black pepper

4oz (115g) fresh shelled
or frozen peas

1½ tbsp chopped thyme

4 tomatoes, quartered

½ tsp smoked paprika

sprig of flat-leaf parsley and
lemon wedges, to garnish

crusty bread and green
salad, to serve

OPTIONAL SHELLFISH

12oz (350g) package (approx.)
frozen mixed seafood

1 Put the saffron in the stock to infuse. Heat the oil in a paella pan or large frying pan and fry the leek, onion, garlic, red pepper, and carrot, stirring, for 3 minutes until softened but not browned. Add the rice and stir until coated in oil and glistening.

2 Add the wine and boil until it has been absorbed, stirring. Stir in the saffron-infused stock, mushrooms, nuts, and some salt and pepper. Bring to a boil, stirring once, then reduce the heat, cover, and simmer very gently for 10 minutes.

3 Add the peas and thyme, stir gently, then distribute the tomatoes over the top. Cover and simmer very gently for a further 10 minutes until the rice is just tender and has absorbed most of the liquid but is still creamy.

4 Sprinkle the paprika over and stir through gently, taking care not to break up the tomatoes. Taste and adjust the seasoning, if necessary.

5 Garnish with a sprig of parsley and lemon wedges and serve hot with crusty bread and a green salad.

IF ADDING SHELLFISH, omit the cashew nuts, mushrooms, and half the peas and add the package of mixed seafood at step 3.

Beet risotto

SERVES 4   **PREPARATION 30 MINS**   TO COOK **1 HR**

The deep, earthy flavor of the beet and the sharp tang of goat cheese combine beautifully in this deep purple, rich risotto, laced with fragrant sage.

INGREDIENTS

1lb 2oz (500g) beets,
  peeled and diced
2 tbsp extra virgin olive oil,
  plus extra for tossing
salt and freshly ground
  black pepper
6 tbsp sunflower or
  vegetable oil
20 sage leaves
2 onions, finely diced
2 garlic cloves, crushed
12oz (350g) risotto rice
3½ cups vegetable stock
2oz (60g) Parmesan
  cheese, grated
7oz (200g) firm goat cheese,
  cut into ½in (1cm) cubes

OPTIONAL FISH

2 fillets smoked mackerel,
  skinned and flaked
¼ cup crème fraîche

1 Preheat the oven to 400°F (200°C). Toss the beets in a little olive oil and some salt and pepper. Wrap in foil and cook in the oven for 30–40 minutes until soft.

2 In a small pan, heat the vegetable oil over high heat until smoking. Drop in most of the sage leaves, a few at a time, and deep-fry for 5 seconds, or until they stop fizzing. Remove and drain.

3 Remove the beets from the oven and purée in a food processor with ¼ cup water, the remaining sage leaves, and some salt and pepper. Set aside.

4 In a large, heavy-based pan, fry the onions in olive oil over medium heat for 3 minutes until soft. Add the garlic and cook for 1 minute. Pour in the rice and stir so that the grains are coated in oil. Meanwhile, bring the stock to a low simmer in a separate pot.

5 Keeping the stock on a low simmer, add a ladle at a time to the rice, stirring continuously until each ladleful is absorbed, for about 15 minutes until the rice is almost cooked. Add the beet purée to the risotto and cook for another 5–10 minutes until the rice is just tender.

6 Remove the rice from the heat and season. Stir in two-thirds of the Parmesan and fold in the goat cheese. Serve garnished with the deep-fried sage leaves and the remaining Parmesan.

IF ADDING FISH, omit the goat cheese. Fold the smoked mackerel into the risotto at the end of step 5 and allow to heat through for 2 minutes. Top each portion with a spoonful of crème fraîche before garnishing with sage leaves and Parmesan.

Traffic-light risotto

SERVES 4–6   **PREPARATION 12 MINS**   TO COOK **30 MINS**

This is a fantastic, colorful dish that is very easy to prepare. It is quite filling, so will serve up to six people, depending upon their appetites.

1 Cut the squash into ½in (1cm) cubes and discard the seeds and skin. Melt the butter in a large pan and fry the onions until transparent. Add the red pepper and squash and continue to cook for a further 2 minutes.

2 Add the rice and stir until the grains are coated in butter, then add the wine (if using), or a cup of stock, and stir. Add the herbs and salt and pepper, and simmer until the wine (or stock) has evaporated.

3 Stir in 2 ladlefuls of stock and simmer until the liquid has evaporated again. Continue adding 2 ladlefuls of stock at a time, allowing it to evaporate until the rice is tender but al dente—about 20 minutes.

4 Add a further ladle of stock, the spinach, and the tomatoes, and simmer for a further 2 minutes. Stir, taste, and season again, if necessary. Serve the grated cheese separately, if using.

IF ADDING FISH, gently stir the cubed salmon fillet through the risotto with the last 2 ladlefuls of stock at step 3. Simmer for 2 minutes or until the salmon is just cooked through. Serve with wedges of lemon to squeeze over.

INGREDIENTS

1½lb (675g) any winter squash
5 tbsp butter
2 onions, chopped
2 red bell peppers, seeded
   and chopped
12oz (350g) arborio rice
1 cup white wine (optional)
4 cups hot vegetable stock
large sprig of thyme, leaves
   picked and chopped
8 sage leaves,
   roughly chopped
salt and freshly ground
   black pepper
5½oz (150g) spinach, chopped
8 cherry tomatoes, chopped
   into quarters
2 tbsp grated Parmesan or
   hard goat cheese (optional)

OPTIONAL FISH
10oz (300g) skinned salmon
   fillet, cut into cubes
lemon wedges, to serve

Green peas pilau

SERVES 4   **PREPARATION 10 MINS, PLUS SOAKING**   **TO COOK 20 MINS**

Always use the right amount of water for pilau rice so it is all absorbed when the rice is done. This dish is great served with cucumber raita, a side salad, and naan bread.

INGREDIENTS

14oz (400g) Basmati rice
5 tbsp butter or ghee
1 tsp cumin seeds
½ tsp cloves
1 cinnamon leaf or bay leaf
4 green cardamom pods
1 cinnamon stick
2 red onions, finely sliced
8oz (225g) frozen peas, thawed
1 tbsp salt
¼oz (10g) mint leaves,
   shredded
¼oz (10g) cilantro
   leaves, chopped

OPTIONAL MEAT

6oz (175g) lean ground lamb

1 Wash the rice in cold running water, then soak in cold water for 20–25 minutes, if you have time. Soaking the rice reduces the cooking time and prevents the grains from breaking while cooking.

2 Heat the ghee in a heavy-based Dutch oven over moderate heat and add the whole spices. When they pop, add the onions and sauté until they are golden brown. Add the peas and sauté for 2–3 minutes. Pour in 2½ cups water. Add the salt, cover, and bring to a boil.

3 Drain the rice and add to the Dutch oven. Bring back to a boil and cook, uncovered, for 8 minutes over medium heat until nearly all the liquid has been absorbed, stirring once—stirring it too much can break up the rice grains.

4 When small holes start to appear on the surface of the rice, sprinkle the mint and cilantro over. Cover the Dutch oven tightly and turn the heat to as low as possible. Cook for another 10 minutes. Alternatively, finish cooking the rice in a preheated 250°F (130°C) oven for another 10 minutes.

IF ADDING MEAT, put the ground lamb in the pan with the peas at step 2. Stir until it is no longer pink and the grains of meat are separate, then continue as before.

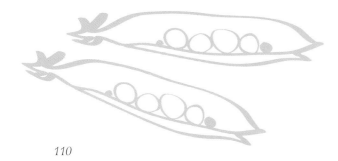

Vegetable biryani

SERVES 6   **PREPARATION 15 MINS, PLUS SOAKING**   **TO COOK 1 HR 5 MINS**

Use any combination of vegetables in season for this colorful, mild curried rice dish. It is equally delicious hot or cold, which is an added bonus.

1 Wash the rice thoroughly in cold running water, then pour in enough water to cover and leave to soak for at least 1 hour. Drain the rice and cook in plenty of salted boiling water for 8 minutes. Drain and set aside.

2 Heat the oil in a saucepan and fry the onions for about 5 minutes, stirring, until golden brown and soft. Remove half and set aside for garnish. Add the ginger and garlic and cook for 1 minute, then stir in the tomatoes, all the spices, the bay leaves, some salt, and the yogurt. Cook for about 10 minutes, or until the oil separates.

3 Add the potatoes, zucchini, carrots, and peas with ½ cup water and cook for 5–8 minutes, or until the vegetables are tender. Remove from the heat.

4 Spread half the cooked rice over the bottom of a large saucepan. Put the cooked vegetables on this layer of rice and sprinkle with cilantro. Cover with the remaining rice.

5 Cover the saucepan with a damp, clean tea towel, then with a tightly fitting lid. Stand the saucepan in a frying pan to reduce the heat further and cook over very low heat for 30 minutes.

6 Mix the rice gently with the vegetables, then spoon into a large, flat dish. Garnish with the reserved onions and serve.

IF ADDING MEAT, add the chicken with the vegetables at step 3 and continue as before.

INGREDIENTS

1lb 2oz (500g) Basmati rice
½ cup sunflower or
   vegetable oil
4 large onions, sliced
1 tsp grated ginger
1 garlic clove, crushed
4 tomatoes, peeled and
   finely chopped
1 tsp red chile powder
1 tsp ground turmeric
1 tsp ground coriander
2 cinnamon sticks
4 black cardamom pods
1 tsp cumin seeds
1 tsp black peppercorns
1 tsp cloves
4 star anise
2 bay leaves
salt
9oz (250g) Greek-style yogurt
2 potatoes, peeled and diced
2 zucchini, diced
5½oz (150g) carrots, diced
5½oz (150g) shelled fresh or
   frozen peas
¼ cup chopped cilantro

OPTIONAL MEAT

10oz (300g) boneless, skinless
   chicken breast, diced

Pan-fries
and fritters

Chinese pumpkin fritters

MAKES 20   **PREPARATION 15 MINS, PLUS CHILLING**   TO COOK **40 MINS**

These crisp, bite-sized fritters, fried in a beer batter, make a light supper accompanied by rice. Use only all-purpose flour for the batter, if preferred.

INGREDIENTS

1lb 2oz (500g) pumpkin or butternut squash, peeled, halved, seeded, and grated
2in (5cm) piece fresh ginger, grated
½ tsp turmeric
1 red chile, seeded and finely chopped
1 tbsp all-purpose flour, plus extra for dusting
salt and freshly ground black pepper
vegetable oil, for deep-frying
soy sauce and rice, to serve

For the batter

½ cup beer
¼ cup all-purpose flour
½ cup gram (chickpea) flour
¼ cup carbonated water

OPTIONAL SHELLFISH

9oz (250g) cooked, peeled shrimp

1 Put the pumpkin in a colander or steamer basket and sit it over a pan of simmering water, covered, for 10–15 minutes until the pumpkin is tender. Remove, leave to cool slightly, then squeeze out any excess water. Place in a bowl and mix in the ginger, turmeric, chile, and all-purpose flour. Season with salt and pepper.

2 Dust your hands with flour, then take a tablespoonful of the pumpkin mixture and shape it into a ball. Repeat to make 19 more round balls. Place them on a lightly floured baking sheet and chill in the refrigerator for at least 30 minutes to firm.

3 For the batter, place all the ingredients in a bowl and season. Stir until combined, but still lumpy. If the batter is thin, add more of the flours in equal amounts—it should be the consistency of thick cream.

4 Pour the oil to a depth of 2in (5cm) into a wok or a large, deep-sided, non-stick frying pan and place over medium-high heat until hot. Don't leave the wok or pan unattended. Take off the heat when not using, and keep a fire blanket nearby in case of fire.

5 Dip the pumpkin balls into the batter one at a time, making sure they are well coated. Fry them in the hot oil, about 5 at a time, cooking each side for 2–3 minutes until golden and crisp. Remove and place on paper towels to drain. Serve with a small bowl of soy sauce and some rice.

IF ADDING SHELLFISH, drain the shrimp and dry well on paper towels, then mince or chop them finely. Use only 9oz (250g) pumpkin and add the shrimp before the flavorings at the end of step 1. At step 2 use wet hands to shape the mixture into balls, then dust with a little flour before chilling.

Sweet corn fritters with tomato salsa

SERVES 4   **PREPARATION 20 MINS**   TO COOK **10 MINS**

If you're lucky enough to obtain **newly harvested corn**, there is no need to blanch them—they will be sweet and tender enough used fresh.

1 If using fresh corn cobs, remove the husks and silk and cut off the kernels (see p321). Blanch the kernels in boiling water for 3 minutes. Drain, rinse with cold water, and drain again.

2 Sift the flour and baking powder into a bowl. Mix the eggs and milk together in a measuring cup and gradually whisk them into the flour to make a thick batter. Add the corn, paprika, the white parts of the scallions, 2 tbsp cilantro, and the chile (if using). Mix well and season with salt and pepper.

3 Heat the sunflower oil in a large frying pan and add tablespoonfuls of the batter mixture. Use the back of the spoon to spread the fritters out slightly, and fry for 2–3 minutes on each side until puffed up and golden brown. Fry in batches until all the mixture is cooked, adding a little more sunflower oil if necessary.

4 Put the tomatoes, the remaining cilantro and scallion, the olive oil, and the Tabasco or chili sauce into a food processor or blender, and process until blended but still quite chunky. Check the salsa for seasoning. Serve the hot fritters with the salsa on the side.

IF ADDING MEAT, use only 1 corn cob and add the chicken to the mixture with the corn kernels at step 2.

INGREDIENTS

2 large corn cobs, or 9oz (250g) fresh or frozen kernels
¾ cup self-rising flour
1 tsp baking powder
2 large eggs
¼ cup milk
1 tsp smoked paprika
2 scallions, finely chopped, green and white parts separated
¼ cup chopped cilantro
1 red chile, seeded and finely chopped (optional)
salt and freshly ground black pepper
2 tbsp sunflower or vegetable oil
2 ripe tomatoes, peeled and roughly chopped
2 tbsp extra virgin olive oil
dash of Tabasco or chili sauce

OPTIONAL MEAT
5½oz (150g) cooked chicken, finely diced

Thai-style beansprout and shredded vegetable fritters

MAKES 8   **PREPARATION 15 MINS**   TO COOK **25 MINS**

If egg rings (or large metal pastry cutters) are not available, **mix the vegetables into the batter and drop ladlefuls into the hot oil**. Serve two for a light lunch.

INGREDIENTS

½ carrot
2oz (60g) asparagus tips
    (approx. 6in/15cm long)
½ small red bell pepper, seeded
    and cut into thin strips
¾ cup all-purpose flour
1 tsp baking powder
¼ tsp ground turmeric
¾ tsp salt
1 tsp grated fresh ginger
1 tsp finely chopped lemongrass
    (or lemongrass purée)
1 garlic clove, crushed
1 thin red chile, seeded
    and finely chopped
4 scallions, chopped
3½oz (100g) beansprouts
1 tbsp chopped cilantro
sunflower or vegetable oil,
    for frying
1 tbsp snipped chives, plus
    extra to garnish
noodle and beansprout salad
    and sweet chili sauce,
    to serve

OPTIONAL SHELLFISH
16 raw, peeled large shrimp

1 Peel the carrot into thin ribbons with a potato peeler. Cut the asparagus in half lengthways and then widthways. Set both aside with the red pepper.

2 Mix the flour with the baking powder, turmeric, salt, ginger, lemongrass, garlic, and chile. Whisk in 1 cup cold water to form a batter the consistency of thick cream. Stir in the scallions, beansprouts, and cilantro.

3 Place 4 egg rings in a large frying pan. Add about ¼in (5mm) oil and heat until hot but not smoking.

4 Add about an eighth of the batter (a small ladleful) to one of the egg rings and quickly top with a few strips of each vegetable, pressing gently into the uncooked batter. Repeat with the other rings, using half the ingredients in all. Fry for 2–3 minutes until the batter is puffed up, set, and brown underneath.

5 Lift off the rings with tongs. Flip the fritters over with a metal spatula and fry for a further 2 minutes to brown and cook the vegetables. Lift out with a metal spatula and drain, vegetable side up, on paper towels. Keep warm while cooking the remaining fritters in the same way.

6 Transfer the fritters to serving plates and garnish with a few snipped chives. Serve with a noodle and beansprout salad and some sweet chili sauce for dipping.

IF ADDING SHELLFISH, omit the carrot and pepper and press 2 large shrimp into the batter with the asparagus at step 4.

Cauliflower pakoras with carrot raita

SERVES 4–6   **PREPARATION 20 MINS**   TO COOK **8 MINS**

These delicious morsels make a great starter or, served with a salad, a light meal. For a variation, use chopped broccoli, onions, or mushrooms instead of cauliflower.

INGREDIENTS

½ small cauliflower, white part
   only (approx. 10oz/300g)
¾ cup gram (chickpea)
   or whole wheat flour
1 tsp ground cumin
1 tsp ground coriander
¼ tsp baking soda
2 scallions, finely chopped
1 large green chile, seeded
   and finely chopped
sunflower or vegetable oil,
   for frying

For the raita

1 tsp cumin seeds
7oz (200g) thick plain yogurt
1 large carrot, coarsely grated
2 tbsp chopped cilantro
1 small green chile, seeded
   and finely chopped
generous pinch of sugar
salt and freshly ground
   black pepper

OPTIONAL MEAT

5½oz (150g) cooked lamb,
   finely chopped

1 First, make the raita. Toast the seeds in a dry frying pan for 30 seconds until fragrant. Pour into a small bowl and add the yogurt. Stir in the carrot, cilantro, chile, and sugar and season with salt and pepper. Chill until ready to serve.

2 To make the pakoras, cut the cauliflower into slices about ¼in (5mm) thick, then chop them into cubes measuring about ½in (1cm). Mix the flour with the cumin, coriander, baking soda, ½ tsp salt, and ⅔ cup water to form a thick batter. Stir in the cauliflower, scallions, and chile.

3 Heat about ½in (1cm) oil in a deep-sided frying pan to 350°F (180°C), or until a tiny portion of batter dropped into it sizzles furiously and rises to the surface immediately. Using about a third of the batter, drop heaped teaspoonfuls of the mixture into the oil and fry for 2–3 minutes until golden, turning once. Remove with a slotted spoon and drain on paper towels. Keep warm while cooking the remainder. Pile on a plate and serve hot with the raita.

IF ADDING MEAT, use half the amount of cauliflower and add the lamb to the mixture at step 2.

Crushed pea fritters in beer batter with a tomato tartare sauce

SERVES 4–8   **PREPARATION 20 MINS**   TO COOK **10 MINS**

Serve these crispy, fresh-tasting little balls with fries or as a starter. For a nibble with drinks, make each ball a bit smaller and use the sauce as a dip.

1 Cook the potatoes in lightly salted boiling water for 5 minutes. Add the peas and mint and cook for a further 4–5 minutes until both vegetables are really tender. Drain thoroughly, return to the pan, and mash the vegetables with a potato masher. Season with salt and pepper and set aside to cool.

2 To make the sauce, finely chop the tomatoes and mix with the mayonnaise, capers, and sugar, then season with salt and pepper. Transfer to a small bowl and chill until ready to serve.

3 Shape the cooled pea mixture into 24 small balls, each about the size of a golf ball, and coat in the all-purpose flour.

4 In a deep-sided frying pan, heat the oil to 350°F (180°C), or until a tiny portion of the batter dropped into the oil sizzles furiously and rises to the surface immediately.

5 Make the batter while the oil is heating. Mix the self-rising flour and cornstarch with a generous pinch of salt and chilled lager. Whisk the egg white until stiff and fold into the batter.

6 Dip the pea balls in the batter to coat completely. Gently drop into the hot oil, in batches, and fry for about 3 minutes until crisp and golden, turning once. Drain on paper towels and serve immediately with the tomato tartare sauce.

IF ADDING FISH, use only 4oz (115g) peas and add the fish to the mixture at the end of step 1. If using thawed, frozen fish, dry on paper towels first.

INGREDIENTS

2 large potatoes, peeled and
   cut into small chunks
12oz (350g) fresh shelled or
   frozen peas
1 large sprig of mint, chopped
salt and freshly ground
   black pepper
¼ cup all-purpose flour
sunflower or corn oil,
   for deep-frying
⅓ cup self-rising flour
⅓ cup cornstarch
⅔ cup chilled lager
1 large egg white

For the tomato
tartare sauce

4 tomatoes, peeled and seeded
6 tbsp mayonnaise
2 tsp pickled capers, chopped
pinch of sugar

OPTIONAL FISH

8oz (225g) raw white fish,
   such as whiting or pollock,
   minced or finely chopped

Bean patties

MAKES 8   **PREPARATION 20 MINS, PLUS CHILLING**   **TO COOK 50 MINS**

Mashed bean patties are a **great alternative to burgers**. If making for children, omit the chile and replace half the onion with grated carrot for sweetness.

INGREDIENTS

1 onion, quartered

2 tbsp chopped
  flat-leaf parsley

14oz (400g) can lima beans,
  drained and rinsed

14oz (400g) can kidney beans,
  drained and rinsed

1 tsp cayenne pepper

2 tbsp all-purpose flour

1 large egg, lightly beaten

salt and freshly ground
  black pepper

3 tbsp olive oil

green salad, to serve

For the avocado salsa

2 ripe avocados, pitted
  and diced (see pp324–5)

1 large garlic clove, grated

1 red chile, seeded and
  finely chopped

2 tbsp olive oil

1 tbsp finely chopped
  cilantro leaves

juice of 1 lime

1 tsp sugar

OPTIONAL MEAT

9oz (250g) lean ground beef

1 Place the onion in a food processor and pulse until roughly chopped. Add the parsley and pulse again a couple of times, then add the beans and pulse again. Transfer to a large bowl and stir in the cayenne pepper, flour, and egg. Season with salt and pepper and mix well. Shape the mixture into 8 patties and chill in the refrigerator until firm.

2 For the salsa, place all the ingredients in a bowl and combine well. Leave for 15 minutes, then stir and season to taste.

3 Heat the oil in a large frying pan over medium-high heat. Add the patties, cooking in 2 batches if necessary and adding more oil as required. Fry for 5 minutes on each side until crisp and golden, then drain on paper towels. Serve with a green salad and the salsa on the side.

IF ADDING MEAT, omit the lima beans. Add the beef to the pulsed mixture at step 1 and mix well with the hands before adding the cayenne pepper and remaining ingredients. Cook as before.

Mushroom burgers with chips and dip

MAKES 4   **PREPARATION 20 MINS, PLUS CHILLING**   **TO COOK 50 MINS**

Served with miso-roasted sweet potato chips and tahini dip, these burgers have **plenty of gutsy flavors**. Mini versions can be made for children.

1 Preheat the oven to 400°F (200°C). Heat 1 tbsp oil in a large frying pan, add the onion, and cook over low heat for 3–4 minutes. Add the mushrooms and cook for 6 minutes, or until they start to release their juices. Add the mushroom ketchup and soy sauce to taste and cook for 1 minute. Transfer to a large bowl. Add the breadcrumbs, then trickle in the egg until the mixture binds well. Add some more breadcrumbs if it's too wet and season well with salt and pepper.

2 Make 4 large balls from the mixture and form into burgers. Place them on a baking sheet lined with parchment paper and chill for 30 minutes.

3 For the chips, toss the potatoes with the oil and soy sauce and spread out in a roasting pan. Roast in the oven for 20 minutes until the chips begin to turn golden and the thinner ones are crisp.

4 For the tahini dip, grind the garlic and salt with a mortar and pestle. Add the soy sauce and mix. Add about 2 tbsp water to loosen it. Stir in the lemon juice.

5 To cook the burgers, heat 1 tbsp oil in a large frying pan over medium heat. Add the burgers, 2 at a time if necessary, and cook for 3–5 minutes on each side until golden. Drain on paper towels. Serve with the sweet potato chips and tahini dip.

IF ADDING MEAT, fry the pancetta slices in a little hot vegetable oil until they crisp and curl up. Drain on paper towels. Serve 2 curls on top of each burger.

INGREDIENTS

2 tbsp olive oil
1 onion, finely chopped
1lb 2oz (500g) crimini
    mushrooms, pulsed in
    a food processor
1 tbsp mushroom ketchup
    or tomato paste
2–3 tbsp soy sauce
1 cup breadcrumbs
1 large egg, lightly beaten
salt and freshly ground
    black pepper

For the miso chips

4 sweet potatoes, peeled
    and cut into thin slices
1 tbsp olive oil
1 tbsp soy sauce

For the tahini dip

2 garlic cloves, grated
pinch of salt
3 tbsp soy sauce
juice of 1 lemon

OPTIONAL MEAT

8 thin pancetta slices
1 tbsp sunflower or
    vegetable oil

Falafel with dill and cucumber dip

SERVES 4   **PREPARATION 20 MINS**   TO COOK **9 MINS**

These falafel balls are particularly appetizing when served with plenty of greens in split, warm pita bread, with the dip spooned in, too.

INGREDIENTS

1 onion, roughly chopped
14oz (400g) can chickpeas,
   drained
1 small garlic clove, crushed
1 tsp ground cumin
1 tsp ground coriander
2 tbsp roughly
   chopped parsley
salt and freshly ground
   black pepper
½ tsp baking powder
1 large egg, separated
splash of milk, if needed
1½ cups fresh breadcrumbs
sunflower or vegetable oil,
   for frying

For the dip
5½oz (150g) Greek-style yogurt
2in (5cm) piece cucumber,
   peeled, seeded, and grated
1 tsp white balsamic vinegar
¼ tsp granulated sugar
2 tbsp chopped dill

OPTIONAL MEAT
handful of ground lamb

1 To make the falafel, put the onion, chickpeas, garlic, spices, parsley, salt and pepper, and baking powder in a food processor and blend to a thick paste, stopping and scraping down the sides as necessary.

2 Mix in the egg yolk to bind. Add a splash of milk, if necessary, but don't make the mixture too wet.

3 Shape the mixture into 12 small balls and flatten slightly. Coat in lightly beaten egg white, then in the breadcrumbs. Chill, if time allows, until ready to cook.

4 Meanwhile, mix the dip ingredients together and chill until ready to serve.

5 Shallow-fry the falafel in hot oil for about 3 minutes, turning once, until crisp and golden. Drain on paper towels. Serve warm or cold with the dip.

IF ADDING MEAT, brown the lamb in a dry frying pan, stirring until no longer pink and all the grains are separate. Add to the processed mixture at step 1 and work in with the hands before shaping into 24 small balls.

Pan-fries and fritters
Lentil and carrot rissoles

MAKES 8   **PREPARATION 20 MINS**   **TO COOK 8–12 MINS**

In these tasty rissoles, other roots can be used instead of carrots. **Try a large parsnip to add a sweet earthiness,** or a small celery root for a subtle celery flavor.

1 Using a food processor or hand blender, purée the lentils to a rough paste.

2 Heat the oil in a saucepan. Add the onion, garlic, and carrots and fry, stirring, for 3 minutes until softened and the onion is lightly golden.

3 Remove from the heat, add the lentils and sage, mix well, and season with salt and pepper.

4 Whisk the egg and yogurt together and add to the mixture to bind. It will be quite wet. Shape the mixture into 8 patties and coat thoroughly in the breadcrumbs, pressing them on firmly as you shape the patties. Place on a plate and chill for at least 30 minutes or overnight, if possible, to firm.

5 Heat about ¼in (5mm) oil in a large frying pan and shallow-fry the patties for 2–3 minutes on each side until crisp and golden, turning once. Cook in two batches.

6 Drain on paper towels and serve hot with chutney and a large mixed salad.

IF ADDING MEAT, use just 1 can of lentils and add the chicken to the blended lentils, mixing them well with your hands. Fry for 3–4 minutes on each side until cooked through, crisp, and browned.

INGREDIENTS

2 × 14oz (400g) cans green
   lentils, rinsed and drained
1 tbsp sunflower or vegetable
   oil, plus extra for frying
1 small onion, finely chopped
1 large garlic clove, crushed
2 large carrots, grated
2 tbsp chopped sage
salt and freshly ground
   black pepper
1 egg
1 tbsp plain yogurt
2 cups fresh breadcrumbs
chutney and large mixed
   salad, to serve

OPTIONAL MEAT
9oz (250g) ground chicken

Veggie burgers with melting cheese

MAKES 4   **PREPARATION 15 MINS, PLUS CHILLING**   TO COOK **10 MINS**

It's best to use ready-sliced Gruyère or Emmental cheese for this dish—the slices will **melt perfectly to a lovely gooey finish and add a sweet, nutty tang**.

INGREDIENTS

14oz (400g) can aduki
  beans, drained
2 carrots, grated
1 small onion, grated
1oz (30g) chopped mixed nuts
1½ cups fresh breadcrumbs
1 tsp dried mixed herbs
1 tbsp mushroom ketchup
  or Worcestershire sauce
salt and freshly ground
  black pepper
1 small egg, beaten
sunflower or vegetable oil,
  for frying
4 burger buns, cut in half
tomato ketchup or sweet
  chili sauce
4 slices Swiss cheese
2 tomatoes, sliced
a little shredded lettuce
French fries and coleslaw,
  to serve

OPTIONAL MEAT

4 strips bacon, cooked

1 Mash the beans well in a bowl with a potato masher or fork. Add the carrots, onion, nuts, breadcrumbs, mixed herbs, mushroom ketchup, and some salt and pepper. Combine thoroughly, then mix with just enough of the beaten egg to bind the mixture together.

2 Shape the mixture into 4 burgers, place on parchment paper on a plate, and chill for 30 minutes to firm up.

3 Heat enough oil to cover the base of a large non-stick frying pan. Fry the burgers over a moderate heat for 6–7 minutes on each side until golden brown. Drain on paper towels.

4 Preheat the broiler. Toast the buns on the cut sides only. Spread with some tomato ketchup. Remove the bun tops from the broiler pan, place the burgers on top of the bases, then add a slice of cheese. Flash under the broiler until the cheese starts to melt. Top with some sliced tomatoes and a little shredded lettuce.

5 Quickly place the bun tops in place, either completely on top or at a jaunty angle, and serve with French fries and coleslaw.

IF ADDING MEAT, put a cooked strip of bacon on top of the melted cheese for each burger at step 4 before adding the bun tops.

Crêpes with mushrooms, garlic, and cheese

MAKES 8   **PREPARATION 15 MINS, PLUS STANDING**   TO COOK **15 MINS**

These flavorful crêpes make a delicious light lunch or supper. For added color, try substituting halved cherry tomatoes for some of the mushrooms.

INGREDIENTS

¾ cup all-purpose flour
pinch of salt
1 large egg
1¼ cup milk
a little olive oil, for frying
salad, to serve

For the filling
2 tbsp olive oil
2 large garlic cloves, crushed
1lb (450g) button
   mushrooms, sliced
7oz (200g) soft white cheese
2–3 tbsp milk
2 tbsp chopped parsley
salt and freshly ground
   black pepper

OPTIONAL MEAT
4oz (115g) bacon, diced
1 tbsp olive oil

1 To make the crêpe batter, sift the flour and salt into a bowl. Add the egg, then gradually work in the milk and beat to form a smooth batter. Leave to stand for 30 minutes.

2 Meanwhile, make the filling. Heat the oil in a saucepan. Add the garlic and mushrooms and fry, stirring, for 2 minutes. Cover, reduce the heat, and cook gently for 5 minutes. Remove the lid and boil rapidly until only about 1 tbsp liquid is left.

3 Stir in the cheese until melted, thinning with enough milk to coat the mushrooms in a smooth sauce. Stir in the parsley and season with salt and pepper. Set aside, ready to heat through when the crêpes are cooked.

4 To make the crêpes, heat a little oil in a non-stick crêpe pan or omelet pan and pour off excess into a bowl to reuse. Add about 3 tbsp batter and swirl around to coat the base. Cook for 1–2 minutes until the base is golden and the top is set. Flip over and briefly cook the other side. Slide out onto a plate and keep warm while cooking the remaining crêpes, reheating and oiling the pan between each one.

5 Reheat the filling, stirring gently. Spoon an eighth of the mushroom mixture on one quarter of a crêpe then fold it in four. Repeat with the remaining crêpes. Serve hot with salad.

IF ADDING MEAT, reduce the quantity of mushrooms to 12oz (350g). Fry the diced bacon in oil at step 2 before adding the mushrooms, then continue as before.

Zucchini, carrot, and Gruyère crêpes

MAKES 8   **PREPARATION 10 MINS, PLUS STANDING**   TO COOK **25 MINS**

For variety, use any melting cheese for these crêpes and experiment with a quarter of a small celery root, grated, cooked with the zucchini instead of the carrots.

1 Make the crêpe batter (see p126, step 1) and leave to stand for 30 minutes. Meanwhile, heat the oil in a saucepan. Add the zucchini and carrots and fry on medium heat for 5–8 minutes, stirring, until softened and lightly golden. Stir in the crème fraîche, cheese, thyme, and salt and pepper to taste. Set aside, ready to heat through when the crêpes are cooked.

2 Make the crêpes (see p126, step 4). Reheat the filling, stirring gently. Spoon an eighth of the filling on one quarter of a pancake, then fold it in four. Repeat with the remaining crêpes. Serve hot with a tomato salad.

IF ADDING MEAT, use 1 zucchini and 1 carrot and add the chopped ham to the cooked vegetables before adding the crème fraîche in step 1. Stir the Dijon mustard into the mixture, too.

INGREDIENTS

1 quantity crêpe batter (see p126)
2 tbsp olive oil, plus a little extra for frying
2 small zucchini, grated
2 young carrots, grated
3½oz (100g) crème fraîche
5½oz (150g) Gruyère cheese, grated
1 tbsp chopped thyme
salt and freshly ground black pepper
tomato salad, to serve

OPTIONAL MEAT

5½oz (150g) cooked ham, finely chopped
½ tsp Dijon mustard

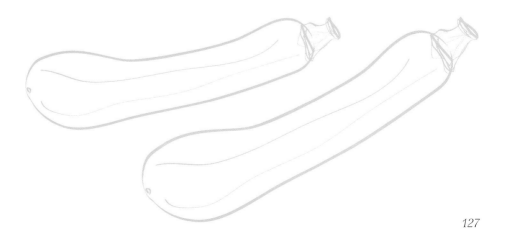

Four ways with
Potatoes

Dauphinoise potatoes ▷

TAKES 2 hrs **SERVES** 4

Preheat the oven to 350°F (180°C). Put 2lb (900g)
red potatoes, peeled and cut into slices ⅛in
(3mm) thick, 1¼ cups **heavy cream**, and 1¼ cups
milk in a large pan. Season with **salt** and freshly
ground **black pepper**. Bring to a boil, cover, and
simmer for 10–15 minutes, or until the potatoes
begin to soften. Using a slotted spoon, transfer the
potatoes to a shallow 2 quart ovenproof dish.
Sprinkle over 3 grated **garlic cloves** and season.
Strain the cream and milk mixture, then pour over
the potatoes. Cover with foil and bake for 1 hour.
Remove the foil and cook for 30 minutes more, or
until the top turns golden.

◁ Egg and fennel potato salad

TAKES 25 mins **SERVES** 4

Boil 4 **large eggs** for 9 minutes—less if you
prefer a runnier yolk. Cook 9oz (250g) **new
potatoes** in a large pan of lightly salted boiling
water for 15–20 minutes, or until soft. Drain them
well and transfer to a serving plate. Drizzle over
some **olive oil** while the potatoes are still hot,
then season with **salt** and freshly ground
black pepper. Mix in a handful of finely
chopped **flat-leaf parsley** and 1 trimmed and
finely chopped **fennel bulb**. Shell and quarter
the hard-boiled eggs and add to the potato
salad. Serve immediately.

Choose floury potatoes for **mashes, fries, baking, and roasting**, and waxy varieties **for gratins, salads, boiling, and steaming**. All-purpose potatoes are mid-way in texture, which makes them **extremely versatile**.

Cajun-spiced potato wedges ▶

TAKES 45 mins–1 hr SERVES 6

Preheat the oven to 400°F (200°C). Cut 4 unpeeled **floury potatoes** into thick wedges. Cook in boiling salted water for 3 minutes; drain. Place on a baking sheet with 1 **lemon**, cut into 6 wedges, 12 **garlic cloves**, 3 **red onions**, cut into 8 wedges, and 4 **bay leaves**. Whisk together 3 tbsp **lemon juice**, 1 tbsp **tomato paste**, **salt** and freshly ground **black pepper**, ½ tsp each **cayenne pepper** and **ground cumin**, 1 tsp each **paprika**, **dried oregano,** and **dried thyme**, and 6 tbsp each **olive oil** and water. Pour evenly over the potatoes and toss. Roast for 30–40 minutes, turning the potatoes frequently. Serve hot.

◀ Potato cakes

TAKES 35 mins SERVES 4

Boil 1lb (450g) peeled **floury potatoes** in a pan of salted water for 15–20 minutes until soft. Drain, then mash. Mix the mashed potatoes with 1 peeled and grated **onion**, a handful of fresh **chives**, finely chopped, 4½oz (125g) **feta cheese**, crumbled, and 1 lightly beaten **large egg**. Season with **salt** and freshly ground **black pepper**. Heat 1 tbsp **olive oil** in a non-stick frying pan over medium heat. Using floured hands, scoop up large balls of the potato mixture, roll, and flatten slightly. Carefully add to the hot oil and fry for 2–3 minutes on each side until golden, adding more oil, if needed. Serve hot.

Potato, celery, and walnut cakes with mushrooms

MAKES 12   **PREPARATION** **15 MINS**   TO COOK **1 HR 30 MINS**

These golden, crisp cakes are delicious served with celery root remoulade (see p284) or just with pickled beets instead of the mayonnaise and mushrooms.

INGREDIENTS

3 Russet potatoes
salt and freshly ground
   black pepper
olive oil, for frying
butter, for frying
1 onion, peeled and
   finely chopped
2 celery stalks, finely chopped
1½oz (45g) walnuts,
   finely chopped
2 tbsp all-purpose flour
2 large eggs
pinch of nutmeg
1 garlic clove, chopped
8oz (225g) mixed
   mushrooms, sliced
dash of lemon juice
2 tbsp thyme leaves
2 tbsp chopped parsley
¼ cup mayonnaise, to serve

OPTIONAL FISH

7oz (185g) can tuna,
   drained and flaked
squeeze of lemon

1 Place the potatoes in a large pan of cold, salted water and cover. Bring to a boil, then simmer for 3 minutes. Drain, cool, and peel off the skins. Grate the potato and put into a bowl. Set aside.

2 Heat a little oil and butter in a frying pan and fry the onion for 5 minutes. Add the celery and cook gently for 5 minutes to soften. Allow to cool, then add the potatoes along with the walnuts, flour, eggs, and nutmeg, and season with salt and pepper. Mix together well.

3 In a non-stick frying pan, melt a knob of butter and some oil. When sizzling hot, add heaped tablespoons of the mixture, pressing down to flatten into round discs. Cook for 5 minutes on each side, turning once. Drain on paper towels and keep warm in a low oven until needed. Repeat this process until 12 cakes are made.

4 Heat a little more oil and butter in the wiped-out frying pan. Add the garlic and cook over low heat until softened, then add the mushrooms and cook for 5 minutes, or until soft and sizzling hot. Season well and add the lemon juice, thyme, and parsley.

5 Divide the cakes between 4 plates, then spoon over the mushrooms and top with a dollop of mayonnaise.

IF ADDING FISH, use just 1 small stalk of celery, omit the walnuts, and add the tuna to the mixture at step 2. Season to taste and spike with a squeeze of lemon.

Warm pea pancakes with grilled asparagus

SERVES 4   **PREPARATION 10 MINS**   TO COOK **30 MINS**

A deceptively simple dish to prepare, the **bright colors of the peas and asparagus** contrast beautifully with the golden yolk of the poached egg.

1 Put the peas in a pan and blanch in boiling water for 1–2 minutes. Drain and leave to cool.

2 Put the peas and mint into a food processor and pulse together to get a rough texture. Add the melted butter, flour, cream, Parmesan, and 2 eggs, and season with salt and pepper. Process the mixture to a stiff paste.

3 Heat some butter or oil in a large frying pan and add 2 tablespoonfuls of the mixture for each pancake. Cook over medium heat and use the back of a spoon to smooth the top of the mixture. After 3–4 minutes, the edges of the pancakes will change color. Carefully turn them over and cook for another 2 minutes.

4 Meanwhile, bring a large pot of water to a boil and lightly poach the remaining eggs until just set. Remove them with a slotted spoon.

5 As the eggs are cooking, grill the asparagus spears in a hot grill pan with oil for 4–6 minutes until tender, seasoning with salt and pepper while cooking.

IF ADDING MEAT, omit the grilled asparagus and grill the bacon strips until golden. Serve with the pancakes and eggs.

INGREDIENTS

14oz (400g) fresh peas (podded weight) or frozen
large handful of mint leaves, chopped
4 tbsp melted butter, plus extra for frying
¼ cup all-purpose flour
¼ cup heavy cream
2 tbsp grated Parmesan cheese
6 large eggs
sea salt and freshly ground black pepper
large bunch of asparagus spears, woody ends removed
1 tsp extra virgin olive oil

OPTIONAL MEAT

8 strips bacon

Parsnip and walnut pancakes with maple butter

MAKES 8 PREPARATION **20 MINS** TO COOK **30 MINS**

These are perfect for breakfast or brunch. For speed, cook and purée the parsnips the night before so that they are ready for making the pancakes in the morning.

INGREDIENTS

1 large parsnip (approx. 8oz/225g), cut into small chunks
salt
¾ cup self-rising flour
1 tsp baking powder
2 tbsp granulated sugar
1 large egg
1 cup milk
2oz (60g) walnuts, finely chopped
sunflower or vegetable oil, for frying

For the maple butter
3 tbsp butter
3 tbsp maple syrup

OPTIONAL MEAT
4–8 slices thick-cut bacon

1 Cook the parsnips in lightly salted boiling water for about 10 minutes or until soft. Drain and return to the pan, then purée with a hand blender or mash well and beat with a wooden spoon until smooth. Allow to cool a little.

2 In a bowl, mix the flour, baking powder, sugar, and a generous pinch of salt. Gradually beat in the egg and milk and continue to beat until smooth. Stir in the walnuts, then beat in the puréed parsnip.

3 Put the butter and syrup in a small saucepan and melt, whisking until thoroughly blended. Set aside.

4 Heat a little oil in a non-stick frying pan until very hot, then pour off the excess. Ladle in 3–4 tbsp batter to make a pancake about 5in (12cm) in diameter. Reduce the heat to medium and cook for 1½–2 minutes until bubbles pop on the surface and the pancake is golden brown underneath and almost set. Flip over and brown the other side. Slide out onto a plate and keep warm while cooking the remaining pancakes in the same way, oiling and heating the pan between batches.

5 Reheat and whisk the maple butter again. Serve the pancakes hot with the maple butter drizzled over.

IF ADDING MEAT, either broil or fry the bacon and serve alongside the pancakes and maple butter.

Buckwheat galettes with cheese and caramelized onions

MAKES 8   PREPARATION **10 MINS, PLUS STANDING**   TO COOK **35 MINS**

Cook the onions first, then reheat them just before serving. They will keep in the refrigerator for several days. For the best results, use pre-sliced cheese.

1 First, cook the onions. Heat the oil and butter in a saucepan. Add the onions and fry, stirring, for 2 minutes. Reduce the heat to low, cover, and cook for 15 minutes, stirring occasionally, until softened and lightly golden. Increase the heat, add the sugar, and cook, stirring for a few minutes, until richly golden. Add 6 tbsp water and cook, stirring, until it evaporates. Remove from the heat, season with a little salt and pepper, and set aside.

2 Mix the flour with a generous pinch of salt in a bowl. Make a well in the center and add the egg and half the milk. Beat well until smooth. Stir in the melted butter and remaining milk. Leave to stand for 30 minutes, if time allows.

3 Reheat the onions gently. Heat a little oil in a non-stick frying pan and pour off the excess. Add about 3 tbsp batter to make a thin pancake covering the base of the pan, swirling the pan quickly to spread out the batter. Fry for 1–2 minutes until holes appear in the surface and the pancake is almost set and golden brown underneath. Flip over and cook the other side.

4 Slide out of the pan, top with a slice of cheese, then a spoonful (about an eighth) of the hot onions. Fold in the sides to wrap like a parcel and invert on a warmed plate. Keep warm while cooking and filling the remainder in the same way. Serve warm.

IF ADDING MEAT, add a thin slice of ham before adding the cheese to each galette.

INGREDIENTS

¾ cup buckwheat flour
1 large egg, beaten
1¼ cups milk
3 tbsp butter, melted
sunflower or vegetable oil,
   for frying
8 thin slices Leerdammer
   or Emmental cheese

For the onions

1 tbsp sunflower or vegetable oil
knob of butter
4 large red onions, halved
   and thinly sliced
2 tsp granulated sugar
salt and freshly ground
   black pepper

OPTIONAL MEAT

8 thin slices of ham

Beet and caraway blinis with sour cream

SERVES 4–6   **PREPARATION 20 MINS**   TO COOK **40 MINS**

Blinis are usually made with yeast, but **these are just as light and much quicker to make**. They are best eaten fresh but can be made in advance and reheated.

INGREDIENTS

¾ cup all-purpose flour
pinch of salt
2 tsp granulated sugar
2 large eggs, separated
1 cup milk
1 tbsp caraway seeds
3 large or 6 small cooked
  beets, grated
1 large onion, finely chopped
1 tbsp chopped cilantro
  or tarragon
7fl oz (200ml) sour cream
  or crème fraîche
sunflower or vegetable oil,
  for frying

OPTIONAL FISH

4–8 slices gravalax

1 Sift the flour, salt, and sugar into a bowl. Add the egg yolks and half the milk and beat well until smooth.

2 Stir in the remaining milk and add the caraway seeds and a quarter of the beets. Whisk the egg whites until stiff and fold in with a rubber spatula.

3 Mix the onion with the cilantro and place in a small serving dish. Put the remaining beets in a second serving dish and the sour cream in a third. Chill until ready to serve.

4 Heat a little oil in a non-stick frying pan. Pour off the excess. Add 3 tbsp batter and spread out to make a pancake about 4in (10cm) in diameter (you may be able to make 2 or 3, depending on the size of the pan). Cook over medium-high heat for 1–2 minutes, or until golden underneath and bubbles have risen and popped to the surface. Flip over and briefly cook the other side. Remove and keep warm while cooking the remainder.

5 Serve the stack of blinis with the beet, onion, and cilantro mixture and sour cream. To eat, take a blini, add a spoonful of beets, then a little onion mixture, and top with a dollop of sour cream. The blinis may also be made much smaller to serve as canapés.

IF ADDING FISH, serve with 1–2 curled slices of gravalax alongside the blinis on each plate.

Stuffed crêpes with spinach, ricotta, and pine nuts

MAKES 8　　**PREPARATION 30 MINS, PLUS STANDING**　　**TO COOK 25–30 MINS**

Here, the classic combination of spinach and ricotta is enhanced with the sweet tang of sun-dried tomatoes and the crunch of toasted pine nuts.

INGREDIENTS

1 quantity crêpe batter
  (see p126)
14oz (400g) spinach
9oz (250g) ricotta cheese
1–2 tbsp chopped rosemary
grated nutmeg
¼ cup toasted pine nuts
squeeze of lemon juice
4 sun-dried tomatoes in oil,
  drained and chopped
salt and freshly ground
  black pepper
4oz (115g) Cheddar
  cheese, grated

OPTIONAL MEAT

2½oz (75g) diced pancetta

1 Make the crêpe batter (see p126, step 1) and leave to stand for 30 minutes. Meanwhile, preheat the oven to 375°F (190°C). Wash the spinach well and shake off excess water. Place in a large saucepan and cook, stirring, for about 2 minutes until the spinach has wilted. Drain in a colander, then squeeze to remove as much moisture as possible and chop, using scissors.

2 Pour the spinach into a bowl and mix with the ricotta cheese, rosemary, plenty of nutmeg, nuts, lemon juice, tomatoes, and salt and pepper to taste.

3 Make the crêpes (see p126, step 4), then divide the spinach mixture among them. Roll up and pack into a lightly greased, shallow, ovenproof dish that will hold the crêpes in a single layer. Sprinkle with Cheddar cheese and bake for about 30 minutes until the cheese melts and is slightly golden, and the crêpes are hot through and crisp at the edges.

IF ADDING MEAT, dry-fry the pancetta, drain, and add to the spinach mixture at step 2. Use 2 tbsp pine nuts instead of 4.

Ratatouille in tomato crêpes

MAKES 8   **PREPARATION** **20 MINS, PLUS STANDING**   TO COOK **25–35 MINS**

To prepare these crêpes in advance, roll them up and place in a baking dish. Sprinkle with grated Cheddar cheese and reheat in a medium-hot oven.

1 Make the crêpe batter (see p126, step 1) and whisk in the tomato paste, 2 tbsp water, and the dried basil. Leave to stand for 30 minutes.

2 Meanwhile, heat the oil in a large saucepan. Add the onion, garlic, red and green peppers, eggplant, and zucchini. Fry, stirring, for 5–10 minutes until they begin to soften, then add the tomatoes, tomato paste, wine or 2 tbsp water, sugar, and salt and pepper to taste. Cover and cook over medium heat for 10 minutes, stirring occasionally, then stir in the chopped basil.

3 Make the crêpes (see p126, step 4). Reheat the ratatouille and use to fill the crêpes. Roll up and serve right away, dusted with grated Parmesan cheese.

IF ADDING MEAT, stir the saucisson sec or salami into the ratatouille in step 2 for the last few minutes of cooking.

INGREDIENTS

1 quantity crêpe batter
   (see p126)
2 tbsp tomato paste
1 tsp dried basil
¼ cup olive oil, plus extra
   for frying the pancakes
1 onion, halved and sliced
1 large garlic clove, crushed
1 red bell pepper, halved,
   seeded, and cut into thin strips
1 green bell pepper, halved,
   seeded, and cut into thin strips
1 eggplant, sliced
2 zucchini, sliced
2 large tomatoes, chopped
1 tbsp tomato paste
2 tbsp red wine
generous pinch of
   granulated sugar
salt and freshly ground
   black pepper
2 tbsp chopped basil
¼ cup grated Parmesan cheese

OPTIONAL MEAT

a few slices of saucisson
   sec or salami, chopped

Potato pancakes with applesauce and chive yogurt

SERVES 4　　**PREPARATION 20 MINS**　　TO COOK **40 MINS**

Enjoy these pancakes as a delicious light lunch on their own or, for a more substantial meal, **add some grilled halloumi slices** and serve with a tomato salad.

INGREDIENTS

1 small onion, grated
2 large potatoes, peeled
　and grated
1 tbsp fennel seeds
3 tbsp all-purpose flour
2 large eggs, beaten
sunflower or vegetable oil,
　for frying

For the applesauce

2 sweet apples, peeled, cored,
　and chopped
1 tbsp lemon juice
knob of butter
granulated sugar, to taste

For the chive yogurt

5$\frac{1}{2}$oz (150g) Greek-style yogurt
2 tbsp snipped chives
salt and freshly ground
　black pepper

OPTIONAL MEAT

4 pork chops

1 First, make the applesauce. Put the apples in a saucepan with the lemon juice and 3 tbsp water. Bring to a boil, reduce the heat, cover, and cook gently for 10 minutes until really tender, stirring occasionally. Beat in the butter, then sweeten to taste with sugar. Put in a small bowl and set aside.

2 Mix the yogurt with the chives and season with salt and pepper. Put in a separate small bowl and set aside.

3 Mix the onion and potatoes together in a bowl. Put into a colander, then squeeze out excess moisture with your hands. Return to the bowl and stir in the fennel seeds, flour, and some salt and pepper, then mix in the eggs.

4 Heat enough oil to just coat the base of a large frying pan over medium heat. Divide the mixture into 12 portions. Add 4 portions of the mixture to the pan and press out to make pancakes about 4in (10cm) in diameter. Cook for 3–4 minutes on each side until golden brown and cooked through. Drain on paper towels and keep warm while cooking the remainder in the same way. Serve with the applesauce and the chive yogurt.

IF ADDING MEAT, serve with grilled pork chops. Brush the chops with oil. Season with salt and pepper, then either cook in a hot grill pan or under a preheated broiler for 3–4 minutes each side until browned and the meat feels firm when pressed. Wrap in foil and leave to rest in a warm place for 10 minutes before serving with the juices poured over.

Mediterranean vegetable fritters with aioli

SERVES 4–6   PREPARATION **15 MINS, PLUS STANDING**   TO COOK **20 MINS**

These vegetables have a wonderful summery flavor. Blanching the pepper ensures it is tender when cooked, but if you prefer a little more crunch, omit this step.

1 Place the eggplant and zucchini in a colander and sprinkle with salt. Toss well and leave to stand for 15 minutes to remove excess moisture. Rinse and dry well on plenty of paper towels.

2 Meanwhile, mix the aioli ingredients together, season with salt and pepper, and chill until ready to serve.

3 Blanch the red and yellow pepper pieces in boiling water for 1 minute. Drain and pat dry on paper towels.

4 Mix the all-purpose flour with plenty of pepper and use to coat all the vegetables.

5 Heat the oil for deep-frying. Meanwhile, mix the self-rising flour with a generous pinch of salt and ²/₃ cup very cold water to form a creamy batter. The oil is ready when a tiny portion of the batter dropped in rises immediately to the surface and sizzles furiously.

6 Dip pieces of vegetable in the batter, allow the excess to drain off, and fry for about 4 minutes until crisp and golden, turning occasionally. Cook in batches and reheat the oil between batches. Drain on paper towels and keep warm while cooking the remainder. Serve the fritters hot with the bowl of aioli for dipping.

IF ADDING FISH, replace the eggplant with the squid rings. Fry just until crisp and lightly golden—take care not to overcook them or they will be tough.

INGREDIENTS

1 small eggplant, halved
 and sliced
1 large zucchini, sliced
salt and freshly ground
 black pepper
1 red bell pepper, halved,
 seeded, and cut into chunks
1 yellow bell pepper, halved,
 seeded, and cut into chunks
¼ cup all-purpose flour
sunflower or vegetable oil,
 for deep-frying
¾ cup self-rising flour

For the aioli
3 garlic cloves, crushed
5¹/₂oz (150g) mayonnaise

OPTIONAL FISH
7oz (200g) squid rings

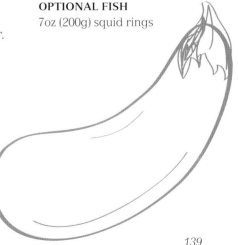

Vegetable spring rolls

MAKES 10 **PREPARATION 30 MINS** **TO COOK 15–20 MINS**

Fry these spring rolls ahead of time and crisp them in a hot oven to serve. Rice paper can be obtained in Asian stores. Use bought chili sauce if preferred.

INGREDIENTS

½oz (15g) dried shiitake
  mushrooms, soaked in
  boiling water for 20 mins
1 small carrot, cut
  into matchsticks
3 scallions, cut
  into matchsticks
3oz (85g) white cabbage,
  shredded
2 garlic cloves, crushed
¾in (2cm) piece fresh
  ginger, grated
2 tbsp soy sauce
1 tbsp Chinese cooking wine
½ tsp Chinese five-spice powder
1 tbsp vegetable oil, plus extra
  for deep-frying
2oz (60g) beansprouts
20 rice paper wrappers

For the chile sauce

¼ cup granulated sugar
⅓ cup rice wine vinegar
2 garlic cloves, chopped
2 red chiles, seeded and
  finely chopped

OPTIONAL MEAT

3oz (85g) sliced roast pork,
  cut in fine shreds

1 Drain and finely chop the mushrooms and mix together with the carrot, scallions, cabbage, garlic, and ginger. In a small measuring cup, mix the soy sauce, wine, and five-spice powder. Heat the oil in a frying pan or wok. Add the vegetable mix and beansprouts and stir-fry for 1 minute. Add the soy sauce mix and simmer for 30 seconds Remove from the heat and leave to cool.

2 For the chile sauce, place all the ingredients in a medium saucepan with ¼ cup water, boil, then simmer for 5 minutes, or until slightly thickened. Cool.

3 Dip a rice paper wrapper in a bowl of warm water for 10–15 seconds, or until soft. Lay it on a damp tea towel and blot until slightly sticky. Place a heaped tablespoonful of filling in the center. Fold the bottom of the wrapper up over the filling, then fold in the sides, rolling up the wrapper tightly. Soak a second wrapper. Wrap it around the first layer and set aside. Repeat until the filling is used up.

4 Heat some oil in a deep-fat fryer or large pan until it reaches 350°F (180°C). Cook the spring rolls in the hot oil, 2 at a time, for 3–4 minutes or until golden. Remove with a slotted spoon and drain on paper towels. Keep the rolls warm while frying the remainder. Serve hot with the chile dipping sauce.

IF ADDING MEAT, omit the cabbage at step 1 and add the pork instead.

Mixed root tempura with dipping sauce

SERVES 4–6   **PREPARATION 25 MINS**   **TO COOK 12–18 MINS**

Here, sturdy Western root vegetables and leeks are given a Japanese treatment and served as tempura with a hot, sweet, piquant dipping sauce.

1 Mix all the dipping sauce ingredients together in a small saucepan. Heat gently, stirring, until the honey dissolves, then bring to a boil. Pour into a small bowl and leave to cool.

2 Blanch all the prepared vegetables in boiling water for 2 minutes. Drain and dry well on paper towels. Put in a large bowl. Sprinkle with the cornstarch and toss to coat.

3 Whisk all the batter ingredients together in a bowl until fairly smooth (the mixture will be quite runny). Heat the oil for deep-frying until a cube of day-old bread browns in 30 seconds when added to it.

4 Dip about a sixth of the vegetables into the batter. Drain off any excess from each piece before carefully dropping it into the oil – it should have only a thin coating. Fry for 2–3 minutes until tender, crisp, and golden, turning over as necessary. Drain on paper towels on a large baking sheet and keep warm while frying the remaining batches. Skim off any floating pieces of batter between batches. Serve with the dipping sauce.

IF ADDING SHELLFISH, replace the rutabaga with shrimp, dried well first on paper towels.

INGREDIENTS

1 parsnip, cut into
   short fingers
½ small rutabaga
½ small celery root, cut into
   small chunks
1 large carrot, cut into
   short fingers
1 leek, cut into thick slices
2 tbsp cornstarch
vegetable oil, for deep-frying

For the dipping sauce
3 tbsp honey
3 tbsp balsamic vinegar
1 tsp grated ginger
1 garlic clove, finely chopped
¼–½ tsp dried chile flakes
3 tbsp soy sauce

For the batter
½ cup self-rising flour
⅔ cup cornstarch
¾ cup sparkling mineral water
2 tsp sunflower or vegetable oil
½ tsp salt
¾ tsp cumin seeds

OPTIONAL SHELLFISH
7oz (200g) raw, peeled shrimp
   (thawed if frozen)

Curries, stews, and casseroles

Kadhai paneer with peppers

SERVES 4–6   **PREPARATION 25 MINS**   TO COOK **30 MINS**

A kadhai is an Indian wok, and **this is the Indian answer to a stir-fry.** The sauce can be used with any vegetables or lentils, so make extra and keep it in the refrigerator.

INGREDIENTS

1 tbsp ghee or vegetable oil
½ tsp dried chile flakes
2 red bell peppers, seeded and
    cut into strips
1 red onion, thickly sliced
1lb 2oz (500g) paneer, cut into
    ½in (1cm) batons
1 bunch of cilantro, chopped
juice of 1 lemon
2in (5cm) piece fresh ginger,
    cut into julienne

For the kadhai sauce

3 tbsp ghee or vegetable oil
2 garlic cloves, finely chopped
2 tsp coriander seeds, crushed
2 red chiles, seeded and finely
    chopped
2 onions, finely chopped
2 tsp grated fresh ginger
1lb (450g) tomatoes, chopped
1 tbsp crushed dried
    fenugreek leaves
salt
1 tsp sugar (optional)

OPTIONAL MEAT

1lb 2oz (500g) lamb loin,
    trimmed and cut into ¼in
    (5mm) thick slices

1 To make the sauce, heat the ghee or oil in a pan, add the garlic, and let it color but not burn. Stir, then add the coriander seeds and red chiles. When they release their aromas, add the onions and cook until they begin to turn light golden. Stir in the grated ginger and tomatoes. Reduce the heat to low and cook until excess moisture has evaporated and the fat starts to separate, stirring frequently. Add the fenugreek. Taste and add salt and some sugar if needed.

2 For the stir-fry, heat the ghee or oil in a kadhai, wok, or large frying pan. Add the chile flakes, pepper strips, and red onion. Stir and sauté over high heat for 2 minutes. Add the paneer and stir for another minute. Now add the sauce and mix well. Once everything is heated through, check for seasoning, adding a touch of salt if required. Finish with the cilantro and lemon juice. Garnish with the ginger and serve.

IF ADDING MEAT, omit the paneer. Stir-fry the lamb instead of the paneer in step 2 for 2–3 minutes until cooked through and tender, then continue as before.

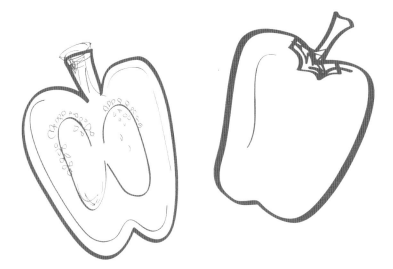

Seasonal vegetables in spinach and garlic sauce

SERVES 4–6   **PREPARATION 25 MINS**   TO COOK **20 MINS**

For this dish, **parboil hard vegetables first and add the delicate and green ones later.** Cut all the vegetables to more or less the same shape and size.

1 Parboil the carrots, cauliflower, and green beans until al dente (3 minutes for the cauliflower and green beans, 4 minutes for the carrots). Drain well, refresh in iced water, and drain again.

2 Blanch the spinach in boiling salted water until wilted, then drain and cool quickly in iced water. Squeeze dry. Blend in a food processor to make a smooth paste, adding a little water if required.

3 In a heavy-based saucepan, heat the ghee or oil over medium heat. Stir in the cumin seeds for 30 seconds until fragrant, then add the garlic and sauté until golden. Add the onion, reduce the heat to low, and cook, stirring, until soft and golden brown. Stir in the ginger and chiles and sauté for 2–3 minutes.

4 Stir in the carrots and cauliflower and cook for 2–4 minutes before adding the coriander and salt. Then add the mushrooms and sauté, stirring, for 2–3 minutes or until they soften. Add the baby corn and sauté for 1–2 minutes. Next add the beans and peas, mixing together well. Add the chickpea flour and stir for 2–3 minutes, then add the spinach paste and bring to a boil, stirring in the butter and half-and-half.

5 As soon as the vegetables are boiling, check for seasoning and correct if necessary. Finish with the fenugreek leaves and garam masala. Do not cook for too long after adding the spinach paste as it will discolor and make the dish look unappetizing. Serve with rice.

IF ADDING MEAT, stir-fry the chicken at the end of step 3 with the ginger and chiles, then continue as before.

INGREDIENTS

2 young carrots, diced
¼ cauliflower, cut into
  small florets
3½oz (100g) thin green beans,
  cut into short lengths
2¼lb (1kg) baby spinach leaves
5 tbsp ghee or vegetable oil
2 tsp cumin seeds
2 garlic cloves, finely chopped
1 large onion, finely chopped
1in (2½cm) piece fresh ginger,
  finely chopped
6 green chiles, seeded and
  finely chopped
1½ tsp ground coriander
2 tsp salt
3½oz (100g) button mushrooms
1¾oz (50g) baby corn, cut into
  short lengths
2oz (60g) fresh or frozen peas
1 tbsp gram (chickpea) flour
2 tbsp butter
¼ cup half-and-half
1 tsp crushed dried
  fenugreek leaves
1 tsp garam masala

OPTIONAL MEAT

2 large boneless, skinless
  chicken breasts, cut into
  strips

Snow pea, sweet potato, and cashew red curry

SERVES 4   **PREPARATION 10 MINS**   TO COOK **20 MINS**

Cooking the green vegetables quickly retains their color and texture. Butternut squash or pumpkin can be substituted for sweet potato and tofu for cashews.

INGREDIENTS

2 tbsp sunflower or vegetable oil

1 bunch scallions, cut into short lengths

1 sweet potato (approx. 1lb 5oz/600g), peeled and cut into walnut-sized pieces

1 garlic clove, crushed

1 tsp grated fresh ginger or galangal

1 tsp finely chopped lemongrass (or lemongrass purée)

3 tbsp Thai red curry paste

14oz (400ml) can coconut milk

6oz (175g) snow peas, trimmed

2 zucchini, cut into batonettes (see p320)

12 cherry tomatoes

4oz (115g) raw cashews

1 tbsp chopped cilantro

squeeze of lime juice

jasmine rice, to serve

1 fat red chile, seeded and cut into thin strips, to garnish

OPTIONAL MEAT

2–3 boneless, skinless duck breasts, cut into cubes

1 Heat the oil in a large saucepan or wok. Add the scallions and stir-fry gently for 2 minutes until softened but not colored. Add the sweet potato and cook, stirring, for 1 minute.

2 Stir in the garlic, ginger, lemongrass, curry paste, and coconut milk. Bring to a boil, reduce the heat, cover, and simmer gently for 10 minutes or until the sweet potato is tender.

3 Meanwhile, cook the snow pea and zucchini batonettes in boiling water for 2–3 minutes until just tender. Drain.

4 Stir the snow peas and zucchini into the curry with the tomatoes, nuts, and cilantro. Spike with a squeeze of lime juice and simmer for 2 minutes until the tomatoes are softened slightly but still hold their shape. Spoon the curry over jasmine rice served in bowls and garnish with strips of red chile.

IF ADDING MEAT, fry the duck cubes with the scallions at step 1 and omit the cashews.

Mixed vegetable curry

SERVES 4   **PREPARATION 15 MINS**   TO COOK **25–30 MINS**

In this popular South Indian dish, **mixed vegetables are cooked in a delightful spicy tomato masala**. The coconut milk makes it creamy and slightly sweet.

INGREDIENTS

1 large carrot
1 potato
3½oz (100g) green beans, fresh or frozen
3 tbsp vegetable oil
2 onions, cut into small pieces
1 green chile, slit lengthways and seeded
½ tsp chile powder
½ tsp ground coriander
½ tsp ground turmeric
salt
¼ small cauliflower, separated into florets
½ cup coconut milk

For the spice paste
2 garlic cloves, peeled
¾in (2cm) piece fresh ginger, finely chopped
1 green chile, seeded and finely chopped
½ tsp fennel seeds
3½oz (100g) tomatoes, chopped

OPTIONAL MEAT
4 boneless, skinless chicken thighs, cut into bite-sized pieces

1 Grind all the ingredients for the spice paste in a mortar and pestle or a blender until fine. Set aside.

2 Cut the carrots, potatoes, and green beans into 1in (2½cm) pieces and set aside.

3 Heat the oil in a large pot, add the onions and green chile and cook for about 5 minutes until the onions are soft. Add the carrots, chile powder, coriander, turmeric, and salt to taste. Mix well. Lower the heat and add the potatoes and 3 tbsp water. Cover and cook very gently for 10 minutes.

4 Add the cauliflower and beans together with the spice paste and mix well. Cook, covered, for a further 10–15 minutes, adding a dash of water, if necessary, to prevent the mixture sticking to the pan.

5 Remove the pan from the heat and slowly add the coconut milk, stirring to blend well. Serve hot.

IF ADDING MEAT, serve as a side dish with any chicken or meat curry, or add the bite-sized chicken pieces with the cauliflower and green beans at step 4 and cook as before.

Spinach and yogurt curry

SERVES 4   **PREPARATION 10 MINS**   **TO COOK 15 MINS**

This is a **mild dish, but can be made spicier** if preferred. Avoid boiling it after adding the yogurt or it will curdle. A yogurt curry is best eaten with rice.

1 Heat the oil in a large saucepan and add the mustard seeds. As they begin to pop, add the fenugreek seeds. Then add the garlic, dried chiles, and curry leaves and sauté for 1 minute. Add the shallots, green chiles, and ginger and cook, stirring occasionally, until the shallots turn brown.

2 Add the green lentils, tomatoes, turmeric, and some salt to taste. Mix thoroughly, then add the spinach and cook for 5 minutes, stirring occasionally.

3 Remove the pan from the heat and gradually add the yogurt, stirring slowly and constantly. Set the pan on a low heat and warm gently for 3 minutes, stirring constantly. Serve the curry warm with Basmati rice.

IF ADDING FISH, omit the lentils. Poach the fish fillets in a little water with a bay leaf added for 5 minutes or until the flesh is opaque and flakes easily with a fork. Drain. Place on a bed of rice on serving plates or in bowls and spoon the spinach and yogurt curry over.

INGREDIENTS

2 tbsp vegetable oil
½ tsp mustard seeds
pinch of fenugreek seeds
2 garlic cloves, finely chopped
3 dried red chiles
10 curry leaves
3½oz (100g) shallots, chopped
3 green chiles, slit lengthways
   and seeded
1in (2½cm) piece fresh ginger,
   finely chopped
2 × 14oz (400g) cans
   green lentils
2 tomatoes, finely chopped
½ tsp ground turmeric
salt
3½oz (100g) spinach, chopped
10oz (300g) plain yogurt

OPTIONAL FISH
4 × 5½oz (150g) white
   fish fillets
1 bay leaf

Vegetable dahl with tandoori paneer

SERVES 4   **PREPARATION 20 MINS, PLUS MARINATING**   TO COOK **35 MINS**

Presentation is key to this dish. Choose the loosest iceberg you can find, cut off the stump, then carefully peel off four good, bowl-shaped leaves.

INGREDIENTS

3 cups vegetable stock
8oz (225g) red lentils
1 tsp ground cumin
1 tsp ground turmeric
½ tsp ground coriander
1 cinnamon stick
2 tbsp sunflower or vegetable oil
1 onion, chopped
1 garlic clove, crushed
2 tbsp Madras curry paste
2 carrots, diced
2 potatoes, diced
5½oz (150g) green beans, cut in short lengths
2 tomatoes, roughly chopped
4 large iceberg lettuce leaves
paprika, to garnish
mango chutney, to serve

For the paneer

9oz (250g) block paneer
2 tbsp tandoori paste
4oz (115g) plain yogurt
1 large garlic clove, crushed
1 tbsp chopped cilantro
salt and freshly ground black pepper

OPTIONAL MEAT

4 small boneless, skinless chicken breasts

1 First, prepare the paneer. Cut the block into 4 strips widthways, then cut each strip in half horizontally to make 8 thinner slabs. Make slashes on each side with a sharp knife, just cutting the surface. Mix the tandoori paste with the yogurt, garlic, coriander, and a pinch of salt. Add the paneer, turn to coat completely, then cover and chill for 2 hours.

2 About 40 minutes before you intend to eat, pour the stock into a saucepan. Bring to a boil and add the lentils and spices. Season well. Bring to a boil, reduce the heat, and simmer for 25–30 minutes until the lentils are tender, stirring occasionally. If necessary, boil rapidly for 1–2 minutes to evaporate any remaining liquid.

3 Meanwhile, in a separate pan, heat the oil and fry the onion and garlic for 3 minutes, stirring, until softened and slightly browned. Add the curry paste and fry for 30 seconds, then gently stir in the carrots, potatoes, and beans. Add ⅔ cup water and salt and pepper. Bring to a boil, reduce the heat, cover, and simmer gently for 10–15 minutes until the vegetables are tender. Remove the lid and boil rapidly to evaporate any remaining liquid, if necessary.

4 Stir the vegetable mixture into the cooked lentils and season to taste. Gently fold in the tomatoes. Cover and keep warm.

5 Oil and preheat a grill pan. Shake excess marinade off the paneer. Grill for 1–2 minutes on each side, pressing down with a metal spatula, until striped and brown in places. Remove from the grill.

6 Spoon the curry into the lettuce on serving plates. Add the paneer. Dust the plates with paprika and serve with mango chutney.

IF ADDING MEAT, use chicken instead of paneer. Prepare in the same way but grill for 6–8 minutes on each side until striped brown and cooked through.

Potato and green bean stew

SERVES 4   **PREPARATION 10 MINS**   TO COOK **35 MINS**

This is a wonderful dish, **so easy to make and with a lovely flavor.** The vegetables can be replaced according to seasonality and to make the dish more colorful.

INGREDIENTS

2 tbsp sunflower or
   vegetable oil
1 tsp mustard seeds
2 dried red chiles
a few curry leaves
2 onions, chopped
½ tsp ground coriander
½ tsp ground garam masala
½ tsp ground turmeric
¼ tsp chile powder
2 tomatoes, quartered
2 potatoes, peeled and cut
   into wedges or cubes
3½oz (100g) green beans,
   fresh or frozen, cut into 1in
   (2½cm) pieces
salt
¾ cup coconut milk
pinch of crushed black
   peppercorns, to garnish

OPTIONAL MEAT
10oz (300g) chicken
   breast, diced

1 Heat the oil in a large saucepan and add the mustard seeds. When they begin to pop, add the dried chiles and curry leaves and sauté for 2 minutes. Stir in the onions and cook over moderate heat for 5 minutes, or until the onions are soft.

2 Stir in the coriander, garam masala, turmeric, and chile powder. Add the tomatoes and cook for 5 minutes. Add the potatoes and mix well, then cook over gentle heat for a further 5 minutes.

3 Add the beans and salt to taste. Cook for another minute, then reduce the heat to very low. Pour in the coconut milk and ½ cup water. Stir well to combine. Cook for 15–20 minutes, or until all the vegetables are tender. Garnish with the black peppercorns and serve hot.

IF ADDING MEAT, stir in the diced chicken breast with the onions at step 1 and continue as before.

Curries, stews, and casseroles
Black-eyed peas with spinach and tomato curry

SERVES 4   **PREPARATION 10 MINS**   TO COOK **12 MINS**

A refreshing and light curry, this is **easy to make and very versatile**. Double the quantity of peas for a more substantial meal. Take care not to overcook the yogurt.

INGREDIENTS

3 tbsp vegetable oil
½ tsp mustard seeds
2 garlic cloves, finely chopped
10 curry leaves
1 large onion, chopped
2 green chiles, slit lengthways
½ tsp chile powder
1 tsp ground coriander
½ tsp ground turmeric
3 tomatoes, chopped
3½oz (100g) spinach, chopped
14oz (400g) can black-eyed
  peas, rinsed and drained
salt
10oz (300g) plain yogurt
naan bread, to serve

OPTIONAL SHELLFISH

8oz (225g) cooked, peeled
  shrimp (thawed if frozen)

1 Heat the oil in a large saucepan and add the mustard seeds. When they start to pop, add the garlic, curry leaves, and onion. Cook over medium heat for 5 minutes, or until the onion is soft.

2 Add the green chiles, chile powder, coriander, and turmeric. Mix well and add the tomato pieces. Stir, then add the spinach. Cook over low heat for 5 minutes.

3 Add the black-eyed peas with salt to taste. Cook for another minute, or until everything is hot. Remove the pan from the heat and slowly add the yogurt, stirring well. Serve warm with plenty of naan bread.

IF ADDING SHELLFISH, replace the black-eyed peas with shrimp at step 3.

Okra and eggplant spicy masala

SERVES 4   **PREPARATION 10 MINS**   **TO COOK 20–25 MINS**

Okra and eggplant blend well here with aromatic spices for a fairly mild curry. This can be eaten as a main dish with chapattis or as a fantastic side dish.

1 Heat the oil in a saucepan and add the fenugreek seeds, fennel seeds, cardamom pods, cinnamon stick, bay leaf, garlic, and onions. Cook, stirring occasionally, until the onions are golden brown.

2 Add the turmeric, chile powder, coriander, and tomato paste and stir well. Cook for another minute. Stir in the tomatoes and 2 cups water. Bring to a boil, then reduce the heat and simmer for about 10 minutes, or until the sauce is thick.

3 Add the okra and eggplant to the sauce with salt to taste and stir thoroughly. Cover and cook over low heat for 5 minutes, or until the eggplant and okra become tender. Garnish with chopped cilantro and serve hot.

IF ADDING MEAT, fry the lamb with the onions at step 1, then continue as before. Alternatively, serve the masala as an accompaniment to any meat or fish curry.

INGREDIENTS

3 tbsp vegetable oil
pinch of fenugreek seeds
pinch of fennel seeds
2–3 cardamom pods
¾in (2cm) cinnamon stick
1 bay leaf
3 garlic cloves, chopped
2 onions, finely chopped
½ tsp ground turmeric
½ tsp chile powder
1 tsp ground coriander
1 tbsp tomato paste
2 tomatoes, finely chopped
5½oz (150g) okra, cut into pieces
5½oz (150g) eggplant,
  cut into pieces
salt
2 tbsp chopped cilantro
  leaves, to garnish

OPTIONAL MEAT

10oz (300g) lamb loin, cut
  into cubes

Potato and green bean stew

SERVES 4   PREPARATION **10 MINS**   TO COOK **35 MINS**

This is a wonderful dish, **so easy to make and with a lovely flavor.** The vegetables can be replaced according to seasonality and to make the dish more colorful.

INGREDIENTS

2 tbsp sunflower or
   vegetable oil
1 tsp mustard seeds
2 dried red chiles
a few curry leaves
2 onions, chopped
½ tsp ground coriander
½ tsp ground garam masala
½ tsp ground turmeric
¼ tsp chile powder
2 tomatoes, quartered
2 potatoes, peeled and cut
   into wedges or cubes
3½oz (100g) green beans,
   fresh or frozen, cut into 1in
   (2½cm) pieces
salt
¾ cup coconut milk
pinch of crushed black
   peppercorns, to garnish

OPTIONAL MEAT

10oz (300g) chicken
   breast, diced

1 Heat the oil in a large saucepan and add the mustard seeds. When they begin to pop, add the dried chiles and curry leaves and sauté for 2 minutes. Stir in the onions and cook over moderate heat for 5 minutes, or until the onions are soft.

2 Stir in the coriander, garam masala, turmeric, and chile powder. Add the tomatoes and cook for 5 minutes. Add the potatoes and mix well, then cook over gentle heat for a further 5 minutes.

3 Add the beans and salt to taste. Cook for another minute, then reduce the heat to very low. Pour in the coconut milk and ½ cup water. Stir well to combine. Cook for 15–20 minutes, or until all the vegetables are tender. Garnish with the black peppercorns and serve hot.

IF ADDING MEAT, stir in the diced chicken breast with the onions at step 1 and continue as before.

Vegetables with lentils

SERVES 4   PREPARATION **15 MINS, PLUS SOAKING**   TO COOK **35–40 MINS**

The lentils add substance and a delicious texture to this curry from South India. Also try it with baby corn or fava beans instead of green beans.

1 To make the spice paste, toast the coconut and spices in a dry frying pan, stirring for 1–2 minutes until brown. Leave to cool, then grind in a food processor, gradually adding about 1 cup water to make a fine paste. Set aside.

2 Bring 1¼ cup water to a boil in a saucepan and add the lentils, turmeric, chile powder, and onions. Simmer for 15–20 minutes until the lentils are well cooked.

3 Add the carrots, beans, tomatoes, and potatoes and stir well. Cover and cook for 10 minutes, or until the vegetables are tender.

4 Add the tamarind paste and salt to the vegetables. Cover and cook for a further 5 minutes. Stir in the spice paste. Bring to a boil, then reduce the heat to medium and cook, uncovered, for 5 minutes, stirring occasionally. Taste and add more salt, if necessary.

5 For tempering, heat the oil in a frying pan and add the mustard seeds. As they begin to pop, add the curry leaves and dried red chiles. Pour this over the curry and gently stir through. Serve hot with rice and/or naan bread.

IF ADDING FISH, mix together the cumin, sweet paprika, smoked paprika, and chile powder. Rub all over the red mullet or mackerel fillets. Brush with oil and grill skin-side up for 5–6 minutes until golden and cooked through. Serve alongside the vegetables and lentils.

INGREDIENTS

3½oz (100g) split yellow lentils
1 tsp ground turmeric
1 tsp chile powder
2 onions, cut into small pieces
1 large carrot, cut into
 1in (2½cm) pieces
3½oz (100g) green beans,
 frozen or fresh, cut into
 1in (2½cm) pieces
3 tomatoes, quartered
3½oz (100g) potatoes, peeled
 and cut into cubes
1 tbsp tamarind paste
pinch of salt
naan bread or rice, to serve

For the spice paste

½ cup unsweetened coconut
2 tsp coriander seeds
1 dried red chile

For tempering

1 tbsp vegetable oil
1 tsp mustard seeds
10 curry leaves
3 dried red chiles

OPTIONAL FISH

1 tsp each ground cumin, sweet
 paprika, and smoked paprika
½ tsp chile powder
4 red mullet or mackerel fillets

Chickpea and spinach masala with bhatura

SERVES 4   PREPARATION **10 MINS**   TO COOK **30 MINS**

Bhatura is a puffy fried bread traditionally served with chole—spicy chickpeas. **It tastes good with any spiced dish** and makes a lovely change from naan or chapatti.

INGREDIENTS

vegetable oil
2 large onions, chopped
1 large garlic clove, crushed
1 tsp ground cumin
1 tsp ground coriander
1 tsp grated fresh ginger
¼ tsp ground cloves
½ tsp chile powder
14fl oz (400ml) vegetable stock
1 tsp granulated sugar
3 potatoes, cut into large cubes
2 × 14oz (400g) cans chickpeas, drained
salt and freshly ground black pepper
14oz (400g) spinach
4 tomatoes, cut into wedges
¼ cup plain yogurt and 1 tbsp snipped chives, to garnish

For the bhatura

⅓ cup whole wheat flour
⅓ cup all-purpose flour, plus extra for dusting
1 tsp baking powder
¼ tsp baking soda
½ tsp granulated sugar
¼ cup plain yogurt
2–3 tbsp milk

OPTIONAL MEAT

8oz (225g) pork tenderloin, diced

1 Heat 2 tbsp oil in a pan, add the onions, and stir-fry for 2 minutes. Add the garlic and all the spices and fry for 30 seconds.

2 Pour in the stock and stir in the remaining ingredients except the spinach and tomatoes. Season with salt and pepper. Bring to a boil, stir, partially cover, and simmer for 15 minutes. Stir in the spinach until beginning to wilt, then add the tomatoes, partially cover, and cook for 5 minutes, until the spinach is tender and everything is bathed in a rich sauce. Taste and adjust the seasoning if necessary.

3 Meanwhile, make the bhatura. Mix the ingredients together with ¼ tsp salt and 2 tsp oil, using enough milk to form a soft but not sticky dough. Working quickly, knead the dough gently on a floured surface and shape into 4 balls. Roll out each to a 4in (10cm) round.

4 Heat the oil for deep-frying to 350°F (180°C) or until a cube of day-old bread browns in 30 seconds. Slide a bhatura into the hot oil and fry for about 2 minutes, turning once, until puffy and golden. Remove from the pan with tongs or a metal spatula, drain on paper towels, then keep warm while cooking the remainder in the same way, reheating the oil each time.

5 Spoon the chickpea masala into bowls. Top each with a spoonful of yogurt, then sprinkle with the chives. Serve with the bhatura.

IF ADDING MEAT, use only 1 can of chickpeas. Fry the diced pork tenderloin in the oil with the onions at step 1 before adding the spices, then continue as before.

Potato and tomato curry

SERVES 4   **PREPARATION 15 MINS**   TO COOK **30 MINS**

Potato curry is an extremely versatile dish—it can be eaten for breakfast, lunch, or dinner, either alone or with bread or rice. Leftovers are great cold, too.

INGREDIENTS

2 tbsp sunflower or vegetable oil
1 large onion, finely chopped
2 large plum tomatoes, peeled
   and chopped
2–3 red chiles, seeded
   and chopped
½ tsp red chile powder
1 tsp cumin seeds
salt
1lb 2oz (500g) potatoes,
   peeled and cut in bite-sized
   chunks, or whole new
   potatoes
chopped cilantro leaves,
   to garnish

OPTIONAL MEAT

4 pork chops
1 tbsp chile oil

1 Heat the oil in a saucepan, add the onion, and cook for 3 minutes or until slightly browned. Add the chopped tomatoes, then stir in the chiles, chile powder, cumin seeds, and salt to taste. Add ½ cup water and cook, stirring, until the excess liquid has evaporated.

2 Add the potatoes, together with another ½ cup water. Stir well to coat the potatoes with the spice mixture, then put the lid on the pan. Cook for 15–20 minutes, or until the potatoes are tender but not breaking up.

3 Remove the lid and continue cooking until the oil separates out. Garnish with chopped cilantro and serve hot.

IF ADDING MEAT, brush the pork chops with chile oil and cook on a hot grill for 3–4 minutes on each side or until the meat feels firm. Wrap in foil and rest in a warm place for 10 minutes before serving. Alternatively, serve the potato curry as an accompaniment to any meat or fish curry.

Red curry of oyster mushrooms and tofu

SERVES 4   **PREPARATION 10 MINS**   **TO COOK 12 MINS**

Tamarind and kaffir limes add tartness to this rustic curry. Reduce the amount of both for a milder flavor, and try the dish with shiitake mushrooms instead.

1 In a saucepan, simmer the red curry paste in the coconut cream, stirring, for 3–5 minutes until fragrant. Season with the sugar, salt, soy sauce, and tamarind paste. Add the coconut milk and bring to a boil, then add the mushrooms, tofu, spinach, and kaffir lime leaves.

2 Cut the kaffir limes in half and seed. Squeeze them and add to the curry along with their juice. Simmer for 5 minutes until the mushrooms and spinach are cooked. Check the seasoning and adjust according to taste, then remove the lime shells and serve the curry spooned over jasmine rice.

IF ADDING FISH, cut the fillets into bite-sized chunks. Add to the curry with the mushrooms in step 1. Retain or omit the tofu as desired.

INGREDIENTS

2½ tbsp Thai red curry paste
½ cup coconut cream
1 heaped tbsp palm sugar or
    brown sugar
pinch of salt
2 tsp light soy sauce
2 tbsp tamarind paste
14oz (400ml) can coconut milk
7oz (200g) oyster mushrooms,
    cut up if large
9oz (250g) firm tofu, drained
    and diced
4oz (115g) baby spinach leaves
7 kaffir lime leaves
2 small kaffir (or ordinary) limes
jasmine rice, to serve

OPTIONAL FISH
9oz (250g) skinned tilapia,
    trout, or other sustainable
    freshwater fish fillets

Heart of palm green curry

SERVES 4 **PREPARATION 10 MINS** **TO COOK 10 MINS**

Heart of palm has a **crunch that offers a wonderful textural contrast to the creamy, spicy sauce**. For added color, throw in some cherry tomatoes in step 2.

INGREDIENTS

5 tbsp coconut cream
¼ cup Thai green curry paste
14oz (400g) can hearts of palm,
  drained and cut into
  bite-sized pieces
4–5 baby corn, each cut
  in half lengthways
light soy sauce, to taste
14oz (400ml) can coconut milk
a few picked pea
  eggplant (optional)
3 kaffir lime leaves, torn
3 green chiles, seeded
  and thinly sliced at an angle
handful of Thai (or ordinary)
  basil leaves, torn
jasmine rice, to serve

OPTIONAL SHELLFISH

5½oz (150g) cooked
  crayfish tails
Thai fish sauce

1 Heat the coconut cream in a saucepan, add the curry paste, and cook over high heat for 3 minutes, stirring regularly. Add the hearts of palm and corn, and fry for a further 3 minutes or until the paste looks scrambled and smells cooked. Season with light soy sauce.

2 Pour in the coconut milk, stirring gently. Bring to a boil and add the remaining ingredients except the basil. Check the seasoning and adjust if necessary. Simmer for 2 minutes, then stir in the basil. Spoon over jasmine rice in bowls and serve.

IF ADDING SHELLFISH, add the crayfish tails with the remaining ingredients at step 2 and simmer as before to heat them through. Use Thai fish sauce instead of soy sauce, if preferred.

Aromatic curry of pumpkin

SERVES 4   PREPARATION **10 MINS**   TO COOK **20 MINS**

Try sweet potato and carrot as alternatives to pumpkin and potato. Cooking the paste first releases its wonderful flavor. Serve this dish over noodles or sticky rice.

1 Blanch the potato in boiling water for 3 minutes, then drain and set aside. Heat the coconut cream in a saucepan, add the curry paste, and cook over medium heat for about 3 minutes, or until it is quite fragrant. Stir regularly to prevent the paste from scorching. Season with the palm sugar and soy sauce.

2 Stir in the coconut milk, salt, pumpkin, and potato, and bring to a boil. Mix in a little water, as this helps to prevent the coconut milk from splitting as the pumpkin cooks. Simmer gently over medium heat for about 10 minutes, or until the vegetables are tender.

3 Meanwhile, heat the oil in a frying pan and fry the onions, stirring over medium heat for about 8 minutes until golden and tender. Drain on paper towels. Serve the curry topped with the onions.

IF ADDING MEAT, put the steak in a plastic bag and beat with a meat mallet or rolling pin to flatten. Cut into thin strips. Omit the potato, if preferred. Simmer the meat gently in the coconut milk in a covered pan for 20 minutes before adding the vegetables at step 2, then continue as before.

INGREDIENTS

1 large potato, peeled and cut
  into bite-sized chunks
¼ cup coconut cream
¼ cup Thai red curry paste
2 tsp palm sugar or
  brown sugar
2 tbsp light soy sauce
2 × 14oz (400ml) cans
  coconut milk
pinch of salt
½ small pumpkin,
  peeled and cut into
  bite-sized chunks (approx.
  12oz/350g prepared weight)
2 tbsp vegetable oil
2 red onions, sliced

OPTIONAL MEAT
9oz (250g) lean sirloin steak

Four ways with
Avocados

Quesadilla with avocado, scallion, and chile ▶

TAKES 25 mins **MAKES** 1

Put 4 finely chopped **scallions**, 1–2 **hot red chiles**, seeded and finely chopped, and juice of ½ **lime** in a bowl. Season with **salt** and freshly ground **black pepper** and mix. Heat 1½ tbsp **olive oil** in a non-stick frying pan, then fry 1 **flour tortilla** for 1 minute. Scatter over ½ sliced **avocado**, leaving some space around the edge. Spoon on the scallion mixture and sprinkle with 1¾oz (50g) **Cheddar cheese**. Top with another tortilla; press down with the back of a spatula. Turn the quesadilla over and cook the other side for 1 minute. Slice in half or quarters and serve.

◀ Avocado with roasted cherry tomatoes and paprika dressing

TAKES 20 mins **SERVES** 4

Preheat the oven to 400°F (200°C). Toss 12oz (350g) **cherry tomatoes** with 1 tbsp **olive oil** on a baking sheet. Add some **thyme** leaves and season with **salt** and freshly ground **black pepper**. Roast for 12–15 minutes. Whisk together ⅓ cup olive oil, 3 tbsp **white wine vinegar**, 1 tsp **paprika**, a pinch of **granulated sugar**, and ½ tsp **mayonnaise**. Season. Halve, pit, and peel 2 ripe **avocados**. Slice lengthways without cutting all the way through, then fan out. Place a fan on each plate with some **wild arugula** leaves and the tomatoes. Spoon the dressing over and serve.

The most widely available types of avocado are the dark, knobby-skinned Hass and the green, smooth-skinned Fuerte. Both have a **nutty flavor, creamy-yellow color, and oily texture**; the latter are easier to peel.

Avocado mousse with lime ▶

TAKES 15 mins, plus chilling **SERVES** 4

Halve and pit 2 large ripe **avocados**. Scoop the flesh into a bowl, add the grated zest and juice of 1 **lime**, and mash until smooth. Beat in 3½oz (100g) **low-fat cream cheese** and season with **salt** and freshly ground **black pepper**. Sprinkle 2 tsp powdered **gelatine** over 2 tbsp water in a small heatproof bowl. Leave for 1 minute, then place the bowl in a pan of hot water and stir the gelatine until it dissolves. Whisk 1 **egg white** in a bowl to form soft peaks. Drizzle the dissolved gelatine into the avocado mixture and stir. Fold in the egg white without knocking out the air. Spoon into ramekins, cover with plastic wrap, and chill for 2 hours.

◀ Avocado, tomato, and mozzarella salad

TAKES 20 mins **SERVES** 4

Preheat the broiler to the highest setting. Put 7oz (200g) small **plum tomatoes** on a baking sheet. Add **salt** and freshly gound **black pepper**, 2 sliced **garlic cloves**, and 2 chopped **scallions**. Drizzle with ¼ cup **extra virgin olive oil**. Broil for 4–5 minutes. Place in a bowl with the juices. Add 2 tbsp **balsamic vinegar**, 2 tbsp **capers**, rinsed, 5½oz (150g) torn **buffalo mozzarella**, and shredded **basil leaves**. Toss gently. Peel, pit, and quarter 2 ripe **avocados**. Place 2 quarters on each plate. Spoon the tomato mixture over and drizzle with balsamic vinegar. Serve immediately.

Vietnamese vegetable and tofu curry

SERVES 4   **PREPARATION 10 MINS**   **TO COOK 25 MINS**

This recipe combines smooth tofu, crunchy bamboo, and slightly smoky eggplant to make a subtle, mild curry. Try it over brown jasmine rice for a change.

INGREDIENTS

1½ tbsp vegetable oil

1 large garlic clove, crushed

1 shallot, thinly sliced

1 tbsp curry powder

2 tsp palm sugar or
   brown sugar

14oz (400ml) can coconut milk

juice of ½ lime

1 tsp annatto seed extract
   or ground turmeric

1 stalk lemongrass, finely
   chopped (or 2 tsp purée)

1 kaffir lime leaf, bruised

salt

1lb 2oz (500g) firm tofu, cut
   into 1in (2½cm) cubes

7oz (225g) can bamboo
   shoots, drained

1 eggplant, halved lengthways
   and cut into 1in (2½cm) pieces

a few cilantro leaves or Thai
   basil leaves, to garnish

OPTIONAL MEAT

1lb 2oz (500g) boneless,
   skinless chicken breast, diced

1 Heat the oil in a saucepan over high heat and stir-fry the garlic and shallot for about 2–3 minutes, or until they are golden. Add the curry powder and sugar and continue to stir-fry for 1 minute, or until fragrant.

2 Add the coconut milk, lime juice, annatto seed extract or turmeric, lemongrass, and kaffir lime leaf. Bring to a boil, then reduce the heat to low. Adjust the seasoning with salt and add the tofu, bamboo shoots, and eggplant. Simmer, covered, for 10–15 minutes, or until the eggplant is tender. Discard the lemongrass. Serve garnished with cilantro or Thai basil.

IF ADDING MEAT, omit the tofu and add the chicken cubes with the bamboo shoots and eggplant at step 2, then continue as before.

Thai-style baby eggplant curry

SERVES 4   **PREPARATION 20–25 MINS**   **TO COOK 40 MINS**

In this **light curry with hot, sweet, and sour flavors,** Thai basil makes a good alternative to cilantro. Non-vegetarians can add Thai fish sauce instead of soy sauce.

1 Heat half the oil in a large, heavy-based saucepan, add the onion, and cook over low heat for 2–3 minutes. Stir in the garlic, cinnamon stick, star anise, chile, lemongrass, and lime leaves, and season with salt and pepper. Add the remaining oil and eggplant. Cook over medium heat for 5 minutes, or until the eggplant begins to turn slightly golden.

2 Add a little coconut milk, sprinkle in the sugar, stir, and bring to a boil. Add the remaining coconut milk and the stock, and bring to a boil. Reduce the heat, add a splash of light soy sauce, and simmer, uncovered, for 20 minutes. In a separate bowl, cook the noodles according to instructions. Drain.

3 Taste the curry and add more soy sauce or sugar if needed. Remove the star anise and cinnamon stick. Chop half the cilantro and stir in. Divide the noodles between 4 bowls and ladle the curry over. Top with the remaining cilantro and serve with the lime wedges.

IF ADDING MEAT, use 4 baby eggplants instead of 8. Fry the duck with the eggplant in the oil at step 1, then continue as before.

INGREDIENTS

2 tbsp sunflower or vegetable oil
1 onion, finely chopped
3 garlic cloves, finely chopped
1 cinnamon stick
1 star anise
1 red chile, seeded and finely chopped
1 tsp finely chopped lemongrass (or use purée)
4 kaffir lime leaves, bruised
salt and freshly ground black pepper
8 baby eggplants, sliced into quarters lengthways, or 2 regular eggplants, roughly chopped
14oz (400ml) can coconut milk
½ tsp palm sugar or brown sugar
2 cups vegetable stock
light soy sauce, to taste
7oz (200g) dried rice noodles
handful of cilantro leaves
lime wedges, to serve

OPTIONAL MEAT

2 boneless, skinless duck breasts, cut into thin strips

Spring vegetable stew with fresh herb dumplings

SERVES 4–6   **PREPARATION 20 MINS**   TO COOK **35 MINS**

This colorful mixture of fresh vegetables, **topped with fluffy dumplings**, has two kinds of dried beans for protein, as well as some grated cheese.

INGREDIENTS

2 tbsp butter

1 tbsp sunflower or vegetable oil

1 bunch scallions, chopped

2 leeks, cut into chunky pieces

2 large red potatoes, peeled and cut into bite-sized pieces

4 young carrots, cut into chunks

1 large turnip, cut into bite-sized pieces

14oz (400g) can chopped tomatoes

2 cups vegetable stock

14oz (400g) can navy beans, drained

14oz (400g) can kidney beans, drained

1 large bay leaf

salt and freshly ground black pepper

1 head escarole, shredded

grated Cheddar or Gruyère cheese, to serve

For the dumplings

¾ cup self-rising flour

4 tbsp butter

2 tbsp chopped parsley

2 tsp chopped thyme

2 tsp chopped sage

OPTIONAL MEAT

4 skinless chicken thighs

1 Melt the butter in a large saucepan with the oil. Add the scallions, leeks, potatoes, carrots, and turnip and fry gently, stirring, for 5 minutes until slightly softened but not browned.

2 Add the tomatoes, stock, beans, bay leaf, and some salt and pepper. Bring to a boil, reduce the heat, cover, and simmer gently for 15 minutes. Discard the bay leaf. Taste and adjust the seasoning, if necessary.

3 To make the dumplings, mix the flour with a pinch of salt in a bowl. Rub in the butter until the mixture resembles breadcrumbs, then stir in the herbs. Using a butter knife, mix in enough cold water to form a soft but not sticky dough. Quickly roll the dough into 8 balls.

4 Add the escarole to the stew and press down well. Bring back to a boil, reduce the heat and drop the dumplings around the top. Cover and simmer for 15 minutes until the dumplings are fluffy and cooked through. Serve hot with grated cheese to sprinkle over.

IF ADDING MEAT, brown the chicken thighs in oil and butter at step 1, then remove before frying the vegetables. Return the chicken to the pan at the beginning of step 2 before adding the tomatoes and stock. Cook as before, but omit one of the cans of beans.

Curries, stews, and casseroles
Chickpea and vegetable goulash

SERVES 4   **PREPARATION 20 MINS**   **TO COOK 30 MINS**

In winter, use root vegetables and shredded white cabbage for a seasonal twist. **For a more substantial meal, add some diced sweet potato, too.**

1 Heat the oil in a large non-stick saucepan. Add the onion and fry, stirring, for 2 minutes to soften. Add the eggplant, yellow and red peppers, and zucchini and cook, stirring, for 2 minutes.

2 Stir in the garlic and both types of paprika, then add the tomatoes, chickpeas, tomato paste, sugar, stock, bay leaf, and a little salt and a generous grinding of pepper. Bring to a boil, reduce the heat, partially cover, and simmer for 30 minutes, stirring occasionally, until everything is tender. If necessary, remove the lid and boil rapidly for a few minutes to thicken the liquid so everything is bathed in a rich, thick sauce. Discard the bay leaf. Stir in the parsley. Taste and adjust the seasoning, if necessary.

3 Spoon the goulash into warmed bowls and top with a dollop of yogurt and a sprinkling of caraway seeds. Serve with plenty of crusty bread and a green salad.

IF ADDING MEAT, brown the pork and chorizo with the onions at step 1, then continue as before.

INGREDIENTS

2 tbsp olive oil
1 large onion, chopped
1 large eggplant, diced
1 yellow bell pepper, seeded and diced
1 red bell pepper, seeded and diced
2 zucchini, thickly sliced
1 large garlic clove, crushed
1 tsp smoked paprika
1 tbsp sweet paprika
14oz (400g) can chopped tomatoes
2 × 14oz (400g) cans chickpeas, drained
2 tbsp tomato paste
½ tsp granulated sugar
²/₃ cup vegetable stock
1 bay leaf
salt and freshly ground black pepper
2 tbsp chopped parsley
¼ cup thick plain yogurt
2 tsp caraway seeds
crusty bread and green salad, to serve

OPTIONAL MEAT
2 pork belly slices, diced
2½oz (75g) diced chorizo

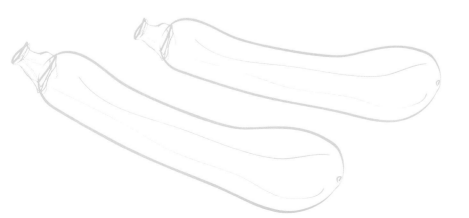

Red bean and chestnut bourguignon

SERVES 4–6   **PREPARATION 25 MINS**   TO COOK **1¼–1½ HRS**

The chestnuts add a wonderful texture to this rich and flavorful stew—elegant enough for a dinner party, but good with comforting baked potatoes, too.

INGREDIENTS

1 tbsp olive oil

2 tbsp butter

2 red onions, quartered

1 garlic clove, crushed

16 baby chantenay carrots
(approx. 4oz/115g), trimmed

8 baby turnips, peeled but
left whole (or 2 larger ones,
cut into chunks)

5½oz (150g) crimini or white
button mushrooms

2 tbsp all-purpose flour

1¼ cups red wine

1¼ cups vegetable stock

2 tbsp brandy

1 tbsp tomato paste

good pinch of granulated sugar

8oz (240g) can cooked,
peeled chestnuts

14oz (400g) can red kidney
beans, rinsed and drained

1 bouquet garni sachet

salt and freshly ground
black pepper

fluffy mashed or baked potatoes
and broccoli, to serve

OPTIONAL MEAT

14oz (400g) lean sirloin steak,
cut into small cubes

1 Preheat the oven to 350°F (180°C). Heat the oil and butter in a Dutch oven and fry the onions for 5 minutes, stirring, until richly browned.

2 Add the garlic, carrots, turnips, and mushrooms and fry for 2 minutes. Stir in the flour and cook for 1 minute. Gradually blend in the wine, stock, brandy, and tomato paste. Bring to a boil, stirring, until slightly thickened.

3 Stir in the sugar, chestnuts, beans, bouquet garni, and salt and pepper to taste. Cover the surface with wet parchment paper, then add the lid and cook in the oven for 1¼–1½ hours until the vegetables are really tender. Discard the bouquet garni, stir gently, then taste and adjust the seasoning if necessary. Serve hot with fluffy mashed or baked potatoes and broccoli.

IF ADDING MEAT, brown the sirloin steak in the oil and butter at step 1, then remove from the pan before adding the onions. Return to the pan at step 3 and omit the beans. Cook for 1½–2 hours until tender.

Creamy bean ragout with shredded kale

SERVES 4   **PREPARATION 15 MINS**   TO COOK **25 MINS**

The slightly bitter flavor of kale blends beautifully with the earthy beans and the sweet taste of celery root. Try different roots such as parsnips, carrots, or turnips, too.

INGREDIENTS

2 tbsp olive oil

1 leek, sliced

2 garlic cloves, chopped

1 tsp ground cumin

1 tsp dried chile flakes

½ tsp ground turmeric

2 star anise

2½ cups vegetable stock

2 × 14oz (400g) cans navy
   beans, drained

1 small celery root, diced

4oz (115g) button mushrooms

1 bay leaf

salt and freshly ground
   black pepper

9oz (250g) kale, finely
   shredded, discarding
   thick stumps

handful of cilantro, chopped

2 tbsp tahini paste

7oz (200g) crème fraîche

dash of lemon juice

OPTIONAL MEAT

1lb (450g) spicy pork sausages

1 Heat the oil in a large saucepan. Add the leek and fry, stirring, for 1 minute. Add the garlic and spices and fry for 30 seconds. Stir in the stock, beans, celery root, and mushrooms. Add the bay leaf, and a little salt and a generous grinding of pepper. Bring to a boil, reduce the heat, partially cover, and simmer gently for 15 minutes.

2 Add the kale, stir, and bring back to a boil. Reduce the heat, cover, and simmer for a further 8 minutes until everything is really tender. Discard the bay leaf and star anise.

3 Gently stir in the cilantro, tahini paste, and all but 2 tsp of the crème fraîche. Add lemon juice to taste and adjust the seasoning, if necessary.

4 Ladle into warmed bowls and add a swirl of the reserved crème fraîche.

IF ADDING MEAT, brown the sausages in a dry frying pan. Drain on paper towels, slice them up, and add to the ragout with the stock. Omit the tahini paste and use just 1 can of beans.

Curries, stews, and casseroles

Sweet potato, roasted pepper, and white bean hotpot

SERVES 4 **PREPARATION 20 MINS** **TO COOK 1 HR 10 MINS**

In this simple casserole, the **sweet potatoes are cooked on top for added texture and flavor**. They can be diced and added to the mixture before cooking, if preferred.

1 Preheat the oven to 375°F (190°C). Heat the oil in a Dutch oven and fry the onion for 3 minutes, stirring, until softened but not browned. Add the garlic and carrots and fry for 1 minute.

2 Add the wine, bring to a rapid boil and cook for about 2 minutes until the wine is well reduced.

3 Add the remaining ingredients except the sweet potatoes and butter. Stir well and season with salt and pepper. Bring to a boil.

4 Layer the sweet potatoes on top and brush liberally with the butter. Cover with the lid or foil and bake in the oven for 30 minutes. Increase the temperature to 425°F (220°C) and cook for a further 20–30 minutes until the potatoes are golden and tender. Serve hot with broccoli and baked potatoes.

IF ADDING MEAT, brown the diced lamb with the onion at step 1. Use just 1 can of navy beans.

INGREDIENTS

2 tbsp olive oil
1 large onion, chopped
2 garlic cloves, crushed
2 carrots, sliced
⅔ cup dry white wine
2 red bell peppers, roasted (see p326) and chopped
4oz (115g) crimini mushrooms, quartered
2 × 14oz (400g) cans navy beans, drained
14oz (400g) can chopped tomatoes
½ cup vegetable stock
2 tbsp oat bran
1 tbsp chopped thyme
generous pinch of granulated sugar
salt and freshly ground black pepper
2 sweet potatoes, cut into ¼in (5mm) slices
1 tbsp butter, melted
broccoli and baked potatoes, to serve

OPTIONAL MEAT
14oz (400g) lamb loin, diced

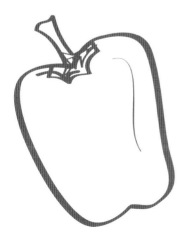

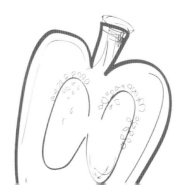

Chile bean and vegetable braise with fried eggs

SERVES 4   PREPARATION **15 MINS**   TO COOK **20 MINS**

Meaty-textured pinto beans in a spicy sauce make a substantial meal when topped with fried eggs and served with rice. Use red kidney beans as an alternative.

INGREDIENTS

olive oil, for frying
1 large onion, chopped
1 large garlic clove, crushed
1 large green bell pepper,
    seeded and diced
1 large yellow bell pepper,
    seeded and diced
½ butternut squash, diced
2 fat red or green chiles,
    seeded and finely chopped
½ tsp ground turmeric
1 tsp ground cumin
¼ tsp ground cloves
2 × 14oz (400g) cans pinto
    beans, rinsed and drained
14oz (400g) can chopped
    tomatoes
½ cup vegetable stock
2 tbsp tomato paste
1 tsp granulated sugar
a few pitted black or
    green olives, halved
handful of raisins
2 tsp red wine vinegar
4 large eggs
plain rice and a green salad,
    to serve
chopped cilantro and lime
    wedges, to garnish

OPTIONAL MEAT

2 handfuls of ground beef

1 Heat 2 tbsp of oil in a large frying pan or wok. Add the onion and fry, stirring, for 3 minutes until starting to soften and turn lightly golden. Add the garlic, green and yellow peppers, and squash, and fry for a further 2–3 minutes until starting to soften.

2 Add the remaining ingredients except the eggs. Bring to a boil, then reduce the heat to medium. Partially cover and simmer, stirring occasionally, for 15 minutes or until thick and pulpy and the vegetables are tender. Taste and adjust the seasoning, if necessary.

3 In a frying pan, fry the eggs in a little oil until cooked to your liking. Spoon the bean mixture onto plain rice in shallow bowls. Top with the eggs. Garnish with a sprinkling of cilantro and lime wedges and serve with a green salad.

IF ADDING MEAT, add the ground beef to the fried onions at step 1 and fry, stirring, until the grains are separate and no longer pink. Add the garlic, peppers, and squash and continue as before.

Mushroom and black-eyed pea stroganoff

SERVES 4–6   **PREPARATION 10 MINS**   **TO COOK 20 MINS**

Use mixed wild mushrooms when available, but **crimini or white cultivated varieties also work well**. Avoid large, flat ones as they will discolor the sauce.

INGREDIENTS

2 tbsp sunflower or vegetable oil
knob of butter
1 large onion, chopped
1 leek, chopped
2 garlic cloves, crushed
1½lb (675g) mushrooms,
    quartered
2 tbsp brandy
14oz (400g) can black-eyed
    peas, drained and rinsed
14oz (400g) crème fraîche
salt and freshly ground
    black pepper
handful of chopped parsley
plain rice and green salad,
    to serve

OPTIONAL MEAT

9oz (250g) steak tenderloin

1 Heat the oil and butter in a large pan and fry the onion and leek gently for 5 minutes, stirring, until golden.

2 Add the garlic and mushrooms and cook, stirring, for 1 minute. Cover and cook gently for 10 minutes.

3 Add the brandy and boil, uncovered, until most of the liquid has evaporated. Add the beans and heat through, stirring gently, for 2 minutes.

4 Stir in the crème fraîche and season with salt and pepper. Heat through, then stir in half the parsley.

5 Spoon the stroganoff over plain rice and sprinkle with the remaining parsley. Serve with a green salad.

IF ADDING MEAT, omit the black-eyed peas and replace them with steak. Cut into thin strips (or use flank steak, beaten flat and cut into very thin strips across the grain). Stir-fry in the oil and butter at step 1 before cooking the onion and leek. Remove from the pan with a slotted spoon and set aside. Return to the pan instead of the black-eyed peas at step 3.

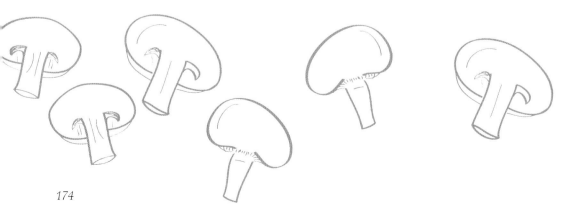

Creamy butternut squash and butter bean stew

SERVES 4   **PREPARATION 15 MINS**   TO COOK **20–25 MINS**

Pumpkin or sweet potato can be used instead of the butternut squash, and **any shredded green cabbage will taste good** in this stew when cavolo nero isn't available.

1 Heat the oil and butter in a large saucepan. Add the onion and fry gently, stirring, for 3–4 minutes until soft but not brown.

2 Add all the remaining ingredients except the cavolo nero, Calvados or brandy, and cream, seasoning with a little salt and plenty of pepper. Bring to a boil, reduce the heat, partially cover, and simmer gently for 8–15 minutes until the potato is tender. Add the cavolo nero and Calvados or brandy and press down in the liquid. Bring back to a boil, partially cover, and simmer for a further 4–5 minutes until everything is tender.

3 Gently stir in the cream and heat through for 1 minute. Ladle into bowls and serve hot with plenty of crusty bread.

IF ADDING MEAT, include the chicken with the vegetables at step 2 and use just 1 can of butter beans.

INGREDIENTS

1 tbsp sunflower or vegetable oil
large knob of butter
1 onion, chopped
1 turnip, cut into
  bite-sized chunks
1 large potato, peeled and
  cut into bite-sized chunks
1 butternut squash (approx.
  1½lb/675g), peeled, seeded,
  and cut into bite-sized chunks
2 × 14oz (400g) cans butter
  beans, drained and rinsed
1¼ cups hard cider
2 cups vegetable stock
1 bay leaf
small handful of chopped
  thyme, plus extra to garnish
1 tart apple, peeled, cored,
  and chopped
salt and freshly ground
  black pepper
6 cavolo nero leaves, shredded
2 tbsp Calvados or brandy
½ cup heavy cream
crusty bread, to serve

OPTIONAL MEAT

9oz (250g) boneless, skinless,
  chicken breast, diced

Vegetable choucroute garni

SERVES 4–6   **PREPARATION 15 MINS**   TO COOK **1 HR 20 MINS**

This version of a traditionally meat-based dish has an **abundance of flavor and color**. Roast frozen vegetables when time is short.

INGREDIENTS

1 eggplant, sliced

3 tbsp olive oil

1 large red bell pepper, seeded and cut into 6–8 thick strips

1 large green bell pepper, seeded and cut into 6–8 thick strips

9oz (250g) halloumi cheese, drained and cut into cubes

2 tsp smoked paprika

4 carrots, thickly sliced

2 turnips (or ½ daikon), cut into small chunks

2lb (950g) jar sauerkraut

¼ tsp ground cloves

12 juniper berries, crushed

⅔ cup dry white wine

⅔ cup vegetable stock

1 large bay leaf

salt and freshly ground black pepper

large handful of chopped parsley

plain boiled potatoes and mustard, to serve

OPTIONAL MEAT

4 pork belly slices

4 chicken thighs

4 bockwurst

1 Preheat a grill pan. Brush the eggplant slices with a little oil, then toss the red and green peppers in the remainder. Cook in batches for 3 minutes on each side, pressing down with a metal spatula, until charred brown in places and tender.

2 Mix the halloumi with the paprika and set aside. Blanch the carrot and turnip in boiling water for 3 minutes, then drain. Preheat the oven to 350°F (180°C). Rinse and drain the sauerkraut and place in a large casserole dish. Stir in the cloves and juniper berries, then add all the remaining ingredients except the parsley, seasoning well with salt and pepper. Stir gently.

3 Place a piece of parchment paper over the mixture, then cover the casserole with the lid and bake in the oven for 1 hour. Discard the bay leaf. Taste and adjust the seasoning, if necessary. Sprinkle with parsley and serve with plain boiled potatoes and mustard.

IF ADDING MEAT, brown the pork belly and chicken in a little oil for 5 minutes. Add them at step 2, along with the bockwurst. Omit the roasted vegetables, halloumi, and paprika. Alternatively, substitute just the bockwurst for the halloumi and paprika.

Cauliflower, broccoli, and tomato braise with cheese crumble

SERVES 4–6   **PREPARATION 20 MINS**   TO COOK **15–20 MINS**

Broccoli and cauliflower are always a good combination, and **simmered in a light tomato sauce under a blanket of golden cheesy crumbs**, they make a perfect light meal.

1 Cut the cauliflower and broccoli into even-sized florets, discarding the thick stump. Tear off any green leaves from the cauliflower stalks to cook with the florets, if liked.

2 Heat the oil in a Dutch oven and fry the onion, stirring, for 3 minutes until softened but not browned. Add the stock and bring to a boil.

3 Add the cauliflower and broccoli, cover, and cook for 3–5 minutes. Add the tomatoes, cover, and cook for a further 2 minutes or until the vegetables are tender. Stir in the remaining ingredients, season with salt and pepper, and simmer for a further 1 minute.

4 Meanwhile, preheat the broiler. Mix the crumble ingredients together and spoon over the braised vegetables. Place the Dutch oven under the broiler and cook for about 5 minutes until golden and the cheese is bubbling. (If need be, turn the vegetables into a shallow ovenproof dish to fit under the broiler.) Serve hot with crusty bread and a green salad.

IF ADDING MEAT, include the ham with the vegetables at step 3.

INGREDIENTS

1 small cauliflower
head of broccoli
   (approx. 10oz/300g)
1 tbsp sunflower or vegetable oil
1 onion, chopped
1¾ cups vegetable stock
4 ripe beefsteak tomatoes,
   peeled and chopped
2 tbsp tomato paste
generous pinch of
   granulated sugar
2 tbsp chopped basil
5 tbsp ground almonds
salt and freshly ground
   black pepper
crusty bread and green
   salad, to serve

For the crumble
2 tbsp butter, melted
1 cup whole wheat
   breadcrumbs
3oz (85g) sharp Cheddar
   cheese, grated
1oz (30g) Parmesan
   cheese, grated

OPTIONAL MEAT
large handful of chopped
   ham pieces

Pizzas, wraps, and quesadillas

Cheese, tomato, and mushroom pizza

MAKES 2 LARGE OR 4 SMALL PIZZAS   **PREPARATION** **20 MINS, PLUS PROOFING**   **TO COOK 35 MINS**

This pizza is delicious with the addition of a **handful of arugula on top to add a cool, peppery finish** to each bite. For a classic Margherita pizza, omit the mushrooms.

INGREDIENTS

2½ cups bread flour, plus extra
   for dusting
1 tsp salt
1 tsp granulated sugar
2 tsp fast-acting dried yeast
2 tbsp olive oil, plus extra for
   greasing and drizzling

For the topping
2 tbsp olive oil
1 small onion, finely chopped
2 garlic cloves, crushed
14oz (400g) can diced tomatoes
1 tbsp tomato paste
2 tsp dried oregano
pinch of sugar
salt and freshly ground
   black pepper
4oz (115g) crimini
   mushrooms, sliced
10oz (300g) fresh buffalo
   mozzarella, drained and
   torn into pieces
large handful of black olives
a few basil leaves

OPTIONAL MEAT
a few slices of pepperoni

1 Mix the flour, salt, sugar, and yeast together in a large bowl. Gradually add 1¼ cups warm water and 2 tbsp oil and stir until combined. Mix with your hands to bring it into a ball, then place on a lightly floured surface and knead for at least 5 minutes, adding a little more flour if needed, until the dough is springy to the touch, but not sticky. Shape into a ball and place in a large lightly oiled bowl. Cover with lightly oiled plastic wrap and leave to proof for 1 hour in a warm place, or until it has doubled in size.

2 Meanwhile, make the topping. Heat the oil in a saucepan, then add the onion and sauté over medium heat for 5 minutes. Stir in the garlic and cook for 1 minute. Add the tomatoes, tomato paste, oregano, and sugar. Season with salt and pepper and simmer uncovered for 10 minutes until pulpy. Set aside.

3 Preheat the oven to 425°F (220°C). Knead the risen dough again, then roll out to two 12–14in (30–35cm) rounds or 4 smaller rounds (about 8in/20cm). Place on oiled pizza plates or baking sheets and press out to rounds again with floured fingers. Alternatively, roll out to 2 large rectangles to just fit the baking sheets and press them into shape once transferred.

4 Divide the tomato sauce, sliced mushrooms, mozzarella, and olives between the pizzas. Season with pepper and drizzle with a little oil. Bake each pizza for 18–20 minutes until crisp and golden around the edges. Scatter with a few basil leaves before serving.

IF ADDING MEAT, scatter a few slices of pepperoni over the pizzas with the mushrooms.

Spinach, fresh tomato, and blue cheese pizza

MAKES 2 LARGE OR 4 SMALL PIZZAS   **PREPARATION 20 MINS, PLUS PROOFING**   TO COOK **20 MINS**

Try topping each pizza with six quail eggs 5 minutes before the end of the cooking time, making tiny wells in the surface of the pizza first.

1 Make and proof the pizza dough (see p180, step 1). While the dough is proofing, put the tomatoes in a bowl and cover with boiling water. Leave for 30 seconds, drain, plunge in cold water, then remove the skins and chop the flesh. Mix with the tomato paste, sugar, and some salt and pepper.

2 Shake the excess water from the spinach. Cook the spinach in a pan with no extra water for about 3 minutes until wilted, stirring. Drain thoroughly. Leave to cool, then squeeze out the excess liquid.

3 Preheat the oven to 425°F (220°C). Knead the risen dough again, then roll out to two 12–14in (30–35cm) rounds or 4 smaller rounds (about 8in/20cm). Place on oiled pizza plates or baking sheets and press out to rounds again with floured fingers. Alternatively, roll out to 2 large rectangles to just fit the baking sheets and press them into shape once transferred.

4 Spread the tomato mixture over the dough, not quite to the edges. Scatter the spinach and cheeses over. Sprinkle with the chopped sage, drizzle with a little more oil, and season with pepper. Bake each pizza for 18–20 minutes until the dough is golden brown.

IF ADDING MEAT, scatter the strips of Parma ham over the pizzas with the cheeses, then bake as before.

INGREDIENTS

1 quantity pizza dough
  (see p180)
8 ripe tomatoes
6 tbsp tomato paste
1 tsp granulated sugar
salt and freshly ground
  black pepper
1lb (450g) spinach, well washed
7oz (200g) blue cheese,
  crumbled
7oz (200g) mozzarella
  cheese, grated
12 sage leaves, chopped

OPTIONAL MEAT

4 slices Parma ham, cut
  into thin strips

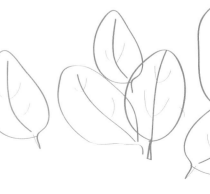

Beet, zucchini, and goat cheese pizzas

MAKES 2 LARGE OR 4 SMALL PIZZAS   **PREPARATION** **25 MINS, PLUS PROOFING**   TO COOK **20 MINS**

When time is short, use two 10oz (290g) pizza crust mixes. **Try this with peppers instead of zucchini** and slices of baby Camembert for a variation on goat cheese.

INGREDIENTS

1 quantity pizza dough
  (see p180)
5 tbsp olive oil
4 small zucchini, sliced
1 red onion, halved and
  thinly sliced
1 large garlic clove,
  finely chopped
2 tbsp chopped rosemary
$2/3$ cup tomato sauce
2 tbsp tomato paste
2 cooked beets (in
  natural juices), diced
4 handfuls of arugula,
  plus extra to garnish
2 × 4¼oz (120g) cylinders goat
  cheese, sliced
coarse sea salt
freshly ground black pepper

OPTIONAL MEAT
3½oz (100g) chopped bacon

1 Make and proof the pizza dough (see p180, step 1). While it is proofing, heat 3 tbsp oil in a frying pan. Add the zucchini, onion, garlic, and rosemary and cook, stirring, for 3 minutes until softened but not browned. Set aside.

2 When the dough has proofed, preheat the oven to 425°F (220°C). Knead the risen dough. Roll out to two 12–14in (30 –35cm) rounds or four 8in (20cm) rounds and place on oiled pizza plates or baking sheets. Press out the rounds again with floured fingers, then place in the oven and bake for 10 minutes to cook them partially.

3 Mix the tomato sauce with the tomato paste. Remove the pizzas from the oven and spread the tomato mixture over, followed by the zucchini and onion mixture. Scatter with the beets and arugula, then arrange the goat cheese slices on top. Sprinkle with a little salt and add a good grinding of pepper to each.

4 Bake in the oven for a further 10 minutes until the crust is golden brown, the cheese is melting, and everything is hot through.

5 Top with a little arugula and drizzle each pizza with the remaining oil before serving.

IF ADDING MEAT, dry-fry the bacon at step 1 before cooking the zucchini in the bacon fat, adding a little oil if necessary. Use only 2 zucchini instead of 4.

Pizzas, wraps, and quesadillas
Vegetable-stuffed pizzas

MAKES 4   **PREPARATION 25 MINS, PLUS PROOFING**   TO COOK **20 MINS**

Vary the vegetables according to what you have on hand—cooked carrots, potatoes, or shredded greens could be added, or use peas instead of corn.

INGREDIENTS

1 quantity pizza dough
  (see p180)
¼ cup tomato paste
9oz (250g) mozzarella cheese,
  torn into pieces
¼ cup grated
  Parmesan cheese
4 small tomatoes, chopped
4 button or crimini
  mushrooms, chopped
7oz (200g) can corn, drained
1 tbsp pickled capers
  (optional)
4 generous pinches
  of dried basil
1 tsp smoked paprika
salt and freshly ground
  black pepper
2 tbsp olive oil, plus extra
  for greasing
⅔ cup tomato sauce, to serve

OPTIONAL FISH
2oz (50g) can anchovies, drained

1 Make and proof the dough (see p180, step 1). Preheat the oven to 425°F (220°C). Cut the dough evenly into 4 pieces and shape into balls. Roll out each ball into a circle about 8in (20cm) in diameter. Spread a little tomato paste on each circle, leaving a 1¼in (3cm) border all around. Divide the mozzarella cheese between the circles and sprinkle each with ½ tbsp Parmesan cheese.

2 Top with the tomatoes, mushrooms, corn, capers (if using), and basil. Season with paprika and salt and pepper, then drizzle with half the oil.

3 Brush the edges with water, draw the dough up over the filling, and press the edges together to seal. Invert on an oiled baking sheet. Brush with the remaining oil and bake in the oven for about 20 minutes until crisp and golden.

4 Meanwhile, heat the tomato sauce in a saucepan. Place the stuffed pizzas on warmed plates. Spoon the tomato sauce over and sprinkle with the remaining grated Parmesan.

IF ADDING FISH, chop the anchovies and add to the pizzas at step 2.

Broccoli rabe, ricotta, and rosemary calzones

MAKES 4   **PREPARATION 30 MINS, PLUS PROOFING**   TO COOK **25 MINS**

The dough of a calzone is folded over the filling and the edge sealed before baking, so **all the flavor is encased in the dough**.

1 Make and proof the dough (see p180, step 1). Preheat the oven to 425°F (220°C). Steam or boil the broccoli rabe for 3–4 minutes until it is just tender. Drain, rinse with cold water, and drain again. Chop into bite-sized pieces and set aside.

2 Cut the dough into 4 equal pieces and roll out to 8in (20cm) rounds on a lightly floured surface. Mash the butter, garlic, rosemary, ricotta, and salt and pepper together and spread over the rounds of dough, leaving a 1¼in (3cm) border all around.

3 Add the chopped broccoli, tomatoes, mozzarella, and olives, leaving the border clear. Drizzle with half the oil.

4 Brush the edges with water. Using lightly floured hands, fold the calzones in half and press the edges together, then roll over the edge to seal. Transfer to an oiled baking sheet and brush the tops with oil. Bake in the oven for 18–20 minutes, or until crisp and golden. Garnish with a dusting of grated Parmesan cheese.

IF ADDING FISH, use dill instead of rosemary and sprinkle in the salmon in step 2.

INGREDIENTS

1 quantity pizza dough
  (see p180)
7oz (200g) broccoli rabe, thick
  stalks removed
flour, for dusting
4 tbsp butter, softened
2 large garlic cloves, crushed
2 tbsp chopped rosemary
5½oz (150g) ricotta cheese
salt and freshly ground
  black pepper
2 large tomatoes, chopped
3oz (85g) mozzarella cheese,
  torn into pieces
¼ cup sliced black olives
2 tbsp olive oil, plus extra
  for greasing
2 tbsp grated Parmesan
  cheese, to garnish

OPTIONAL FISH
2 tbsp chopped dill
4½oz (120g) pack of smoked
  salmon trimmings, chopped

Asparagus, mushroom, and garlic sauce pizzas

MAKES 2 LARGE OR 4 SMALL PIZZAS   **PREPARATION** **30 MINS, PLUS PROOFING**   TO COOK **20 MINS**

When asparagus isn't in season, try this pizza with strips of eggplant sliced lengthways and broiled. Fresh, green garlic works particularly well here, too.

INGREDIENTS

1 quantity pizza dough (see p180)

5½oz (150g) thin asparagus spears, trimmed

5–6 tbsp olive oil

2 shallots, chopped

9oz (250g) mixed speciality mushrooms such as shiitake, enoki, and nomeku, sliced if large

4 leaves escarole or green cabbage (approx. 3½oz/100g), finely shredded, discarding any thick stalks

2 tbsp butter

3 tbsp all-purpose flour

1 cup milk

2 large garlic cloves, crushed

3oz (85g) Cheddar cheese, grated

salt and freshly ground black pepper

2 tbsp chopped tarragon or basil

4½oz (125g) mozzarella cheese, grated

2 tbsp snipped chives

OPTIONAL MEAT

8 thin slices of pancetta, cut in half

1 Make and proof the pizza dough (see p180, step 1). While the dough is proofing, preheat a grill pan. Brush the asparagus with a little oil and cook on a grill pan for 2 minutes on each side, until bright green with brown stripes and just tender. Cut in diagonal short lengths. Set aside.

2 Heat 2 tbsp oil and sauté the shallots and mushrooms for 2 minutes until softened. Remove from the pan and set aside. Add a further 1 tbsp oil to the pan and stir-fry the greens for 2 minutes, stirring until slightly softened. Set aside.

3 When the dough has proofed, preheat the oven to 425°F (220°C). Knead the risen dough. Roll out to two 12–14in (30–35cm) rounds or four 8in (20cm) rounds and place on oiled pizza plates or baking sheets. Press out the rounds again with floured fingers, then place in the oven and bake for 10 minutes to partially cook them.

4 Meanwhile, melt the butter in a small saucepan. Work in the flour with a wire whisk and cook, stirring, for 1 minute. Remove the pan from the heat and whisk in the milk. Return to the heat, bring to a boil, and cook for 2 minutes, whisking constantly until thickened. Stir in the garlic, Cheddar cheese, and salt and pepper to taste.

5 Spread the garlic sauce over the pizzas. Top with the greens, mushrooms, and asparagus. Sprinkle with the tarragon or basil, then the mozzarella. Drizzle with a little oil and sprinkle with the chives. Bake for 15–20 minutes until the pizzas are golden around the edges and crisp. Serve hot, cut into wedges.

IF ADDING MEAT, scatter the pancetta pieces over the mozzarella at step 5 before drizzling with oil, so they crisp and brown as the pizza cooks.

Spicy lentil and pepper pizzas

MAKES 2 LARGE OR 4 SMALL PIZZAS   **PREPARATION 30 MINS, PLUS PROOFING**   TO COOK **25 MINS**

The roast pepper adds a lovely sweetness to the spices and lentils. If time is short, use a roasted pepper from a jar or simply a raw fresh pepper.

INGREDIENTS

1 quantity pizza dough (see p180)

1 large red bell pepper, roasted, peeled, and seeded (see p326)

2 tbsp olive oil, plus extra for greasing and drizzling

1 garlic clove, chopped

1 small onion, finely chopped

4 tomatoes, chopped

¼ cup tomato paste

14oz (400g) can green lentils, rinsed and drained

2 tsp smoked paprika

½ tsp chile powder

½ tsp granulated sugar

salt and freshly ground black pepper

2 tbsp pickled jalapeño peppers, sliced

1 tsp dried oregano

4½oz (125g) mozzarella cheese, grated

a few black olives

OPTIONAL MEAT

9oz (250g) ground beef

1 Make and proof the pizza dough (see p180, step 1). While the dough is proofing, cut the pepper into thin strips.

2 Heat the oil in a saucepan. Add the garlic and onion and fry gently, stirring, for 2 minutes to soften. Add the tomatoes, tomato paste, lentils, paprika, and chile powder and cook, stirring, for 2 minutes. Add the sugar and season with salt and pepper to taste.

3 Preheat the oven to 425°F (220°C). Knead the risen dough again, then roll out to two 12–14in (30–35cm) rounds or 4 smaller rounds (about 8in/20cm). Place on oiled pizza plates or baking sheets and press out to rounds again with floured fingers. Alternatively, roll out to 2 large rectangles to just fit the baking sheets and press them into shape once transferred.

4 Spread the lentil mixture over the dough, leaving a ½in (1cm) border all around. Sprinkle with the pepper strips, jalapeños, oregano, and mozzarella. Dot with a few black olives and drizzle with a little oil.

5 Bake for 18–20 minutes or until the dough is crisp and lightly golden brown and the cheese has melted.

IF ADDING MEAT, replace the lentils with the beef. Fry with the onion and garlic until the meat is brown and all the grains are separate, then continue as before.

Pizza primavera

MAKES 2 LARGE OR 4 SMALL PIZZAS   PREPARATION **30 MINS, PLUS PROOFING**   TO COOK **20 MINS**

These are **sumptuous pizzas packed with vegetables**. The vegetables are cooked first, then added to the part-baked pizza so they retain all their goodness, color, and flavor.

1 Make and proof the pizza dough (see p180, step 1). While the dough is proofing, heat the oil and butter in a large saucepan or wok. Add the garlic and onion and fry, stirring, for 2 minutes. Add the cauliflower, carrot, mushrooms, and a splash of water and stir-fry for about 3 minutes until softened, but still with some bite.

2 Add the zucchini slices and stir-fry for another 1–2 minutes. Add a pinch of salt, plenty of pepper, rosemary, and a good squeeze of lemon juice and mix well. Set aside.

3 Preheat the oven to 425°F (220°C). Knead the risen dough again, then roll out to two 12–14in (30–35cm) rounds or 4 smaller rounds (about 8in/20cm). Place on oiled pizza plates or baking sheets and press out to rounds again with floured fingers. Alternatively, roll out to 2 large rectangles to just fit the baking sheets and press them into shape once transferred. Bake for 10 minutes.

4 Remove from the oven and spread quickly with the tomato paste, then top with the tomato slices and sprinkle with oregano. Divide the vegetable mixture between the baking sheets and spread out evenly. Sprinkle the cheeses over. Return to the oven for 10 minutes until golden around the edges and the cheese is melted and slightly brown.

IF ADDING SHELLFISH, scatter the shrimp over each pizza at step 4 before adding the cheeses.

INGREDIENTS

1 quantity pizza dough (see p180)
¼ cup olive oil, plus extra for greasing
1 tbsp butter
2 large garlic cloves, crushed
1 red onion, halved and sliced
¼ cauliflower, white only, cut into tiny florets
2 young carrots, thinly sliced
4oz (115g) button or crimini mushrooms, sliced
2 small zucchini, sliced
salt and freshly ground black pepper
1½ tbsp chopped rosemary
wedge of lemon
¼ cup tomato paste
4 large tomatoes, sliced
2 tsp dried oregano
4½oz (125g) mozzarella cheese, grated
¾oz (20g) Parmesan cheese, grated

OPTIONAL SHELLFISH
handful of cooked, peeled large shrimp (thawed if frozen)

Avocado, baby spinach, and chile wraps

MAKES 2   **PREPARATION 5 MINS**

Packed with flavor and nutrients, **these wraps make a tasty lunch or snack.** Peppery arugula or watercress make delicious alternatives to baby spinach.

INGREDIENTS

1 small avocado
1 tsp lemon or lime juice
1 large flour tortilla
2 tbsp mayonnaise
large handful of
   baby spinach
½ red bell pepper, seeded
   and cut into thin strips
½ tsp dried chile flakes
6 slices pickled jalapeño
   chile pepper
freshly ground black pepper

OPTIONAL MEAT
small handful of chopped
   cooked chicken

1 Peel and halve the avocado and remove the pit (see pp324–5). Slice thinly and toss in the lemon or lime juice.

2 Put the tortilla on a board. Spread with the mayonnaise, then add the spinach, avocado, red pepper, chiles, and jalapeño chile pepper, one after the other. Season with plenty of pepper. Fold in the sides and roll up firmly, then cut in half and serve.

IF ADDING MEAT, add the chicken before the avocado at step 2.

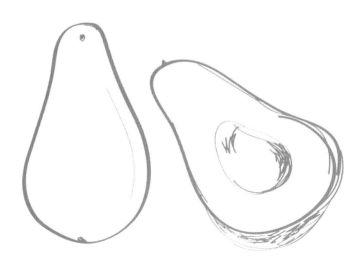

Chile bean fajitas

MAKES 8   **PREPARATION 20 MINS**   **TO COOK 20 MINS**

Fajitas are perfect for a colorful, informal meal. To turn them into enchiladas, smother with grated cheese in an ovenproof dish and bake in a hot oven until melted.

1 Heat the oil in a large frying pan or wok. Add all the vegetables, cover, and cook for 5–10 minutes until fairly soft, stirring occasionally.

2 Add the garlic and spices and fry for 30 seconds, then stir in the oregano, tomatoes, and tomato paste. Cover and cook, stirring occasionally, for a further 5 minutes until just tender. Add salt and pepper to taste.

3 Put the refried beans in a separate pan and heat through, stirring. Warm the tortillas briefly in the microwave, if liked.

4 Taking each tortilla in turn, spread with a little of the refried beans, then some of the vegetable mixture. Top with 1 tbsp crème fraîche and a little cheese and roll up. Serve immediately with a crisp green salad.

IF ADDING MEAT, omit the refried beans, if preferred, and cook the beef stir-fry strips with the vegetables at step 1.

INGREDIENTS

2 tbsp olive oil
1 large onion, halved
   and sliced
2 red bell peppers, halved,
   seeded, and sliced
2 green bell peppers, halved,
   seeded, and sliced
2 zucchini, sliced
4½oz (150g) green
   cabbage, shredded
1 large garlic clove, crushed
2 tsp ground cumin
1 tsp dried chile flakes
1 tsp dried oregano
4 tomatoes, chopped
2 tbsp tomato paste
salt and freshly ground
   black pepper
14oz (435g) can refried beans
8 flour or corn tortillas
½ cup crème fraîche
4oz (115g) Cheddar
   cheese, grated
crisp green salad, to serve

OPTIONAL MEAT
9oz (250g) beef stir-fry strips

Grilled zucchini and sun-dried tomato wraps

MAKES 2   **PREPARATION 5 MINS**   TO COOK **4–6 MINS**

For this recipe, use either store-bought hummus or make your own (see p313). Slices of eggplant may be substituted for the zucchini.

INGREDIENTS

2 zucchini, cut into ¼in (5mm) slices lengthways
2 tbsp olive oil
2 large flour tortillas
6 tbsp hummus
8 pieces sun-dried tomatoes in oil, drained and chopped, oil reserved
handful of arugula
lemon juice
freshly ground black pepper

OPTIONAL FISH
6 tbsp taramasalata

1 Preheat a grill pan. Brush the zucchini slices with oil, then grill for 2–3 minutes on each side or until tender and striped brown. Set aside.

2 Put the tortillas on a board and spread with the hummus. Lay the zucchini strips on top and scatter with the sun-dried tomatoes.

3 Scatter the arugula on top, drizzle with the tomato oil and a squeeze of lemon juice, then add a good grinding of pepper. Fold in the sides, roll up each tightly, and cut in half.

IF ADDING FISH, substitute taramasalata for the hummus.

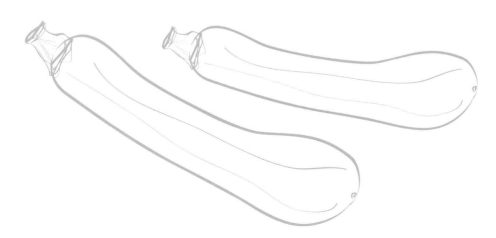

Zucchini and pea mini wraps

MAKES 10   **PREPARATION 20 MINS**   **TO COOK 5 MINS**

Pea shoots—the first tendrils of the young plants—can be enjoyed raw. Combine them with **fresh baby peas and raw zucchini in this vibrant, healthy dish.**

INGREDIENTS

9oz (250g) zucchini, grated
handful of baby
  spinach leaves
grated zest and juice of
  1½ lemons
4½oz (125g) young
  peas, shelled
scant 1oz (25g) toasted
  pine nuts
salt and freshly ground
  black pepper
1–2 tbsp mayonnaise, plus
  extra for spreading
5 flour tortillas, halved
handful of pea shoots

OPTIONAL MEAT

2oz (60g) cooked
  ham, chopped

1 In a large bowl, mix together the zucchini, spinach, lemon zest and juice, peas, and pine nuts. Season with salt and pepper, then moisten with a little mayonnaise.

2 Heat a dry frying pan over high heat. Add the tortilla halves, 2 at a time, and toast for about 15 seconds on each side. Set aside the tortilla halves under a clean tea towel to keep warm.

3 Lay one of the tortilla halves flat on a cutting board and spread lightly with a scraping of mayonnaise. Take some of the zucchini filling and place in the center. Arrange some of the pea shoots on top, so that they stick out at one end, then gently roll up the mini wrap. Repeat this process until 10 wraps have been made.

4 To serve, arrange the mini wraps on individual serving plates, allowing 2 per person.

IF ADDING MEAT, use 7oz (200g) zucchini and add the ham to the mixture at step 1.

Rainbow pepper Mexican tacos

SERVES 4   **PREPARATION 10 MINS**   **TO COOK 10 MINS**

These easy-to-make tacos are delicious with a dollop of guacamole instead of the sour cream. The filling tastes equally good in crispy corn tacos.

1 Heat the oil in a wok or large frying pan and sauté the onions and peppers, stirring, for 6–8 minutes until soft. Stir in the garlic and corn and cook, stirring, for a further 1–2 minutes.

2 Add all of the spices and fry for 30 seconds, stirring. Remove the wok or frying pan from the heat and stir in the lime juice and chopped cilantro. Season with salt and pepper to taste.

3 Divide the filling between the tortillas, add a spoonful of sour cream to each, and roll up. Serve immediately while still hot.

IF ADDING MEAT, fry the chicken with the onions and just 1 red pepper in step 1, then continue as before.

INGREDIENTS

2 tbsp sunflower or vegetable oil
2 red onions, sliced
1 red bell pepper, seeded
   and cut into thin strips
1 green bell pepper, seeded
   and cut into thin strips
1 yellow bell pepper, seeded
   and cut into thin strips
1 orange bell pepper, seeded
   and cut into thin strips
1 garlic clove, crushed
4oz (115g) baby corn,
   halved lengthways
1 tsp ground cumin
1 tsp ground coriander
1 tsp paprika
½ tsp dried chile flakes
juice of 1 lime
handful of chopped cilantro
salt and freshly ground
   black pepper
8 flour tortillas
½ cup sour cream

OPTIONAL MEAT

 4 small boneless, skinless
   chicken breasts, cut into
   thin strips

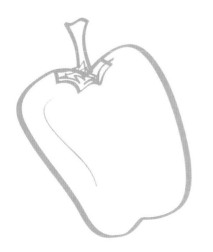

Maki sushi wraps

MAKES 24   **PREPARATION 40 MINS**   TO COOK **20 MINS, PLUS STANDING AND COOLING**

Sushi is fun to make. Vary the fillings with strips of pepper or batonettes of zucchini. Choose sweet, pink pickled ginger rather than the salty beige-colored type.

INGREDIENTS

8oz (225g) sushi rice
¼ cup rice vinegar
2 tsp granulated sugar
2 tsp sesame oil
½ tsp salt
4 nori sheets (dried seaweed)
wasabi paste, pink pickled
  ginger, and tamari or light
  soy sauce, to serve

For the filling

1 small avocado
1 tsp rice vinegar
1 tomato, seeded and
  cut into thin strips
4 strips carrot, peeled with
  a potato peeler
1 scallion, cut into short
  lengths and shredded
2in (5cm) piece cucumber,
  peeled, seeded and
  cut into batonettes

OPTIONAL FISH AND SHELLFISH

a few smoked salmon strips
a few cooked, peeled small
  shrimp (thawed if frozen)

1 Cook the sushi rice according to the package directions. Mix the vinegar, sugar, oil, and salt together and sprinkle over the cooked rice. Cover and leave to stand for 20 minutes.

2 For the filling, halve, pit, and peel the avocado (see pp324–5). Slice the flesh thinly and toss in the vinegar to prevent browning.

3 Place a nori sheet, shiny side down, with the lines in the nori sheet horizontal to you, on a sushi mat or a square of heavy-duty foil. Spread the surface with a quarter of the sushi rice, leaving a ¾in (2cm) strip of nori uncovered at the edge furthest away from you.

4 Mark a line across the center of the rice. Lay a line of avocado slices and a line of tomato strips all along it and press gently into the rice. Using the mat or foil to help, start to roll the sushi away from you firmly, checking that the roll is tucking under and making sure the filling does not pop out. Press gently while rolling but do not squash the filling. Dampen the end strip of nori so that it sticks when it is completely rolled. Wrap in plastic wrap. Make another avocado and tomato wrap the same way.

5 Repeat the process with the remaining rice and nori sheets, using a row of carrot strips topped with a row of shredded scallions (white and green shreds evenly distributed) and a row of cucumber for the filling in each one. Chill all the wrapped rolls until ready to serve.

6 To serve, remove the plastic wrap and cut each roll into 6 pieces. Place on a serving platter with wasabi paste, pickled ginger, and tamari or light soy sauce to add to the sushi before eating.

IF ADDING FISH AND SHELLFISH, use salmon strips instead of the carrot, and shrimp instead of tomatoes. If the shrimp are thawed from frozen, make sure they are well dried.

Tabbouleh lettuce wraps

MAKES 16   **PREPARATION 30 MINS, PLUS COOLING**

Using lettuce leaves instead of flour tortillas, **these low-calorie wraps make an excellent lunchtime snack** or a refreshing starter.

INGREDIENTS

4oz (115g) bulgur wheat
1¼ cups boiling
   vegetable stock
1 large garlic clove, crushed
large handful each of cilantro,
   mint, and parsley, chopped
2 tomatoes, finely chopped
2in (5cm) piece cucumber,
   finely chopped
2 tbsp chopped black olives
1 tbsp lemon juice, plus
   more if needed
2 tbsp olive oil
salt and freshly ground
   black pepper
16 large, soft, round
   lettuce leaves

OPTIONAL MEAT
handful of finely chopped
   cooked lamb

1 Put the bulgur wheat in a bowl and stir in the boiling stock. Leave to stand for 20–30 minutes until swollen and all the liquid is absorbed. Stir in the garlic and herbs and leave to cool.

2 When nearly ready to serve, mix in the tomatoes, cucumber, and olives and add the lemon juice and oil. Season with salt and pepper and add more lemon juice, if liked.

3 Divide the mixture equally among the lettuce leaves on serving platters. Roll up each wrap like a tortilla and serve.

IF ADDING MEAT, add the chopped lamb to the mixture with the tomatoes and cucumber and omit the olives.

Spicy potato and mango chutney chapatti wraps

MAKES 8   **PREPARATION 10 MINS**   **TO COOK 20 MINS**

If you need to make only one wrap at a time, **store the filling in the refrigerator to use over the next few days**—it is just as good served cold.

1 Boil the potatoes in lightly salted water for about 10 minutes until just tender but still holding their shape. Drain.

2 Heat the oil in the rinsed-out pan and fry the spices over medium heat, stirring, for 30 seconds. Stir in the tomatoes and sugar and fry for 2–3 minutes.

3 Add the potatoes, then stir and turn gently until they are coated in the tomatoes. Sprinkle with a little salt. Cook for 5 minutes, stirring occasionally, until the juice has been absorbed. Add the cilantro, then stir and turn one more time. Crush the potatoes with the back of a spoon to break them up. Set aside until just warm.

4 Lay the chapattis on a board and spread the mango chutney down the center. Top with the crushed potatoes and sprinkle with shredded lettuce. Roll up tightly and cut into halves to serve.

IF ADDING MEAT, use a little less potato for each wrap and add it cold. Scatter some chopped chicken tikka over the potato at step 4 before adding the lettuce.

INGREDIENTS

3 potatoes (approx. 12oz/350g), peeled and cut into walnut-sized pieces
salt
1½ tbsp sunflower or vegetable oil
1 tsp dried chile flakes
½ tsp ground cumin
½ tsp ground coriander
¼ tsp ground turmeric
2 large tomatoes, chopped
generous pinch of granulated sugar
1 tbsp chopped cilantro
4 chapattis
4 tbsp mango chutney
4 handfuls shredded iceberg lettuce

OPTIONAL MEAT

1–2 pre-cooked chicken tikka breasts, chopped

Four ways with Tomatoes

Tomato soup ▶

TAKES 1 hr 15 mins **SERVES** 4

Heat 1 tbsp **olive oil** in a large saucepan over medium-low heat. Add 1 chopped **onion**, 1 sliced **garlic clove**, and 2 sliced **celery** stalks, then fry, stirring, until soft but not colored. Add 1 sliced **carrot**, 1 chopped **potato**, and stir for 1 minute. Add two 14oz (400g) cans **chopped tomatoes** with their juice, 2½ cups **vegetable stock**, 1 **bay leaf**, and 1 tsp **sugar**. Add **salt** and freshly ground **black pepper**, bring to a boil, reduce the heat, cover, and simmer for 45 minutes. Remove from the heat and allow to cool slightly, then process in a blender or food processor until smooth. Taste and adjust the seasoning, then reheat and serve.

◀ Baked stuffed tomatoes

TAKES 1 hr, plus standing **SERVES** 4

Cut 4 large ripe **beefsteak tomatoes** in half horizontally. Scoop out the insides and discard. Sprinkle the tomatoes with **salt** and drain upside down for 30 minutes. Preheat the oven to 425°F (220°C). Heat 1 tbsp **olive oil** in a pan, then add 2 finely chopped **anchovies** and 1 crushed **garlic clove**. Cook for 30 seconds. Stir in ¼ cup fresh **breadcrumbs** and cook for 2 minutes. Mix ¼ cup **mascarpone** cheese, 4¹/₂ oz (125g) **ricotta** cheese, and 2 tbsp finely chopped **basil leaves**. Season with freshly ground **black pepper**. Fill each tomato with the cheeses and top with the breadcrumb mixture. Bake for 15–20 minutes.

For salads, choose classic roma tomatoes, cherry tomatoes, or the beefsteak variety (for slicing). For sauces, soups, grilling, and roasting, **plum and beefsteak tomatoes have the best flavor**.

Tomato, red onion, and mozzarella salad ▶

TAKES 10 mins **SERVES** 4

Put 8 ripe **plum tomatoes**, sliced, 6 **cherry tomatoes**, halved, 1 small **red onion**, peeled and sliced, and a small handful of torn **basil leaves** in a large bowl. Drizzle over plenty of **extra virgin olive oil**, season well with **salt** and freshly ground **black pepper**, and toss. Arrange 2 handfuls of **arugula** on a plate, drizzle over a little oil and some **balsamic vinegar**, and season. Spoon over the tomato and basil mixture. Add 2 balls of **mozzarella**, torn. Scatter some basil leaves over and drizzle with a little oil and balsamic vinegar. Serve immediately.

◀ Chunky tomato sauce

TAKES 35 mins **MAKES** 2 cups

Heat ¼ cup **sunflower or vegetable oil** in a large saucepan over medium heat. Add 1 chopped **onion** and 1 chopped **garlic clove**. Fry, stirring occasionally, for 5–8 minutes, or until soft and golden. Stir in ¼ cup **tomato paste**, two 14oz (400g) cans **chopped tomatoes** with their juice, 4 torn **basil leaves**, and **salt** and freshly ground **black pepper** to taste. Lower the heat and simmer, uncovered, for 20 minutes, or until the sauce has thickened. Stir in a few more torn basil leaves just before serving.

Vietnamese vegetable and beansprout summer rolls

MAKES 8   **PREPARATION 50 MINS**

These colorful rolls make a **healthy, tasty light lunch or supper, or serve one each as a starter**. Ideally, use a lettuce with small round leaves, or halve larger ones.

INGREDIENTS

3oz (85g) fresh rice vermicelli
1 tbsp light soy sauce
1 tsp grated fresh ginger
1 tsp light brown sugar
  or palm sugar
8 small soft, round, green
  lettuce leaves, thick stalk
  ends cut off
handful of beansprouts
2in (5cm) piece cucumber,
  peeled, seeded, and cut
  in julienne strips
2 scallions, cut into short
  lengths and shredded
½ carrot, peeled with a potato
  peeler into thin ribbons
8 red radishes, sliced
a few sprigs of cilantro,
  leaves picked
8 large (8½in/22cm) rice-
  paper wrappers

OPTIONAL SHELLFISH

24–32 (approx. 7oz/200g)
  cooked, peeled shrimp
  (thawed if frozen)

1 Soak the vermicelli in boiling water for 5 minutes. Drain, rinse with cold water, and dry on paper towels.

2 Mix the soy sauce, ginger, and sugar together until well-blended. Add the noodles and toss until completely coated and all the liquid has been absorbed.

3 Arrange all the vegetables and the cilantro in neat piles for easy access. Place a large plate on the work surface and have a large shallow dish of warm water to one side, ready to soak the rice wrappers.

4 Put a wrapper into the water and soak for 5 seconds. Remove and lay on the plate. Put a lettuce leaf, bright green side down, on the edge of the rice paper nearest to you. Put an eighth of the noodles alongside it, then add a few beansprouts, strips of cucumber, shreds of scallions, and a carrot ribbon.

5 Fold the edge of the wrapper nearest to you (with the filling on) up over the filling to make the beginnings of the roll. Lay a row of radish slices, well tucked in, along the line where the rolled bit meets the unrolled bit of wrapper. Lay 3 or 4 cilantro leaves alongside.

6 Now fold in the sides of the rice wrapper, then roll it up into a tight cylinder and place, radish-side up, on a serving plate. Cover with a clean, damp cloth while making the remainder, then cover with plastic wrap and keep covered at room temperature until ready to serve. These are best eaten within a couple of hours.

IF ADDING SHELLFISH, substitute the shrimp for the radish slices in each roll at step 5.

Sage and onion quesadillas

MAKES 2   **PREPARATION 5 MINS**   TO COOK **5 MINS**

Sage, onion, and cheese is the perfect combination for a simple quesadilla filling. Grated Cheddar cheese is convenient and often no more expensive than a block.

1 Heat a large non-stick frying pan and place a tortilla in it. Scatter half the onion over it, followed by half the cheese and half the sage.

2 Cover with the second tortilla and press down well with a spatula. Cook for 2–3 minutes over medium heat until the base is crisp and brown and the cheese is beginning to melt, pressing down all the time.

3 Carefully flip over the tortilla sandwich and cook the other side for about 2 minutes, pressing down again until the cheese has melted and the base is crisp and brown. Slide the quesadilla out of the pan and cut in quarters. Keep warm while you cook the second tortilla in the same way.

IF ADDING MEAT, add a thin slice of roast pork over the onion at step 1 before adding the cheese and sage.

INGREDIENTS

4 flour tortillas
1 small onion, halved
   and thinly sliced
3½oz (100g) Cheddar
   cheese, grated
12 sage leaves, chopped,
   or 1 tsp dried sage

OPTIONAL MEAT
2 thin slices of roast pork

Roasted eggplant, feta, and tomato quesadillas

MAKES 2   **PREPARATION 10 MINS**   TO COOK **40–50 MINS, PLUS COOLING**

The eggplant may be roasted in advance, perhaps when the oven is already on, and used in the next day or two, or frozen. Alternatively, use a jar of roasted eggplant.

INGREDIENTS

1 small eggplant, approx. 9½oz
    (275g)
1 small garlic clove, crushed
1 tbsp olive oil
squeeze of lemon juice
salt and freshly ground
    black pepper
4 large flour tortillas
1 tomato, chopped
3½oz (100g) feta
    cheese, crumbled
½ tsp dried oregano

OPTIONAL MEAT

2 thin slices raw cured ham,
    such as Serrano

1 Preheat the oven to 400°F (200°C). Roast the eggplant whole for 30–40 minutes, turning occasionally until soft. Place in a plastic bag and leave to cool.

2 Remove the stalk, peel off the skin, and chop the flesh. Place in a bowl and add the garlic, oil, lemon juice, and some salt and pepper. Mash well.

3 Heat a large non-stick frying pan and place a tortilla on it. Spread with half of the eggplant mixture, then scatter over the chopped tomato and half the crumbled feta. Sprinkle with half the oregano.

4 Cover with a second tortilla and cook over medium heat, pressing down well with a spatula, for 2–3 minutes until crisp and brown underneath. Carefully invert onto a plate, then slide back into the pan and cook the other side for 2–3 minutes, still pressing down, until crisp and brown underneath.

5 Slide out onto a plate and keep warm while cooking the remaining quesadilla in the same way. Cut them in quarters and serve.

IF ADDING MEAT, finely chop the ham slices and scatter over the eggplant mixture at step 3 before adding the tomato and cheese.

Corn, Cheddar cheese, and chili sauce quesadillas

MAKES 4   **PREPARATION 5 MINS**   TO COOK **20 MINS**

An easy and nutritious snack, these quesadillas are packed with flavor. **Make sure the corn is drained and dried thoroughly**, or the mixture will be too wet.

1 Drain the can of corn with peppers and dry on paper towels, then pour into a bowl. Mix the cheese and mayonnaise into the corn and peppers.

2 Put 2 tortillas on a board and spread each with 1 tbsp sweet chili sauce. Heat a large frying pan and add 1 tsp oil. Put one of the sauce-topped tortillas in the pan, sauce-side up. Spread with half the corn mixture and top with the second tortilla. Press down with a spatula. Cook over medium heat for 2 minutes until sizzling and golden underneath. Invert onto a plate.

3 Slide the quesadilla back into the pan, browned-side up. Press down again and cook for a further 2 minutes, or until the cheese has melted and everything is brown and sizzling. Slide out of the pan and keep warm while cooking the remaining quesadillas. It is best to cut them in quarters when they have cooled slightly as corn tortillas are quite soft.

IF ADDING MEAT, use half the amount of cheese and add the chicken to the mixture at step 1.

INGREDIENTS

7oz (200g) can corn
  with peppers
4 large handfuls of grated
  aged Cheddar cheese
¼ cup mayonnaise
8 tbsp sweet chili sauce
8 corn tortillas
4 tsp sunflower or vegetable oil

OPTIONAL MEAT
2 handfuls of chopped
  cooked chicken

Guacamole and Cheddar quesadillas

MAKES 2   **PREPARATION 5 MINS**   **TO COOK 5 MINS**

The Pico de Gallo on pp310–11 is excellent with these quesadillas. **Make sure the avocados are ripe** or they may taste bitter.

INGREDIENTS

2 avocados

2 tsp lime juice

1 tsp dried chile flakes,
   or to taste

2 thin scallions,
   finely chopped

2in (5cm) piece cucumber,
   finely chopped

2 tomatoes, seeded and
   finely chopped

salt and freshly ground
   black pepper

4 flour tortillas

2 large handfuls of grated
   Cheddar cheese

2 tbsp chopped cilantro

a few drops of Worcestershire
   sauce or mushroom ketchup

OPTIONAL MEAT

a few thin slices of dry,
   Spanish-style chorizo

1 For the guacamole, halve, pit, and peel the avocados (see pp324–5). Put the flesh in a bowl and mash well with the lime juice, then mix in the chiles, scallions, cucumber, and tomatoes. Add salt and pepper to taste.

2 Heat a large non-stick frying pan. Put one tortilla on a board and spread with half the guacamole. Place in the frying pan and scatter over half the cheese and then half the cilantro. Add a few drops of Worcestershire sauce and top with a second tortilla. Press down well with a metal spatula.

3 Cook for 2–3 minutes over medium heat until the base is crisp and brown and the cheese is beginning to melt, pressing down constantly. Invert the tortilla onto a plate, then slide back into the pan and cook the other side for about 2 minutes, pressing down again, until the cheese has melted and the base is crisp and brown. Transfer to a plate and cut into quarters. Keep warm while making the second quesadilla in the same way.

IF ADDING MEAT, lay the slices of chorizo on the first tortilla before spreading with the guacamole at step 2.

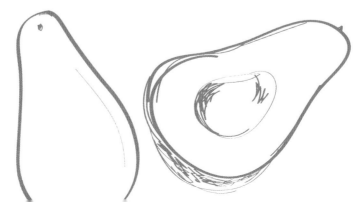

Arugula, pear, blue cheese, and walnut quesadillas

MAKES 2   **PREPARATION** **10 MINS**   TO COOK **10 MINS**

Peppery arugula, sweet pears, tangy blue cheese, and earthy walnuts—a great combination for a sophisticated quesadilla. Chop the nuts finely for the best flavor.

INGREDIENTS

1½oz (45g) soft blue cheese, such as St. Agur or cambazola, cut into small pieces
1oz (30g) Emmental cheese, grated
¾oz (20g) walnuts, finely chopped
2 tbsp crème fraîche
4 large flour tortillas
1 not-too-ripe pear, peeled, cored, and thinly sliced
2 handfuls of arugula

OPTIONAL MEAT
2 crisp strips bacon, crumbled

1 Mash the cheeses with the walnuts and crème fraîche. Spread half over 1 tortilla. Top with half the pear and arugula, then top with a second tortilla. Press down well.

2 Heat a large non-stick frying pan and cook the quesadilla over medium heat, pressing down well with a spatula, for 2–3 minutes until crisp and golden underneath. Carefully turn over and fry the other side for a further 2 minutes, pressing down again, until the cheese has melted and the base is crisp.

3 Slide out of the pan and cut in quarters. Set aside to cool slightly while you cook the second quesadilla in the same way.

IF ADDING MEAT, omit the walnuts and sprinkle the cheese mixture with the bacon at step 1 before adding the pear and arugula.

Cream cheese and roasted pepper quesadillas

MAKES 2   **PREPARATION 20 MINS, PLUS COOLING**   TO COOK **20 MINS**

A drained roasted pepper from a can or jar can be used for these delicious quesadillas, but **a freshly roasted pepper will always give the tastiest result**.

1 Cut the pepper into thin slices. Mix the cheese with the basil and pine nuts and add a good grinding of pepper.

2 Heat 1 tsp oil in a frying pan. Add 1 corn tortilla, then spread with the cheese mixture and top with the pepper slices. Place another tortilla on top and press down well with a spatula. Fry the quesadilla for 2–3 minutes until golden underneath, then slide out onto a plate.

3 Heat the remaining oil in the pan. Invert the plate over the pan so the tortilla is cooked-side up. Fry the other side for about 2 minutes until golden and hot through, pressing down all the time. Slide out of the pan and keep warm while making the second quesadilla. These are softer than flour tortilla quesadillas, so leave to cool slightly before cutting into quarters.

IF ADDING MEAT, scatter the ham over the cheese along with the pepper strips.

INGREDIENTS

1 small red bell pepper, roasted, peeled, and seeded (see p326)
2½oz (75g) cream cheese
2 tbsp chopped basil
2 tbsp pine nuts
freshly ground black pepper
2 tsp olive oil
4 corn tortillas

OPTIONAL MEAT
a few strips of cooked ham

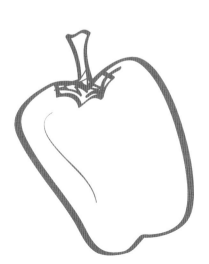

Tortillas, frittatas, and omelets

Spanish tortilla

SERVES 4   **PREPARATION 10 MINS**   TO COOK **45 MINS**

A delicious choice for a light meal with a crisp salad, this tortilla is also great cut into cubes and served as tapas with drinks, Spanish-style.

INGREDIENTS

1¼ cups olive oil, plus
   1 tbsp for frying
5 potatoes, peeled and sliced,
   approx. ¼in (5mm) thick
3 onions, quartered and sliced
sea salt and freshly ground
   black pepper
5 large eggs, beaten

OPTIONAL MEAT
2½oz (75g) Spanish-style dry
   chorizo, finely diced

1 Put the oil in a deep-sided, ovenproof frying pan (preferably non-stick), add the potatoes, and simmer gently for about 15 minutes, or until soft. Remove the potatoes with a slotted spoon and put them in a large bowl to cool.

2 Pour most of the oil out of the pan and add the onions and a pinch of salt. Cook over low heat until soft and beginning to caramelize. Add to the potatoes and leave to cool.

3 Pour the eggs into the cooled potato and onion mixture, season with salt and pepper, and combine gently so that all the potatoes are coated.

4 Heat 1 tbsp oil in the pan until hot, then carefully slide the egg mixture in, spreading it evenly so it covers the base of the pan. Reduce the heat to medium-low and cook for 6–10 minutes, or until almost set. Invert onto a plate and return to the pan to cook the other side. Alternatively, preheat the broiler and put the pan under the broiler for a few minutes to brown and set the top. Remove from the pan, leave to cool and set, then cut into wedges. Serve warm or cold.

IF ADDING MEAT, stir the chorizo into the cooled potato and onion mixture at the end of step 2 before adding the eggs.

Tortillas, frittatas, and omelets
Eggplant and potato tortillas

SERVES 4   **PREPARATION 5 MINS**   TO COOK **15 MINS**

Eggplants soak up a lot of oil, but **blanching them along with the potatoes, as below, will reduce the calorie count**. Alternatively, simply fry them for about 5 minutes.

1 Bring a pot of water to a boil, drop in the eggplant and potato slices, and cook for 2–3 minutes until tender. Drain thoroughly and dry on paper towels.

2 Heat the oil in a large non-stick frying pan. Add the onion and garlic and fry over medium heat for 2 minutes. Add the potato and eggplant and season with salt and pepper and rosemary. Toss gently until thoroughly combined and heated through.

3 Add the beaten eggs. Cook gently, lifting and stirring at first, until the egg has almost set—this should take 4–5 minutes. Loosen the edge, invert onto a plate, slide back into the pan, and cook for a few minutes to brown the other side. Alternatively, preheat the broiler and put the pan under the broiler for a few minutes to brown and set the top. Slide out onto a plate and serve, cut into wedges.

IF ADDING MEAT, fry the ground lamb with the onion and garlic at step 2 and continue as before.

INGREDIENTS

1 small eggplant, thinly sliced
1 large potato, scrubbed, halved lengthways, and thinly sliced
2 tbsp olive oil
1 onion, chopped
1 garlic clove, crushed
salt and freshly ground black pepper
1 tbsp chopped rosemary
6 large eggs, beaten

OPTIONAL MEAT
handful of ground lamb

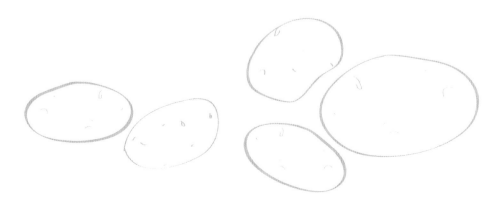

Sweet potato and leek tortilla with fresh tomato sauce

SERVES 4   PREPARATION **15 MINS**   TO COOK **15 MINS**

Tortillas always contain potato, which differentiates them from frittatas. These **use sweet potatoes as they go so well with leeks**, but ordinary potatoes can be substituted.

INGREDIENTS

1 small sweet potato
  (approx. 1lb/450g),
  peeled, halved
  lengthways, and thinly
  sliced crossways
2 tbsp butter
2 tbsp olive oil
2 leeks, thinly sliced
2 tbsp chopped thyme,
  plus extra to garnish
6 large eggs, beaten

For the tomato sauce
1 tbsp olive oil
1 garlic clove, crushed
2 beefsteak tomatoes,
  peeled and chopped
1 tbsp tomato paste
generous pinch of
  granulated sugar
½ tsp ground cinnamon
salt and freshly ground
  black pepper

OPTIONAL MEAT
a few slices of dry, Spanish-style
  chorizo, cut into thin strips

1 First, make the tomato sauce. Heat the oil in a saucepan, add the garlic and tomatoes, and fry, stirring, for 2 minutes until the juices are running. Stir in the tomato paste, sugar, cinnamon, and a little salt and pepper. Cover and simmer gently for 5 minutes. Remove the lid and boil rapidly for about 3 minutes until thick and pulpy, stirring constantly. Remove from the heat, then reheat when ready to serve.

2 Bring a pan of water to a boil, drop in the slices of sweet potato, and cook for 4–5 minutes until they are just tender but still holding their shape. Drain thoroughly.

3 Heat the butter and oil in a large non-stick frying pan. Add the leeks and fry over medium heat for 2 minutes. Add the sweet potatoes, thyme, and salt and pepper. Toss gently until thoroughly combined. Add the beaten eggs and cook gently for 4–5 minutes, lifting and stirring at first, until the egg has almost set.

4 Meanwhile, preheat the broiler. Put the frying pan under the broiler for a few minutes to brown and set the top of the tortilla. Slide onto a plate and garnish with a few thyme leaves. Cut into wedges and serve with the tomato sauce.

IF ADDING MEAT, scatter the chorizo in the pan with the sweet potatoes at step 3, then continue as before.

French bean, garlic, and tomato omelet

SERVES 4   **PREPARATION** **10 MINS**   **TO COOK** **20 MINS**

Packed with fresh vegetables, these omelets are a healthy choice. If the beans are chopped before cooking, the mixture makes a delicious sauce for long pasta, too.

INGREDIENTS

8oz (225g) thin French beans, trimmed
2 tbsp olive oil
2 tomatoes, roughly chopped
¼ cup dry white wine or hard cider
1 tsp tomato paste
1 large garlic clove, finely chopped
pinch of granulated sugar
salt and freshly ground black pepper
1 tbsp chopped parsley
1 tbsp chopped basil
8 large eggs
a little butter

OPTIONAL FISH

2oz (50g) can anchovies, drained
milk, to cover

1 Blanch the beans in boiling water for 3 minutes, then drain. Heat the oil in a saucepan. Add the tomatoes and cook gently, stirring, for 2 minutes until they start to soften. Add the wine, tomato paste, garlic, sugar, and salt and pepper. Bring to a boil. Add the beans, reduce the heat, and simmer gently for 5 minutes, stirring occasionally, until the beans are just tender and bathed in a thick sauce. Add the parsley and basil, taste, and season again. Cover with a lid and keep warm.

2 Beat 2 eggs at a time with a little salt and pepper. Add a dash of cold water. Heat a little butter in an omelet pan until it foams, then pour in the eggs. Cook over medium heat, lifting and stirring until the base is set and golden, and the eggs are almost firm but still slightly creamy.

3 Spoon a quarter of the tomato and bean mixture over one half of the omelet. Tilt the pan over a warmed plate. Flip the other side of the omelet over the beans, then slide out onto the plate. Keep the omelet warm while you quickly make the others in the same way.

IF ADDING FISH, soak the anchovies in enough milk to cover for 5 minutes, then drain and split each in half lengthways. Add to the bean mixture at the end of step 1, before seasoning.

Piperade

SERVES 4   **PREPARATION 5 MINS**   TO COOK **20 MINS**

This savory scrambled egg dish is from the Basque region of southwest France, where it is served as either a main course or a side dish.

1 Heat the oil in a large frying pan and fry the onion over gentle heat until softened. Add the garlic and peppers and fry for 5 minutes, stirring occasionally.

2 Add the tomatoes and simmer for 2–3 minutes, or until any liquid has evaporated.

3 Pour the eggs into the pan and scramble, stirring frequently until creamy and the eggs are just set. Be careful not to let the mixture boil or it will curdle. Season with salt and pepper, sprinkle with parsley, and serve.

IF ADDING FISH, poach the haddock in a little milk or water for 3–5 minutes or until it flakes easily. Drain and flake, removing the skin. Gently stir into the cooked piperade at the end of step 3, before seasoning.

INGREDIENTS

2 tbsp olive oil
1 large onion, finely sliced
  or chopped
2 garlic cloves, crushed
1 red bell pepper, seeded
  and chopped
1 green bell pepper, seeded
  and chopped
4 tomatoes, chopped
8 large eggs, beaten
salt and freshly ground
  black pepper
2 tbsp chopped parsley,
  to garnish

OPTIONAL FISH

6oz (175g) undyed
  smoked haddock
milk for poaching (optional)

Four ways with
Zucchini

Zucchini with golden raisins, red onion, and pine nuts ▶

TAKES 30 mins **SERVES** 4

Preheat the oven to 400°F (200°C). Halve 8 **zucchini** lengthways. Scoop out the flesh, chop, and set aside. Heat 1 tbsp **olive oil** in a frying pan over a low heat. Add 1 finely chopped **red onion** and a pinch of **salt**. Sweat for 5 minutes until soft, then stir in the zucchini flesh and a pinch of **chile flakes**. Cook for 2 more minutes. Stir in a small handful each of toasted **pine nuts** and **golden raisins**. Remove from the heat. Spoon the mixture into the shells. Top with 2½oz (75g) crumbled **feta cheese**. Roast in the oven for 10–15 minutes. Drizzle with olive oil and serve.

◀ Moroccan couscous salad

TAKES 10 mins **SERVES** 4

Put 9oz (250g) **couscous** in a large bowl with enough hot **vegetable stock** to just cover. Seal with plastic wrap and leave for 5 minutes, then fluff up with a fork. Chop 2 **zucchini**. Heat a little **olive oil** in a frying pan and cook the zucchini until golden. Add to the couscous with a good pinch of **paprika**, the juice of 2 **lemons**, and a handful each of finely chopped fresh **flat-leaf parsley** and chopped **olives**. Season well with **salt** and freshly ground **black pepper** and stir to combine.

Zucchini cooks quickly and can be steamed, boiled, sautéed, or baked. Just trim, then slice, cut in batons, or chop. Cook baby zucchini whole, or stuff larger ones. The flowers are also delicious stuffed and fried.

Grated zucchini with goat cheese omelet ▶

TAKES 15 mins **SERVES** 1

Put 3 lightly beaten **large eggs** and 1 small grated **zucchini** in a bowl. Season with **sea salt** and freshly ground **black pepper**. Melt a knob of **butter** in a non-stick frying pan over medium-high heat until foaming, then pour in the egg mixture, swirling it around to cover the base. When it begins to cook around the edges, scatter over 1¾oz (50g) crumbled **soft goat cheese**. Cook until the center is almost cooked, but still a little wet. Remove from the heat and leave for 2 minutes to set. Sprinkle a little pepper over, carefully slide out of the pan, and serve.

◀ Zucchini fritters with dill tzatziki

TAKES 30 mins, plus draining **SERVES** 4

Grate 7oz (200g) **zucchini**, sprinkle with 1 tsp **salt**, and drain in a sieve for 1 hour. Rinse and squeeze dry. Whisk together 3½oz (100g) **ricotta cheese**, 1 **large egg**, and 2 tbsp **all-purpose flour**. Add 2 crushed **garlic cloves** and a small handful each of chopped **basil** and **flat-leaf parsley**. Season well with **salt** and freshly ground **black pepper**. Mix in the zucchini. Fry tablespoons of the batter in **olive oil** for 2–3 minutes on each side. Drain. Serve with tzatziki made with 1 crushed **garlic clove**, 2 tbsp chopped **dill**, 7oz (200g) **Greek-style yogurt**, a squeeze of **lemon juice**, and salt and pepper.

219

Mint, new potato, pea, and lettuce tortilla

SERVES 4   **PREPARATION 15 MINS**   TO COOK **18 MINS**

This fresh, summery tortilla is **delicious eaten cold with a salad as a picnic lunch**. You can also tuck it into soft bread rolls for lunch on the go, adding some salad, too.

INGREDIENTS

12oz (350g) small new
   potatoes, scrubbed
   and sliced
salt and freshly ground
   black pepper
4oz (115g) shelled fresh
   or frozen peas
large knob of butter
1 tbsp sunflower or vegetable oil
4 scallions, chopped
1 head Little Gem lettuce,
   shredded
1 tbsp chopped mint
1 tbsp chopped parsley
6 large eggs, beaten

OPTIONAL MEAT

boneless, skinless duck breast,
   cut into small pieces

1 Cook the potatoes in salted, boiling water for 3 minutes. Add the peas and cook for a further 4 minutes until both are tender. Drain, rinse with cold water, and drain again.

2 Heat the butter and oil in a large frying pan. Add the scallions and fry, stirring, for 2 minutes over medium heat. Add the lettuce and fry for another minute until the lettuce is wilted and the onions are soft, but not brown. Add the potatoes and peas and fry, stirring, for 1 minute. Sprinkle with the mint and parsley and add some salt and pepper.

3 Pour in the eggs and cook, lifting and stirring at first, for 4–5 minutes until the mixture has almost set. Invert on a plate, slide back into the pan, and cook the other side for 2 minutes until brown. Alternatively, preheat the broiler and put the pan under the broiler for a few minutes to brown and set the top. Slide out onto a plate and serve, cut into wedges.

IF ADDING MEAT, sauté the duck in the butter and oil for 2 minutes at step 2 before adding the scallions, or add a handful of chopped cooked duck to the mixture with the lettuce.

Mixed mushroom and garlic omelets

MAKES 4   PREPARATION **5 MINS**   TO COOK **20 MINS**

This is a delicious way to serve wild mushrooms. As many of the wild varieties are now cultivated, you may be able to find them in the store all year round.

1 Melt the butter in a saucepan with the oil. Add the shallot and garlic and fry, stirring, for 2 minutes to soften. Add the mushrooms and cook, stirring, for 3–4 minutes until soft.

2 Add the wine and boil until the liquid has almost disappeared, stirring all the time. Stir in the cream and boil for 1 minute. Season the mixture with salt and pepper and stir in the parsley. Keep hot.

3 Beat 2 eggs with a little salt and pepper. Add a dash of cold water. Heat a little butter in an omelet pan until it foams, then pour in the eggs. Cook over medium heat, lifting and stirring, for 1–2 minutes until the base is set and golden and the eggs are almost firm but still slightly creamy.

4 Spoon a quarter of the mushroom mixture over one half of the omelet. Tilt the pan over a warmed plate. Flip the other side of the omelet over the mushrooms, then slide out onto a plate. Keep warm while quickly making 3 more omelets in the same way.

IF ADDING MEAT, fry the bacon with the shallot at step 1, then continue as before.

INGREDIENTS

knob of butter, plus
    extra for frying
1 tbsp olive oil
1 shallot, finely chopped
2 garlic cloves, chopped
12oz (350g) mixed wild
    mushrooms, cut into
    pieces if large
¼ cup dry white wine
¼ cup heavy cream
salt and freshly ground
    black pepper
1 tbsp chopped parsley
8 large eggs

OPTIONAL MEAT
2 strips bacon, diced

Cheese soufflé omelet with corn and pepper

MAKES 1   **PREPARATION 15 MINS**   TO COOK **6 MINS**

If making more than one omelet, **serve each as it is ready** as their lovely texture is rapidly lost as they cool. Serve with crusty bread and a green salad.

INGREDIENTS

2 eggs, separated
knob of butter

For the sauce
knob of butter
handful of fresh or thawed
   frozen corn kernels
½ small red bell pepper,
   seeded and finely chopped
2 tsp cornstarch
7 tbsp milk
2 tsp snipped chives,
   plus a few extra
   to garnish
¾oz (20g) Gruyère
   cheese, grated
¾oz (20g) Cheddar
   cheese, grated
pinch of cayenne pepper
salt and freshly ground
   black pepper

OPTIONAL MEAT
small handful of chopped
   cooked chicken

1 To make the sauce, heat the butter in a saucepan. Add the corn and red pepper, stir, then cover and cook very gently for 5 minutes or until tender. Stir in the cornstarch, followed by the milk. Bring to a boil and cook for 2 minutes, stirring all the time, until thick. Stir in the chives, cheeses, cayenne, and salt and pepper to taste.

2 Beat the egg yolks with 2 tbsp water and add salt and pepper. Whisk the egg whites until stiff and fold into the yolks with a metal spoon.

3 Preheat the broiler. Heat a knob of butter in an omelet pan, add the egg mixture, and gently spread it out. Cook over medium heat for about 3 minutes until golden underneath. Immediately place the pan under the broiler and cook for 2–3 minutes until risen and golden on top. Meanwhile, reheat the sauce, stirring.

4 Slide the omelet onto a plate. Quickly spread one half with the cheese and corn sauce (don't worry if it oozes over the edge). Flip the uncovered side over the top to fold the omelet in half and garnish with a few snipped chives. Serve immediately.

IF ADDING MEAT, omit the Gruyère cheese and use only half the corn. Add the chicken to the saucepan 3 minutes after adding the corn and red pepper at step 1.

Asparagus and scallion soufflé omelet

SERVES 2   **PREPARATION 10 MINS**   **TO COOK 14 MINS**

To **make individual omelets** instead, simply use an omelet pan, cook half the egg mixture and use half the vegetables, then repeat with the remaining ingredients.

INGREDIENTS

4oz (115g) thin asparagus
   spears, trimmed if necessary
4 thick scallions
1 tbsp olive oil
4 large eggs, separated
salt and freshly ground
   black pepper
1 tbsp chopped thyme
knob of butter

OPTIONAL FISH

handful of chopped smoked
   salmon trimmings
splash of olive oil

1 Steam the asparagus or boil in water for 3–4 minutes until tender. Drain thoroughly and set aside.

2 Trim off most of the green part of the scallions so they are the same length as the asparagus. Cut in halves lengthways. Heat the oil in a non-stick frying pan and sauté the onions over medium heat for 4–5 minutes until they are soft and lightly golden. Remove with a slotted spoon and add to the asparagus. Mix together gently.

3 Beat the egg yolks with a pinch of salt and some pepper, thyme, and ¼ cup water. Whisk the egg whites until stiff and fold into the yolk mixture.

4 Reheat the frying pan and melt the butter, swirling it around the pan. Add the egg mixture, then spread it out and cook over medium heat for 2 minutes until golden underneath. Slide out of the pan onto a plate.

5 Lay the asparagus and scallions in the pan. Invert the plate with the omelet over the pan so the uncooked side of the omelet sits on top of the vegetables. Cook for a further 2 minutes until just firm, then set onto a plate, vegetable-side up. Cut the omelet in half and serve immediately.

IF ADDING FISH, stir-fry the salmon in a splash of oil in the frying pan before cooking the omelet, and set aside. Sprinkle it over the asparagus and scallions in the pan at step 5 before inverting the half-cooked omelet back on top.

Vegetable egg foo yung

SERVES 4   PREPARATION **10 MINS, PLUS SOAKING**   TO COOK **10 MINS**

Beansprouts are key to achieving the desired flavor, but any of the other **vegetables can be substituted as long as they are cut thinly** so they cook in 2–3 minutes.

1 If using dried mushrooms, soak them in hot water for 30 minutes, then drain before use.

2 Heat 2 tbsp oil in a wok or large frying pan. Stir-fry the mushrooms and other vegetables for 2–3 minutes until they are softened, but still have some texture. Pour into a bowl, mix in the beaten eggs, and add the soy sauce, ginger, and five-spice powder.

3 Heat ½ tbsp of the remaining oil in an omelet pan. Add a quarter of the mixture and spread out evenly. Fry for 1–2 minutes until almost set, lifting the edges and tilting the pan so the runny egg flows underneath.

4 Carefully fold the omelet in half and slide it out onto a warmed plate. Keep it warm while cooking the remaining omelets in the same way. Serve warm with sweet chili sauce or soy sauce to drizzle over, if required.

IF ADDING MEAT OR SHELLFISH, add the chicken or shrimp to the vegetable mixture when stir-frying at step 2.

INGREDIENTS

2 heaped tbsp dried sliced
   shiitake mushrooms, or
   4 fresh mushrooms, sliced
4 tbsp sunflower or vegetable oil
1 carrot, cut into
   thin batonettes
2in (5cm) piece cucumber,
   seeded and cut into
   thin batonettes
3oz (85g) cooked fresh peas,
   or frozen peas (thawed)
4 small handfuls
   of beansprouts
2 scallions, chopped
2 heads bok choy, shredded
8 large eggs, beaten
1 tbsp soy sauce
1 tsp grated fresh ginger
½ tsp Chinese five-spice powder
sweet chili sauce or extra soy
   sauce, to serve (optional)

**OPTIONAL MEAT
OR SHELLFISH**
handful of chopped cooked
   chicken or small cooked,
   peeled shrimp (thawed
   if frozen)

Butternut squash, spinach, and goat cheese frittata

SERVES 4   **PREPARATION** **10 MINS**   **TO COOK** **20 MINS**

This fresh-tasting frittata is equally good with chopped Swiss chard or bok choy instead of the spinach. Cottage cheese can replace the soft goat cheese, too.

INGREDIENTS

1 small butternut squash
   (approx. 1lb 2oz/500g),
   halved, peeled, seeded,
   and diced
2 tbsp olive oil
knob of butter
1 small onion, chopped
7oz (200g) spinach
4½oz (125g) soft
   goat cheese
4 pieces of sun-dried
   tomatoes in oil, drained
   and cut into small pieces
2 tbsp grated
   Parmesan cheese
grated nutmeg
2 tbsp chopped tarragon
6 large eggs, beaten
salt and freshly ground
   black pepper

OPTIONAL MEAT
3½oz (100g) blood
   sausage, diced

1 Blanch the squash in boiling water for 2–4 minutes to soften slightly. Drain thoroughly.

2 Heat the oil and butter in a large non-stick frying pan. Add the onion and fry, stirring, for 3 minutes until softened and lightly golden. Add the squash and fry, stirring, for 2 minutes until tender but still holding its shape.

3 Scatter the spinach into the pan and cook, stirring, for 2 minutes to wilt. Boil rapidly for 1–2 minutes to drive off any liquid, stirring gently and spreading the spinach evenly into the squash. Add small spoonfuls or pieces of the goat cheese and sun-dried tomatoes. Sprinkle with Parmesan, dust with nutmeg, and scatter the tarragon over.

4 Season the beaten eggs with a little salt and plenty of pepper. Pour into the pan and cook, lifting and stirring, until beginning to set. Cover the pan and cook gently for about 5 minutes until the eggs are almost set and the base is golden.

5 Meanwhile, preheat the broiler. When the eggs are nearly set, put the pan under the broiler for about 3 minutes to finish setting—the frittata should only just be starting to brown so that all the colors remain vibrant. Remove from the broiler and leave to cool for at least 5 minutes. Serve warm or cold, cut into wedges.

IF ADDING MEAT, omit the goat cheese and scatter the blood sausage over the cooked vegetables at step 3.

Spiced crushed carrot, pine nut, and cottage cheese frittata

SERVES 4   **PREPARATION 5 MINS**   **TO COOK 20 MINS**

The sweet carrots and pine nuts perfectly complement the creamy, soft cottage cheese in this dish, which draws its inspiration from the Middle East.

INGREDIENTS

14oz (400g) young spring
  carrots, trimmed
salt and freshly ground
  black pepper
2 tbsp olive oil, plus extra
  for drizzling
2 tbsp pine nuts
1 tbsp black mustard seeds
2 tsp cumin seeds
6 large eggs
1 tbsp chopped thyme
5½oz (150g) cottage or
  ricotta cheese
2 tbsp chopped cilantro

OPTIONAL MEAT
handful of lean ground beef

1 Halve any fat carrots lengthways so that they cook evenly, then boil the carrots in lightly salted water or steam for about 10 minutes until tender. Drain well, then roughly crush with a potato masher until well broken up but not mushy. Set aside.

2 Heat half the oil in a frying pan. Add the pine nuts, mustard, and cumin and fry, stirring, for about 1 minute until the mustard seeds begin to pop and the pine nuts are golden. Add to the carrots and mix well. Season with plenty of pepper.

3 Preheat the broiler. Beat the eggs in a bowl with the thyme and a little salt and pepper. Heat the remaining oil in the frying pan. Add the crushed carrot mixture and spread out. Dot with small spoonfuls of cheese. Pour the eggs over and sprinkle with the cilantro. Cook over gentle heat for 4–5 minutes, lifting and stirring the mixture gently at first and tilting the pan to allow the uncooked egg to run underneath until the frittata is almost set and the base is golden.

4 When the frittata is almost set, place the pan under the hot broiler for a few minutes to brown and cook the top. Cut into wedges and serve warm.

IF ADDING MEAT, when the pine nuts, mustard, and cumin have been fried and added to the carrots, dry-fry the ground beef until brown and all the grains are separate. Continue to fry for a further 2 minutes. Add the carrots and mix well. Use half the amount of cottage cheese.

Swiss chard, beet, and goat cheese frittata

SERVES 4   PREPARATION **10 MINS**   TO COOK **20 MINS**

When Swiss chard isn't available, use spinach instead. If you have a larger disc of goat cheese, dice it rather than cutting it into slices.

1 Wash the Swiss chard but don't dry it. Shred the leaves and chop the stalks.

2 Heat the oil and butter in a large non-stick frying pan. Add the onion and fry, stirring, for 3 minutes until soft. Add the chard and stir-fry for about 5 minutes until wilted and the stalks are tender, adding a splash of water if necessary—this should all be evaporated when the vegetables are tender. Spread the mixture out in the pan and scatter the beets over.

3 Preheat the broiler. Season the eggs with a little salt and pepper and pour into the pan. Scatter the cheese slices and then the dill over the eggs. Cook over gentle heat for 4–5 minutes, lifting and stirring the mixture gently at first and tilting the pan to allow the uncooked egg to run underneath the omelet.

4 When the base is golden and set but the top is still creamy, put the pan under the hot grill for a few minutes to brown and set the top. Cut into wedges and serve.

IF ADDING FISH, scatter the tuna over the cooked Swiss chard before adding the beets at the end of step 2. Omit the cheese.

INGREDIENTS

7oz (200g) Swiss chard (preferably red-stalked)
2 tbsp olive oil
knob of butter
1 small onion, chopped
2 cooked beets, diced
6 large eggs, beaten
salt and freshly ground black pepper
3½oz (100g) narrow-cylinder goat cheese, thinly sliced
2 tbsp chopped dill

OPTIONAL FISH

7oz (185g) can tuna, drained and flaked

Tarts, pies, and turnovers

Tarts, pies, and turnovers
Caramelized shallot tart

SERVES 4–6   **PREPARATION 20 MINS, PLUS CHILLING**   TO COOK **45 MINS**

The allium family is indispensable to most cooks, yet onions and shallots rarely take center stage. **This simple recipe gives shallots a starring role.**

INGREDIENTS

1 cup all-purpose flour
pinch of salt
8 tbsp butter
2 tbsp olive oil
14oz (400g) shallots, peeled
    and split in half lengthways
2 tbsp balsamic vinegar
a few sprigs of thyme
green salad, to serve

OPTIONAL MEAT
4oz (115g) pancetta, diced

1 For the dough, combine the flour, salt, and 6 tbsp butter in a food processor, and mix to form fine breadcrumbs. With the motor running, add cold water, a tbsp at a time, until the dough starts to stick together. Form the dough into a ball, wrap it in plastic wrap, and leave it in the refrigerator to chill for 30 minutes. Alternatively, use 9oz (250g) store-bought pie dough.

2 Preheat the oven to 400°F (200°C). In a 9–10in (23–25cm) ovenproof frying pan, melt the remaining butter with the oil. Put the shallots in, cut-side down, and cook very gently for 10 minutes or until they are browned. Turn over and cook for another 5 minutes. Add the vinegar and 2 tbsp water, then remove from the heat. Tuck the thyme sprigs between the shallots.

3 Roll out the dough to a circle a little larger than the frying pan. Lay the dough over the shallots, trim, and tuck it in. Transfer the pan to the oven and cook for 30 minutes until the dough is golden brown.

4 Remove the pan from the oven and bang gently to loosen the shallots. Run a knife around the edges of the dough, then put a large plate over the pan and quickly turn it over. Serve warm with a green salad.

IF ADDING MEAT, dry-fry the diced pancetta in the pan, then remove with a slotted spoon. Fry the shallots as in step 2. Scatter the pancetta over the cooked shallots after sprinkling them with the balsamic vinegar and water, then continue as before.

Roasted squash and Gorgonzola tart

SERVES 4–6   **PREPARATION 25 MINS, PLUS CHILLING**   TO COOK **1 HR 30 MINS**

Make this wonderful tart in the early autumn when spinach and squash are readily available. You can use chard in place of the spinach.

1 Preheat the oven to 350°F (180°C). Roll out the dough on a lightly floured surface, to a thickness of about ⅛in (3mm) in a circle a little larger than a 8in (20cm) tart pan with removable bottom. Line the tart pan with the dough. Chill for 30 minutes.

2 Put the squash slices on a baking sheet and brush with oil. Bake for 30 minutes, or until tender. Meanwhile, place the spinach and a little oil in a saucepan and cook over medium heat for 4 minutes until wilted. Drain and leave to cool. Whisk the eggs, egg yolk, cream, Parmesan, and nutmeg together, and season with salt and pepper.

3 Line the tart crust with waxed paper and fill with baking beans. Bake blind for 15 minutes. Remove the beans and paper and bake for another 10 minutes.

4 Squeeze the spinach dry and spread it across the bottom of the tart crust, then add the squash and Gorgonzola. Pour the egg mixture over and bake for 30–40 minutes, or until the filling is set. Remove from the oven and let it sit for 10 minutes before serving.

IF ADDING MEAT, scatter the salami over the cooked tart crust before adding the spinach at step 4.

INGREDIENTS

9oz (250g) store-bought pie dough
all-purpose flour, for dusting
1lb (450g) winter squash, halved, peeled, seeded, and thickly sliced
1–2 tbsp olive oil
14oz (400g) spinach
2 large eggs
1 large egg yolk
1¼ cup heavy cream
1¾oz (50g) Parmesan cheese, grated
pinch of grated nutmeg
salt and freshly ground black pepper
4oz (115g) Gorgonzola cheese, crumbled

OPTIONAL MEAT

2oz (60g) thinly sliced salami, diced

Stuffed portobello mushroom en croûte

SERVES 4   **PREPARATION 30 MINS**   **TO COOK 40 MINS**

Chestnuts make a delicious, meaty-textured filling for mushrooms. These pies are wonderful served with new potatoes and a selection of baby vegetables.

INGREDIENTS

1 tbsp olive oil

knob of butter

1 onion, finely chopped

1 celery stalk, finely chopped

7oz (240g) can cooked chestnuts

2 tbsp chopped
   flat-leaf parsley

2 tbsp chopped thyme

1 tsp grated lemon zest

2 tbsp mushroom ketchup
   or Worcestershire sauce

1 cup whole wheat
   breadcrumbs

salt and freshly ground
   black pepper

2 small eggs

4 large portobello mushrooms,
   peeled and stalks reserved

15oz (450g) package puff pastry

sprigs of parsley, to garnish

For the sauce

2 tbsp sunflower or vegetable oil

6oz (175g) chestnut mushrooms,
   finely chopped

1 garlic clove, crushed

⅔ cup dry, hard cider

¾ cup heavy cream

2 tsp chopped thyme

OPTIONAL MEAT

10oz (300g) pork sausage meat

1 Heat the oil and butter in a saucepan. Add the onion and celery and fry, stirring, for 3 minutes until softened and lightly golden. Remove from the heat, add the chestnuts, and mash with a fork. Work in the herbs, lemon zest, ketchup, breadcrumbs, and salt and pepper. Beat one of the eggs and stir into the mixture. Press into the mushrooms.

2 Preheat the oven to 400°F (200°C). Cut the pastry into quarters and cut a third off each. Roll out the thirds to rounds about ¾in (2cm) larger in diameter than the mushrooms. Line a baking sheet with parchment paper, lay the rounds on it, and place a stuffed mushroom in the center of each. Beat the second egg and brush the edges with it.

3 Roll out the remaining pastry to rounds about 3in (8cm) larger than the mushrooms. Place the pastry over and press the edges to seal. Make small indentations and flute the edges with the back of a knife, then brush all over with beaten egg and make a hole in the center of each to allow steam to escape. Make leaves out of pastry trimmings, if liked, and arrange on top. Brush with the remaining egg. Bake in the oven for 40 minutes or until puffy and golden and the mushrooms are cooked through.

4 Meanwhile, make the sauce. Heat the sunflower oil in a saucepan and add the chestnut mushrooms, finely chopped portobello mushroom stalks, and garlic. Cook, stirring, over medium heat for about 3 minutes until tender and the liquid has evaporated.

5 Add the cider and boil for 2 minutes until reduced by half. Stir in the cream, thyme, and 6 tbsp water. Simmer for 3 minutes until reduced and thickened, stirring. Season with salt and pepper. Transfer the pies to plates, garnish with parsley, and serve with the sauce.

IF ADDING MEAT, omit the chestnuts and breadcrumbs and work the sausage meat into the onion mixture with the flavorings at step 1.

Asparagus cream cheese quiche

SERVES 4–6 **PREPARATION 20 MINS, PLUS CHILLING** TO COOK **45 MINS**

Grilling the asparagus enhances its flavor and keeps the color beautifully green. The cream cheese in the quiche adds a velvety texture and extra goodness.

INGREDIENTS

1 cup all-purpose flour
pinch of salt
6 tbsp cold butter, diced
6oz (175g) green
   asparagus spears
a little olive oil
4oz (115g) cream cheese
2 tsp chopped thyme
freshly ground black pepper
3oz (85g) aged Cheddar
   cheese, grated
2 large eggs
⅔ cup half-and-half

OPTIONAL FISH
4½oz (125g) smoked salmon
   trimmings, chopped if large

1 Sift the flour and salt into a bowl. Add the butter and rub in with the fingertips until the mixture resembles fine breadcrumbs. Mix with 2 tbsp cold water to form a firm dough. Knead gently on a lightly floured surface. Roll out and use to line a 8in (20cm) pie dish set on a baking sheet. Chill for 30 minutes.

2 Preheat the oven to 400°F (200°C). Line the pie crust with waxed paper and fill with baking beans. Bake for 10 minutes. Remove the paper and baking beans, then bake for a further 5 minutes to dry out. Remove from the oven and lower the oven temperature to 350°F (180°C).

3 Toss the asparagus in a little oil and cook on a hot grill pan for 2 minutes on each side until bright green and just tender.

4 Spread the cream cheese over the bottom of the pie crust and sprinkle with thyme, some pepper, and the cheese. Trim the asparagus spears to fit the quiche, as necessary. Scatter the trimmings over the cheese and lay the whole spears attractively on top.

5 Beat the eggs and cream together with a little salt and pepper and pour into the crust. Bake in the oven for about 30 minutes until golden and set. Serve warm or cold.

IF ADDING FISH, scatter the smoked salmon over the cream cheese in the pie crust at step 4 before adding the thyme and seasoning.

Swiss chard and cheese tart

SERVES 6 **PREPARATION 15 MINS** TO COOK **1 HR 20 MINS, PLUS COOLING**

Traditional Swiss chard, with its **succulent, thick white stems, is best for this dish**. When it is not in season, spinach makes an ideal alternative.

1 Preheat the oven to 400°F (200°C). Roll out the dough on a floured surface, into a circle large enough to fit a 9in (23cm) tart pan with a removable bottom. Trim away the excess. Line the dough with waxed paper and fill with baking beans. Bake in the oven for 15–20 minutes until the edges are golden. Remove the beans and paper and brush the bottom of the shell with a little of the egg wash. Return to the oven for 1–2 minutes to crisp up, then set aside. Reduce the oven temperature to 350°F (180°C).

2 Heat the oil in a pan over low heat. Add the onion and a pinch of salt and sweat for 5 minutes until soft. Add the garlic and rosemary and cook for a few seconds, then add the chard. Stir for 5 minutes until it wilts.

3 Spoon the onion and chard mixture into the crust. Sprinkle the Gruyère over and scatter evenly with feta. Season well with salt and pepper. Mix together the cream and the 2 eggs until well combined and carefully pour over the tart filling. Bake in the oven for 30–40 minutes until set and golden. Leave to cool for 10 minutes before releasing from the crust. Serve warm or at room temperature.

IF ADDING MEAT, mix the garlic sausage into the onion and chard mixture at step 3 before spooning into the pie crust. Use only 1 garlic clove and omit the feta cheese if preferred.

INGREDIENTS

9oz (250g) store-bought
   pie dough
all-purpose flour, for dusting
2 large eggs, plus 1 large egg
1 tbsp extra virgin olive oil
1 onion, finely chopped
salt and freshly ground
   black pepper
2 garlic cloves, finely chopped
a few sprigs of rosemary,
   leaves picked and
   finely chopped
9oz (250g) Swiss
   chard, chopped
4½oz (125g) Gruyère
   cheese, grated
4½oz (125g) feta cheese, diced
¾ cup heavy cream

OPTIONAL MEAT
2½oz (75g) cooked garlic
   sausage, diced

Fennel and Gruyère tart

SERVES 6   **PREPARATION 20 MINS, PLUS CHILLING**   TO COOK **45 MINS**

The light anise flavor of the fennel and the sweet tanginess of the Gruyère are a winning combination in this dish—an ideal choice for a summertime lunch.

INGREDIENTS

3 tbsp olive oil

1 onion, sliced

1 large fennel bulb, trimmed, quartered, and sliced

salt and freshly ground black pepper

½ tsp grated nutmeg

4 large eggs

1¼ cups heavy cream

12oz (350g) store-bought pie dough

all-purpose flour, for dusting

3½oz (100g) Gruyère cheese, grated

greens, to serve

OPTIONAL MEAT

4oz (115g) cooked chicken, diced

1 Preheat the oven to 400°F (200°C). For the filling, heat the oil in a frying pan, add the onion, and fry over medium heat for 2–3 minutes. Add the fennel and sauté for 6–8 minutes, stirring occasionally, until golden. Season with salt and pepper and nutmeg and set aside. Beat the eggs and cream together in a bowl.

2 Roll out the dough on a lightly floured surface to a thickness of ¼in (5mm). Lift it over a 9in (23cm) round, 1¼in (3cm) deep, fluted tart pan and press into the base and sides. Trim the edges. Prick the base with a fork, line with waxed paper, fill with baking beans, and bake for 15 minutes. Remove the beans and paper, then return to the oven for another 5 minutes to crisp up.

3 Scatter the onions and fennel over the base and sprinkle with the cheese. Pour the egg and cream mixture into the crust. Return the tart to the oven. Reduce the temperature to 350°F (180°C) and bake for 20–25 minutes, or until the filling is set and golden brown. Serve warm or cold with greens.

IF ADDING MEAT, scatter the chicken over the onions and fennel in the crust at step 3 before sprinkling with cheese. Use a small fennel bulb instead of a large one.

Red pepper and chile tart

SERVES 4–6　　**PREPARATION** **25–30 MINS**　　TO COOK **1 HR 30 MINS**

These hot flavors are tempered with mild sheep cheese. If preferred, swap the cheese for another favorite such as Brie, feta, or a blue cheese.

1 Preheat the oven to 400°F (200°C). For the filling, sit the peppers and chiles on a baking sheet and coat with half the oil. Cook in the oven for 30–40 minutes until the skins begin to char. Transfer the peppers to a plastic bag to cool. Chop and seed the chiles. When the peppers are cool, remove and discard the skins and seeds, roughly chop the flesh, and add to the chiles.

2 Carefully roll out the dough on a lightly floured surface to a thickness of ¼in (5mm). Lift it over a 8in (20cm) round tart pan with a removable bottom and press into the base and sides. Prick the base with a fork, line with waxed paper, fill with baking beans, and bake for 15 minutes. Remove the beans and paper and return to the oven for another 5 minutes to crisp up. Reduce the oven temperature to 350°F (180°C).

3 Heat the remaining oil in a frying pan, add the onion, and cook for 6–8 minutes over medium-low heat until softened. Season with salt and pepper, then stir in half the thyme. Leave to cool a little, then transfer to the crust. Add the peppers and chiles, spreading them out evenly, and scatter the cheese so it covers the whole tart. Mix together the cream and eggs and season with salt and pepper. Add the remaining thyme and the garlic and stir well. Pour the mixture over the tart evenly, place the pan on a baking sheet, and bake for 20–25 minutes, or until the top is set and golden. Remove and leave to cool before releasing from the pan.

IF ADDING MEAT, combine the chorizo with the onion for the last minute of frying at step 3 before stirring in the thyme.

INGREDIENTS

3 red bell peppers
2 red chiles
2 tbsp olive oil
9oz (250g) store-bought
　pie dough
all-purpose flour, for dusting
1 red onion, finely chopped
salt and freshly ground
　black pepper
leaves from a few sprigs
　of thyme
5½oz (150g) soft sheep
　cheese, crumbled
⅔ cup heavy cream
2 large eggs
2 garlic cloves, crushed

OPTIONAL MEAT
2½oz (75g) dry Spanish
　chorizo, finely diced

Leek, sage, walnut, and tomato tartlets

SERVES 4 **PREPARATION** **30 MINS, PLUS CHILLING** **TO COOK** **15 MINS**

Serve these pretty tartlets with new potatoes and a crisp green salad. The crispy sage leaves add an extra dimension but can be omitted if preferred.

INGREDIENTS

1lb 2oz (500g) package puff
 pastry, thawed if frozen
4 tbsp butter
4 leeks, cut into thick slices
12 cherry tomatoes, halved
2oz (60g) walnut pieces,
 roughly chopped
1 tbsp chopped sage, plus
 a small handful of sage
 leaves, to garnish
salt and freshly ground
 black pepper
2 large eggs, beaten
¼ cup mayonnaise
sunflower or vegetable oil,
 for frying

OPTIONAL MEAT

2oz (60g) cooked ham, diced

1 Cut the puff pastry into quarters and roll out to rectangles of about 6 × 7in (15 x 18cm). Place on 2 baking sheets lined with parchment paper. Score a line about ¾in (2cm) from each edge of the rectangles, taking care not to cut right through the pastry. This will form the rims of the tartlets. Chill for at least 30 minutes.

2 Meanwhile, make the filling. Melt the butter in a saucepan. Add the leeks and cook gently, stirring, for 2 minutes to soften slightly but not brown. Reduce the heat, cover, and cook gently for 4 minutes until the leeks are soft but still bright green and holding their shape. Transfer to a bowl and set aside to cool, then add the tomatoes, walnuts, sage, and salt and pepper.

3 Preheat the oven to 400°F (200°C). Brush a little of the beaten egg around the rims of each tartlet. Beat the remainder with the mayonnaise and stir into the leek mixture. Spoon into the centers of the tartlets, leaving the rims free and making sure each tartlet gets a good mixture of leeks, walnuts, and tomatoes. Bake in the oven for about 20 minutes until the centers are set and the edges puffy and golden.

4 Meanwhile, heat about ½in (1cm) oil until hot but not smoking. Put the sage leaves in a slotted spoon and lower into the hot oil. Cook for a few seconds, just until they stop sizzling and are bright green. Remove immediately and drain on paper towels. Scatter a few crispy leaves over each tartlet before serving.

IF ADDING MEAT, omit the walnuts, add the ham to the mixture at step 2, and cook as before.

Wild mushroom and Taleggio tart

SERVES 6   **PREPARATION 20 MINS**   TO COOK **50 MINS**

This is an earthy, robust tart that is excellent for entertaining, served with roasted new potatoes and a lightly dressed watercress and orange salad.

INGREDIENTS

12oz (350g) store-bought
  pie dough
all-purpose flour, for dusting
2 tbsp olive oil
5½oz (150g) mixed wild or
  exotic mushrooms, larger
  ones sliced
5½oz (150g) crimini
  mushrooms, roughly
  chopped
scant 1oz (25g) dried porcini
  mushrooms, soaked
  in boiling water for
  30 minutes and drained
3 garlic cloves, finely chopped
1¾oz (50g) hazelnuts, toasted
  and roughly chopped
salt and freshly ground
  black pepper
handful of flat-leaf parsley,
  finely chopped
3 tbsp heavy cream
1 large egg, lightly beaten
7oz (200g) Taleggio
  cheese, sliced
pinch of sweet paprika

OPTIONAL MEAT

4oz (115g) thick-cut
  bacon, diced

1 Preheat the oven to 400°F (200°C). Roll out the dough on a lightly floured surface to a thickness of ¼in (5mm). Use it to line a 14 × 5in (35 × 12cm) rectangular, 1in (2½cm) deep tart pan with a removable bottom. Trim to neaten. Prick the base with a fork and line with waxed paper. Fill with baking beans and bake in the oven for 15 minutes, or until the edges start turning golden. Remove the beans and paper and return to the oven for 5 minutes to crisp up.

2 Meanwhile, for the filling, heat the oil in a large frying pan. Add all the mushrooms and cook over medium-high heat for 10 minutes. Stir in the garlic and nuts and season with salt and pepper.

3 Transfer the mixture to a large bowl and toss with the parsley, cream, and egg. Spoon the mixture into the tart crust and top with the cheese. Sprinkle with paprika and bake for 15–20 minutes until golden and set. Remove and leave for at least 10 minutes before releasing from the pan.

IF ADDING MEAT, in step 2, dry-fry the diced bacon in the frying pan. Remove with a slotted spoon and set aside. Add just 1 tbsp oil and fry the mushrooms. Stir the bacon in with the garlic and continue as before.

Corn and jalapeño tart

SERVES 4   **PREPARATION 20 MINS**   **TO COOK 45 MINS–1 HR**

The **mix of sweet and hot flavors** in this colorful tart is characteristic of the American Southwest. Pair it with a tomato and avocado salad.

1 Preheat the oven to 400°F (200°C). Roll out the dough on a lightly floured surface to a thickness of ¼in (5mm). Line a 7in (18cm) round, straight-sided tart pan with a removable bottom with the dough, letting it overlap, then trim the surplus. Prick the base with a fork and line with waxed paper, then fill with baking beans and bake for 15 minutes. Remove the beans and paper and return to the oven for a further 5 minutes to crisp up. Reduce the oven temperature to 350°F (180°C).

2 Meanwhile, heat the oil in a large pan, add the scallions, and cook over low heat for 2 minutes. Stir in the cayenne or paprika (if using) and add the red pepper. Cook for a further 5 minutes, add the corn, and season with salt and pepper. Remove from the heat and leave to cool.

3 Stir in the cream and egg to coat the onions and pepper. Spoon the mixture into the tart crust and top with the jalapeños and cheese. Bake for 20–30 minutes or until set and golden. Remove and leave to cool for 10 minutes, then slice and serve.

IF ADDING MEAT, use a 7oz (200g) can corn and add the chicken together with the corn at step 2.

INGREDIENTS

6oz (175g) store-bought pie dough
all-purpose flour, for dusting
2 tbsp olive oil
bunch of scallions, finely chopped
pinch of cayenne pepper or sweet paprika (optional)
1 large red bell pepper, halved, seeded, and finely chopped
14oz (400g) can corn, drained
salt and freshly ground black pepper
⅔ cup heavy cream
1 large egg, beaten
1–2 tbsp sliced green jalapeño chiles, from a jar
2oz (60g) Monterey Jack or Cheddar cheese, sliced or grated
tomato and avocado salad, to serve

OPTIONAL MEAT

5½oz (150g) cooked chicken, diced

Cheese and asparagus turnovers

MAKES 9   **PREPARATION 20 MINS**   TO COOK **20–25 MINS**

These flaky, crumbly parcels are perfect for a light lunch or picnic on a sunny summer's day. Using store-bought puff pastry makes the preparation quick and easy.

INGREDIENTS

salt and freshly ground
   black pepper
3½oz (100g) asparagus spears,
   cut into ½in (1cm) strips
1¾oz (50g) aged Cheddar
   cheese, grated
3 tbsp snipped chives
1lb 2oz (500g) store-bought
   puff pastry
all-purpose flour, for dusting
1 large egg, beaten, to glaze
sweet paprika, for dusting
greens, to serve

OPTIONAL MEAT

2oz (60g) cooked chicken,
   finely chopped

1 Bring a small pan of salted water to a boil and blanch the asparagus spears for 2 minutes. Drain and refresh in cold water. Drain again and cool. Mix the asparagus with the cheese, chives, and plenty of pepper. Set aside.

2 Carefully roll out the dough on a lightly floured surface to form a 12in (30cm) square, ¼in (5mm) in thickness. Trim the edges, then cut out 9 equal squares. Brush the edges of each square with water. Divide the asparagus filling between the squares, heaping it over one diagonal half of each. Fold the pastry over the filling and pinch the edges together to seal. Use a knife to flute and crimp the edges together.

3 Place the triangles well apart on a large, lightly greased baking sheet. Make a steam hole in the top of each, then glaze with beaten egg and dust with paprika. Bake for 20–25 minutes, or until golden and risen. Serve warm or cold with greens.

IF ADDING MEAT, use just 2oz (60g) asparagus and mix it with the chicken at step 1. Add the cheese and chives and continue as before.

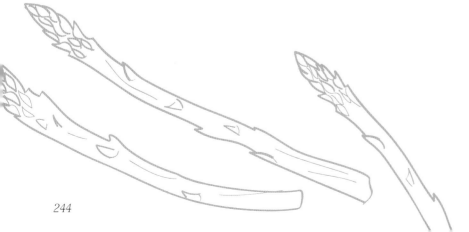

Spanakopita

SERVES 6   **PREPARATION 20 MINS**   **TO COOK 1 HR**

This is a **classic pie, filled with spinach, feta, and a hint of nutmeg.** Brushing the filo with butter between layers gives a really crisp, golden finish when baked.

1 Preheat the oven to 400°F (200°C). Heat the oil in a large frying pan, add the onion, and cook for 2–3 minutes. Season with salt and pepper. In a separate large pan, cook the spinach in 4 batches of 9oz (250g) each over low heat for 4–5 minutes until it wilts. Remove and set aside.

2 In a bowl, stir together the feta, nutmeg, and dill, and season with more pepper. Add the eggs and combine. Squeeze any excess water from the spinach, then add this and the onion to the feta mixture and mix.

3 Brush a 1 quart (1.4 litre) shallow rectangular dish with a little of the butter. Line with 1 sheet of filo and brush again. Lay the second sheet at a right angle to the first and brush again with butter. Repeat with a third sheet at a right angle again.

4 Fill the dish with the spinach mixture. Fold the edges of the filo over the top. Lay one of the remaining sheets of filo on top of the dish, folding the edges underneath so it fits the top of the dish. Brush with butter and lay another sheet on top folded the same way, then the final sheet. Brush the top with any remaining butter. Place the pie on a baking sheet.

5 Bake in the oven for about 20–25 minutes or until crisp and golden brown. Remove from the oven and leave to cool for 5–10 minutes before serving with a tomato salad.

IF ADDING MEAT, fry the lamb with the onion in step 1, cooking until the onion is softened and the meat is no longer pink and all the grains are separate. Use only 14oz (400g) spinach and 4½oz (125g) feta cheese. Add the lamb and onion to the feta mixture at step 2.

INGREDIENTS

1 tbsp olive oil
½ onion, very finely chopped
salt and freshly ground
 black pepper
2¼lb (1kg) spinach
9oz (250g) feta cheese,
 crumbled
pinch of grated nutmeg
handful of dill, finely chopped
3 large eggs
2 tbsp butter, melted
6 sheets filo dough
tomato salad, to serve

OPTIONAL MEAT

1lb 2oz (500g) lean
 ground lamb

Four ways with
Bell peppers

Red pepper salad ▶

TAKES 35 mins **SERVES** 4

Heat 3 tbsp **olive oil** in a large frying pan. Add 6 **red bell peppers**, seeded and cut into large strips, and 2 finely chopped **garlic cloves**. Fry over low heat for 5 minutes, stirring, then add 9oz (250g) ripe **tomatoes**, peeled, seeded, and chopped. Increase the heat, bring to simmering point, then reduce to low, cover, and cook for 12–15 minutes. Stir in 2 tbsp chopped **parsley**, season with **salt** and freshly ground **black pepper**, and cook for 2 minutes. Transfer the peppers to a serving dish. Add 1 tbsp **sherry vinegar** to the pan, increase the heat, and simmer for 5–7 minutes. Pour the sauce over the peppers and allow to cool.

◀ Pasta with roasted peppers

TAKES 35 mins **SERVES** 4

Roast and peel 6 **red bell peppers** (see p326) and cut into strips. Melt a knob of **butter** with 3 tbsp **olive oil** in a frying pan and gently fry 2 chopped **garlic cloves** together with 1 **red chile** and 1 **green chile**, seeded and chopped, for 2 minutes to soften but not brown. Add a generous pinch of **dried oregano** and 1 tbsp **thyme leaves**. Cook 12oz (350g) **dried penne** according to the package directions. Drain, reserving a little of the cooking water. Return to the pan, add the pepper mixture, and toss gently with scant 1oz (25g) grated **Pecorino cheese**. Serve drizzled with **chile oil**.

Bell peppers become sweeter as they ripen from green, through yellow and orange, to red. If you **buy them when glossy and firm** they will store in the fridge for up to 2 weeks, but use them within 24 hours once cut.

Roasted mixed pepper bruschetta ▶

TAKES 1 hr **SERVES** 4

Remove the seeds from 1 **red bell pepper** and 1 **yellow bell pepper**. Then slice the flesh into strips and add to a frying pan with a little **olive oil**. Season with **salt** and freshly ground **black pepper**. Cook until the peppers begin to soften. Increase the heat, add a drop of **balsamic vinegar**, and cook for a couple more minutes. Toast 4 **ciabatta** slices. Peel and cut 1 **garlic clove** in half. Rub the cut side over each slice. Spoon the pepper mixture onto the bread slices and serve hot, garnished with a scattering of **basil** leaves.

◀ Red pepper and walnut dip

TAKES 50 mins **SERVES** 8

Heat ⅓ cup **olive oil** in a heavy-based frying pan over low heat. Add 1 sliced **onion**, then sweat gently for 5 minutes until soft and translucent. Add 4 **red bell peppers**, seeded and sliced, and cook for about 30 minutes until soft, stirring regularly. Stir in 2 crushed **garlic cloves** and cook for a further 30 seconds, or until the garlic has turned white. Transfer the pepper mixture to a blender or food processor. Add 4½oz (125g) toasted and chopped **walnuts** and grated zest and juice of 1 **lemon**, then blend to a chunky purée. Serve with bread or crudités, such as carrot or cucumber batons, for dipping.

Creamy broccoli and blue cheese puffs

SERVES 4   **PREPARATION 20 MINS**   TO COOK **35 MINS**

Broccoli and blue cheese are perfect partners in these tasty, simple-to-make pies, but goat cheese or even Cheddar make an equally good match.

INGREDIENTS

6oz (175g) broccoli, cut into tiny florets

13oz (375g) store-bought puff pastry (approx. 9 × 16in/23 × 40cm)

3½oz (100g) creamy blue cheese, crumbled

6 tbsp crème fraîche, plus extra for glazing

salt and freshly ground black pepper

OPTIONAL MEAT

2oz (60g) ham, chopped

3½oz (100g) Cheddar cheese, grated

1 Cook the broccoli in lightly salted boiling water for 2 minutes until almost tender. Drain, rinse with cold water, and drain again. Preheat the oven to 425°F (220°C).

2 Cut the pastry in quarters. Pile the broccoli at one end of each oblong, leaving a border. Add some cheese and crème fraîche. Season with pepper and a few grains of salt (the cheese is quite strong).

3 Brush the pastry edges with water. Fold over the uncovered halves of the pastry, press the edges together to seal, and transfer to a dampened baking sheet. Make a few slashes in the tops and glaze with crème fraîche. Bake for 30 minutes until puffy, crisp, and golden.

IF ADDING MEAT, use only 4oz (115g) broccoli and pile the chopped ham on top. Use Cheddar cheese instead of the blue cheese.

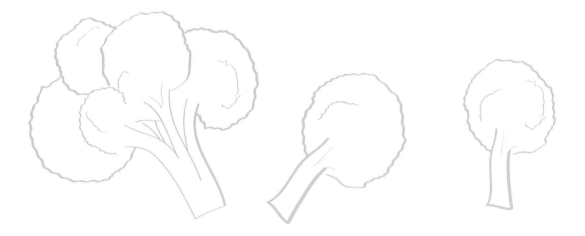

Artichoke, black olive, tomato, and feta tart

SERVES 4–6   **PREPARATION** **15 MINS**   **TO COOK** **1 HR**

This tart is bursting with the wonderful flavors of the Mediterranean. If fresh thyme isn't available, a couple of pinches of dried oregano will work equally well.

1 Preheat the oven to 400°F (200°C). Roll out the dough on a lightly floured work suface and use to line a 13 × 5in (35 × 12½cm) fluted tart pan with a removable bottom. Trim away the excess, line the dough with waxed paper, and fill with ceramic baking beans. Bake in the oven for 15–20 minutes until the edges are golden. Remove the beans and paper, brush the bottom of the shell with a little of the egg wash, and return to the oven for 2–3 minutes to crisp. Remove and set aside. Reduce the oven temperature to 350°F (180°C).

2 Heat the oil in a pan over low heat. Add the onion and sweat gently for about 5 minutes until soft and translucent. Add the garlic and cook for a few seconds more. Spoon the onion mixture evenly over the bottom of the tart crust. Arrange the artichokes down the center with tomatoes and olives alternately along either side, then sprinkle with the feta and thyme leaves.

3 Mix together the cream and 2 eggs and season well with salt and pepper. Carefully pour over the tart filling. Bake in the oven for 25–35 minutes until set, puffed, and golden. Leave to cool for about 10 minutes before releasing from the pan. Serve warm or at room temperature, with an arugula and tomato salad.

IF ADDING MEAT, use just a small, finely chopped onion and fry the pancetta with it at step 2. Continue as before.

INGREDIENTS

9oz (250g) store-bought
  pie dough
all-purpose flour, for dusting
2 large eggs, plus 1 lightly
  beaten for egg wash
1 tbsp olive oil
1 onion, finely chopped
2 garlic cloves,
  finely chopped
14oz (400g) can artichoke
  hearts, drained
6 sun-dried tomato pieces
12 pitted black olives
6oz (175g) feta cheese, diced
a few sprigs of thyme,
  leaves picked
¾ cup heavy cream
salt and freshly ground
  black pepper
arugula and tomato salad,
  to serve

OPTIONAL MEAT

2oz (60g) diced pancetta

Wild mushroom and hollandaise tartlets

SERVES 6   **PREPARATION 35 MINS, PLUS CHILLING**   TO COOK **10 MINS**

Halved **English muffins, hollowed out and baked with butter until golden**, make a delicious alternative to dough for these tartlet crusts.

INGREDIENTS

3 English muffins
7 tbsp butter, melted
2 tbsp unsalted butter
1 small onion, chopped
14oz (400g) fresh wild
   mushrooms, such as
   chanterelle or morel, sliced
1½oz (45g) dried wild
   mushrooms, soaked in
   boiling water for 30 minutes,
   drained, and chopped
2 tbsp chopped tarragon
juice of ½ lemon
salt and freshly ground
   black pepper
6oz (175g) mascarpone cheese
a few chive stalks, to garnish

For the hollandaise
3 large eggs
1½ tbsp lemon juice
12 tbsp butter, melted
pinch of cayenne pepper

OPTIONAL FISH
2–3 thin slices of
   smoked salmon

1 Preheat the oven to 375°F (190°C). Scoop out most of the soft filling from the muffins, leaving a ¼in (5mm) border all around. Brush all over with melted butter. Place on a baking sheet and bake in the oven for 15 minutes until golden but not too crisp. Remove from the oven and set aside.

2 For the filling, melt the unsalted butter in a frying pan and cook the onion and fresh mushrooms over medium heat. Add the dried mushrooms. Once all the mushrooms are soft, increase the heat and boil until the liquid has evaporated. Add the tarragon and lemon juice and season with salt and pepper. Remove from the heat, cool, then put in the food processor with the mascarpone cheese and purée until fairly smooth. Adjust the seasoning.

3 To make the hollandaise, whisk the eggs with the lemon juice in a small pan. Gradually whisk in the melted butter. Cook over very gentle heat, whisking all the time until thick—do not boil or it will curdle. Remove from the heat and season to taste with salt and pepper, and a pinch of cayenne pepper.

4 Spoon the mixture into the muffin tartlets and pour the hollandaise over. Bake for 10 minutes to glaze the tops. Serve hot, garnished with chive stalks.

IF ADDING FISH, line the baked muffin crusts with a thin slice of smoked salmon at step 4, cutting to fit before adding the mushroom mixture.

Tomato and onion tart

SERVES 4–6   **PREPARATION 25 MINS**   TO COOK **25 MINS**

Adding cinnamon to the whole wheat dough adds a **lovely depth of flavor to this simple, rustic tart**. Use good-quality, ripe tomatoes for the best result.

1 Preheat the oven to 400°F (200°C). Mix the flour, salt, and cinnamon together. Rub in the butter until the mixture resembles breadcrumbs, then mix with enough cold water to form a firm dough. Knead gently on a lightly floured surface. Roll out and use to line a 9in (23cm) shallow pie dish. Line with waxed paper, fill with baking beans, and bake in the oven for 10 minutes. Remove the paper and beans and cook for a further 5 minutes to dry out.

2 Meanwhile, fry the onions gently in the oil, stirring, for 5 minutes until soft but not brown. Add the garlic, tomatoes, tomato paste, and sugar, and season with some salt and pepper. Simmer gently, stirring occasionally, for 10 minutes until pulpy. Stir in the parsley, taste, and season again, if necessary.

3 Spoon into the pie crust and spread out. Top with the olives and bake for 10 minutes. Serve warm or cold.

IF ADDING FISH, arrange the anchovies in a lattice pattern over the surface at step 3 before garnishing with the olives.

INGREDIENTS

1 cup whole wheat flour
pinch of salt
1 tsp ground cinnamon
7 tbsp butter, diced
2 Spanish onions,
    roughly chopped
3 tbsp olive oil
1 garlic clove, crushed
1lb (450g) tomatoes, peeled
    and chopped
1 tbsp tomato paste
½ tsp granulated sugar
salt and freshly ground
    black pepper
2 tbsp chopped parsley
a few black olives

OPTIONAL FISH

2oz (50g) can of anchovies,
    drained

Summer squash, fava bean, and fresh pea quiches

SERVES 6 **PREPARATION 15 MINS, PLUS CHILLING** TO COOK **30 MINS**

Yellow summer squash have a slightly sweeter flavor than zucchini and go particularly well with peas. They also add color to this fresh-tasting quiche.

INGREDIENTS

1½ cups all-purpose flour, plus
  extra for dusting
7 tbsp unsalted butter, plus
  extra for greasing
1 large egg yolk
1½oz (45g) Parmesan
  cheese, grated
salt and freshly ground
  black pepper
a little milk
1½lb (675g) fava beans in
  the pod, or 8oz (225g) frozen
7oz (200g) yellow summer
  squash, cut into ½in
  (1cm) cubes
14oz (400g) fresh peas
  (4½oz/125g podded weight)
6 large egg yolks
⅔ cup heavy cream
1 tbsp chopped mint
salt and freshly ground
  black pepper
mixed greens, for serving

OPTIONAL MEAT

4½oz (125g) diced bacon

1 Preheat the oven to 350°F (180°C). In a food processor, pulse the flour for 1 minute, then add the butter in small knobs. Once incorporated, add the egg yolk, Parmesan, and some salt and pepper to season. Transfer to the work surface and bring the dough together with a little milk. Wrap in plastic wrap and rest in the refrigerator for at least 30 minutes until needed.

2 Bring a saucepan of salted water to a boil and drop in the fava beans. Blanch them for 3–4 minutes, then drain under cold running water and pop them out of their skins.

3 Take 6 mini tart pans, 4in (10cm) in diameter and 2in (5cm) deep, and grease with butter, then dust with flour. Roll out the dough on a lightly floured surface and use to line the pans. Chill for 10 minutes, then bake the tart crusts for 8 minutes. Cool and fill with the beans, squash, and peas.

4 Mix together the egg yolks and cream, then add the mint and some salt and pepper. Pour over the tarts, right up to the top, and bake for about 25 minutes until the custard has just set. Let them stand for 5 minutes before serving with a few dressed mixed greens.

IF ADDING MEAT, dry-fry the diced bacon and scatter over the baked tart crusts before adding the remaining filling at step 3. Omit the peas.

Celery root and pecan soufflé pie

SERVES 4   PREPARATION **40 MINS, PLUS CHILLING**   TO COOK **50 MINS**

This light-textured pie is **equally good made with parsnips or sweet potatoes instead of celery root**. Try walnuts or hazelnuts instead of pecans, too.

1 Mix the flour and salt in a bowl. Add the caraway seeds. Rub in the butter until the mixture resembles breadcrumbs. Stir in the cheese. Mix 3 tbsp cold water with the egg yolk and stir into the flour mixture to form a firm dough, adding more water if necessary. Knead gently on a lightly floured surface, then wrap and chill for at least 30 minutes.

2 Meanwhile, cook the celery root in salted boiling water until tender. Drain and return to the pan. Dry out briefly over gentle heat. Mash with the butter and milk. Beat in the pecans, egg yolks and chives. Season well with pepper.

3 Preheat the oven to 400°F (200°C). Roll out the dough and use it to line a 8in (20cm) pie dish. Line with waxed paper and fill with baking beans. Bake blind in the oven for 10 minutes, then remove the paper and beans. Bake for a further 5 minutes and remove from the oven.

4 Whisk the 3 egg whites until stiff. Mix 1 tbsp of the whites into the celery root mixture. Fold in the remainder with a rubber spatula. Spoon into the pie crust and bake for 25 minutes until risen, just set, and golden. Serve immediately.

IF ADDING MEAT, dry-fry the bacon and add with any residual fat to the mashed celery root at step 2. Use only 3 tbsp butter, omit the pecans, then continue as before.

INGREDIENTS

1 cup whole wheat or
  spelt flour
generous pinch of salt
1 tbsp caraway seeds
5 tbsp butter, chilled and diced
3oz (85g) aged Cheddar
  cheese, grated
1 large egg, separated
all-purpose flour, for dusting
1 celery root, approx. 1lb (450g),
  peeled and cut into chunks
4 tbsp butter
¼ cup milk
2oz (60g) pecans, chopped
2 large eggs, separated
2 tbsp snipped chives
freshly ground black pepper

OPTIONAL MEAT
4 slices bacon, diced

Mediterranean vegetable and feta filo pie

SERVES 4   **PREPARATION 35 MINS**   TO COOK **25 MINS**

This pie is delicious hot or cold. Brush the layers of filo with olive oil instead of butter if preferred—although the butter gives a crisper finish to the dish.

INGREDIENTS

2 tbsp olive oil

1 red onion, chopped

1 garlic clove, crushed

1 red bell pepper, seeded
   and cut into small chunks

1 green bell pepper, seeded
   and cut into small chunks

1 eggplant, halved lengthways
   and sliced

1 large zucchini, sliced

4 tomatoes, chopped

1 tsp dried oregano

small handful of pitted black
   olives, halved

salt and freshly ground
   black pepper

4 tbsp butter, melted

6 sheets filo dough

7oz (200g) feta cheese, diced

green salad, to serve

OPTIONAL MEAT

8oz (225g) cooked lamb, diced

1 Heat the oil in a large saucepan. Add the onion and garlic along with the vegetables and fry, stirring, for about 3 minutes until slightly softened. Cover, reduce the heat, and cook gently for 20 minutes, stirring occasionally.

2 Stir in the oregano, olives, and a little salt and pepper (the cheese and olives will be salty when added). Set aside to cool.

3 Preheat the oven to 400°F (200°C). Brush a 1 quart shallow rectangular dish with a little of the butter. Line with a sheet of filo and brush again. Lay a second sheet at right-angles to the first and brush again with butter. Repeat with a third sheet at right-angles again.

4 Fill the dish with the vegetable mixture and scatter the cheese over, pressing it into the surface. Fold the edges of the filo over the top. Lay one of the remaining sheets of filo on top of the dish, folding the edges underneath so it fits the top of the dish. Brush with butter and lay another sheet on top folded the same way, then the final sheet. Brush the top with any remaining butter. Place the pie on a baking sheet.

5 Bake in the oven for about 20–25 minutes or until crisp and golden brown. Remove from the oven and leave to cool for 5–10 minutes before serving with a green salad.

IF ADDING MEAT, omit the eggplant and add the lamb to the mixture instead at step 1.

Limoges potato and onion pie

SERVES 6–8   **PREPARATION** **35 MINS**   **TO COOK** **1 HR 15 MINS**

Flavored with herbs, **this substantial pie makes full use of earthy new potatoes**. When garlic chives are in season, stir in a few chopped leaves instead of the garlic cloves.

INGREDIENTS

2¼lb (1kg) new potatoes,
   scrubbed and sliced
salt and freshly ground
   black pepper
4 tbsp butter
3 onions, halved and
   thinly sliced
2 garlic cloves, chopped
1lb 2oz (500g) puff pastry,
   thawed if frozen
2 tbsp snipped chives
2 tbsp chopped parsley
2 tbsp chopped mint
2 large eggs
1¼ cup half-and-half
pickles and green salad,
   to serve

OPTIONAL FISH
7oz (185g) can tuna, drained
   and flaked

1 Boil the potatoes in salted water for about 5 minutes until tender but still holding their shape. Drain well and leave to cool.

2 Melt the butter in the rinsed-out saucepan. Fry the onions and garlic gently for 5 minutes, stirring, until soft and browning slightly. Set aside.

3 Preheat the oven to 425°F (220°C). Cut the pastry in half, roll out one half, and use to line a deep pie dish, 10in (25cm) in diameter.

4 Layer the potatoes, onions, and garlic, seasoning each layer with salt and pepper and sprinkling with herbs. Repeat 3 times to make 4 layers. Whisk the eggs and half-and-half together with a little salt and pepper. Pour all over the filling and allow it to soak down into the pie. Reserve the dregs of the egg and cream mixture for glazing the pie.

5 Roll out the remaining pastry and use as a lid, pressing it down all around, then trim off excess pastry and crimp the edges together between the finger and thumb to seal and decorate.

6 Brush the top with the dregs of the eggs and cream mixture to glaze. Make leaves out of the pastry trimmings and arrange on the pie. Brush again. Make a hole in the center to allow steam to escape.

7 Place the pie on a baking sheet and bake in the oven for 30 minutes until puffy and golden. Cover the pie loosely with foil to prevent over-browning and cook for a further 30–35 minutes until the custard is set and the pie is well risen and crisp. Cool for a few minutes to allow the flavors to develop before serving the pie with pickles and a green salad.

IF ADDING FISH, reduce the potato quantity to 2lb (900g) and add the tuna when layering the potatoes and onions in the pie dish at step 4.

Root vegetable and fennel pasties with seed pastry

MAKES 4   PREPARATION **30 MINS, PLUS CHILLING**   TO COOK **45–50 MINS**

These well-flavored pasties are **delicious served hot with cauliflower or broccoli in cheese sauce,** or cold with pickles and salad.

1 Mix the flours together in a bowl with a pinch of salt. Add the butter and rub in with the fingertips until the mixture resembles fine breadcrumbs. Stir in the fennel seeds, then mix with about ¼ cup cold water to form a soft but not sticky dough. Wrap in plastic wrap and leave to rest in the refrigerator for 30 minutes.

2 In a large bowl, mix the vegetables together with the thyme, and a little salt and plenty of pepper.

3 Preheat the oven to 375°F (190°C). Knead the dough gently on a lightly floured surface and cut into quarters. Roll out each quarter to rounds, about 7in (18cm) in diameter. Spread the center of each round with 1 tbsp cream cheese and pile the vegetables on top. Brush the edges with a little beaten egg.

4 Working with one pasty at a time, spoon ½ tbsp stock over to moisten, then draw the dough up over the filling and press together to seal. Flute between your finger and thumb to give an attractive edge, then transfer to a non-stick baking sheet. Repeat with the remaining pasties.

5 Brush the pasties with beaten egg to glaze, then bake in the oven for 45–50 minutes until the pasties are golden brown and the vegetables are tender. Cover loosely with foil after 30 minutes if over-browning. Serve hot or cold.

IF ADDING MEAT, crumble the lamb over the diced vegetables in the bowl at step 2 before mixing in the herbs and seasoning. Continue as before, but omit the cheese.

INGREDIENTS

1 cup whole wheat flour
1 cup all-purpose flour,
   plus extra for dusting
salt and freshly ground
   black pepper
12 tbsp butter, cut
   into small pieces
1 tbsp fennel seeds

For the filling

1 small onion, chopped
1 carrot, cut into small cubes
1 small potato, peeled and cut
   into small cubes
1 small turnip, cut into
   small cubes
1 fennel bulb, chopped
2 tbsp chopped thyme
¼ cup cream cheese
1 small egg, beaten
2–3 tbsp vegetable stock

OPTIONAL MEAT

handful of lean ground lamb

Vegetable samosas

SERVES 4   **PREPARATION 45 MINS, PLUS RESTING AND COOLING**   **TO COOK 35–40 MINS**

Serve these Indian pastries hot or cold. In India they would be fried in ghee, a clarified butter that can be heated to a high temperature, but oil works equally well.

INGREDIENTS

2 cups all-purpose flour, plus
    extra for dusting
salt and freshly ground
    black pepper
9 tbsp vegetable oil or ghee,
    plus extra for frying
1lb (450g) potatoes, scrubbed
8oz (225g) cauliflower,
    chopped into small pieces
6oz (175g) peas, thawed
    if frozen
2 shallots, sliced
2 tbsp curry paste
2 tbsp chopped cilantro
1 tbsp lemon juice

OPTIONAL MEAT

8oz (225g) lean ground lamb

1 To make the dough, sift the flour into a bowl with ½ tsp salt. Stir in 6 tbsp oil or ghee and gradually add ½ cup warm water, mixing to make a dough. Knead the dough on a floured surface until smooth. Wrap in plastic wrap and leave to rest for at least 30 minutes.

2 To make the filling, cook the potatoes in a saucepan of boiling water until tender. Drain and cool, then peel and chop into small pieces. Blanch the cauliflower florets in a pan of boiling water for 2–3 minutes, or until just tender, then drain. If using fresh peas, blanch them with the cauliflower.

3 Heat the remaining oil in a large frying pan and fry the shallots for 3–4 minutes, stirring frequently, until soft. Add the potatoes, cauliflower, peas, curry paste, cilantro, and lemon juice and cook over low heat for 2–3 minutes, stirring occasionally. Set aside to cool.

4 Divide the dough into 8 equal pieces. Roll them out so each forms a 7in (18cm) round. Cut each round in half and shape into a cone, dampening the edges to seal. Spoon a little of the filling into each cone, dampen the top edge of the dough, and press down over the filling to enclose it. Repeat with the rest of the dough and filling.

5 Heat the oil for deep-frying to 350°F (180°C), or until a cube of day-old bread browns in 30 seconds. Fry the samosas in batches for 3–4 minutes, or until golden brown on both sides. Drain on paper towels and serve hot or cold.

IF ADDING MEAT, omit the cauliflower and, at step 3, add the lamb to the cooked shallots. Fry, stirring, until no longer pink and all the grains are separate before adding the potatoes and other ingredients.

Corn and pepper empanadas

MAKES 24   **PREPARATION 45 MINS, PLUS CHILLING**   TO COOK **40–50 MINS**

These Spanish pastries make versatile snacks. For a main meal, make fewer, larger pies, using a tea plate as a guide to cut out the dough. The baking time is the same.

1 To make the dough, sift the flour into a large mixing bowl with ½ tsp salt. Add the butter and rub in with your fingertips until it resembles fine breadcrumbs. Add the beaten eggs with 4–6 tbsp water and combine to form a dough. Cover with plastic wrap and chill for 30 minutes.

2 Heat the oil in a frying pan, add the onion, and fry for 3 minutes until softened. Add the green pepper and fry for a further 3 minutes, stirring. Add the tomatoes, tomato paste, and paprika. Season with salt and pepper, partially cover, and simmer, stirring occasionally, for 5 minutes until pulpy. Stir in the chopped egg and parsley.

3 Preheat the oven to 375°F (190°C). Roll out the dough to a thickness of ⅛in (3mm). Cut out 24 rounds with a 3½ in (9cm) round pastry cutter. Put a heaped tsp of the mixture on each, then brush the edges with water, fold over, and pinch together.

4 Place the empanadas on an oiled baking sheet and brush with some beaten egg. Bake for 25–30 minutes, or until golden brown, and serve warm.

IF ADDING FISH, stir in the tuna with the tomatoes at step 2 and continue as before, but omitting the eggs.

INGREDIENTS

2½ cups all-purpose flour, plus extra for dusting
salt and freshly ground black pepper
6 tbsp butter, diced
2 large eggs, beaten, plus extra to glaze
1 tbsp olive oil
1 onion, finely chopped
1 green bell pepper, seeded and finely chopped
2 tomatoes, chopped
2 tsp tomato paste
1 tsp sweet paprika
2 hard-boiled eggs, chopped
2 tbsp finely chopped parsley

OPTIONAL FISH
185g (7oz) can tuna, drained

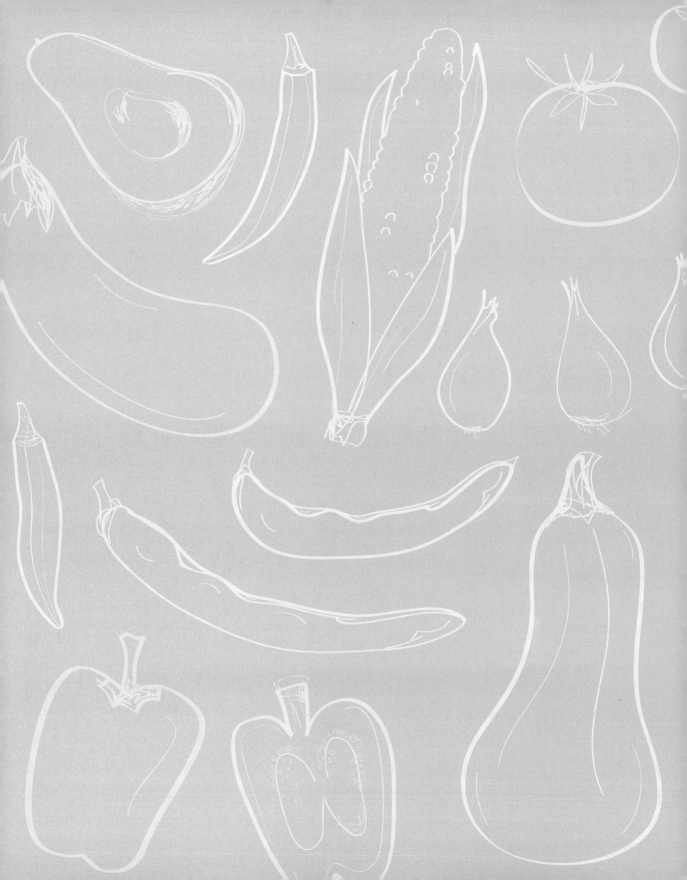

Grills and bakes

Shiitake mushroom and water chestnut teriyaki

SERVES 4   **PREPARATION** **10 MINS**   TO COOK **20–25 MINS**

A simple Japanese-style grill, this is **great with a salad of beansprouts** tossed with some chopped scallion in a dash of soy sauce, rice vinegar, and sesame oil.

INGREDIENTS

6 tbsp tamari (or light soy
   sauce), plus extra to serve
2 tbsp lime juice
2 tsp grated fresh ginger
2 garlic cloves, crushed
1 fat red chile, seeded
   and chopped
3 tbsp honey
1 tsp sunflower or vegetable oil
10oz (300g) shiitake
   mushrooms, halved if large
10oz (250g) can water
   chestnuts, drained
2 red onions, quartered
   and separated into slices
udon noodles, tossed in
   sesame oil and beansprout
   salad, to serve
torn cilantro or flat-leaf
   parsley leaves, to garnish

OPTIONAL MEAT
12oz (350g) boneless, skinless
   chicken breast, diced

1 Put all the ingredients except the mushrooms, water chestnuts, and onions in a saucepan. Stir well, bring to a boil, and continue to boil for 2–3 minutes until syrupy. Remove from the heat and stir in the vegetables until well coated.

2 Preheat the broiler. Spread the coated vegetables on a large baking sheet lined with oiled foil. Grill about 2in (5cm) from the heat source for 15–20 minutes, turning once or twice, until richly browned and glazed.

3 Serve spooned onto noodles, sprinkled with torn cilantro or flat-leaf parsley leaves, with a beansprout salad and extra tamari to sprinkle over.

IF ADDING MEAT, omit the water chestnuts, use half the amount of mushrooms, and add the chicken instead at the end of step 1.

Eggplant koftas with tzatziki

MAKES 8 **PREPARATION 20 MINS** **TO COOK 6–8 MINS**

These kebabs make a delicious main meal served as below or in **pita bread with a salad**. Put 8 wooden skewers in cold water to soak before preparing the dish.

1 Preheat a grill pan. Brush the eggplant slices with oil and grill in two batches for 2–3 minutes on each side until tender and striped brown. Finely chop in a food processor or by hand. Pour into a bowl and mix in all the remaining kebab ingredients. Season with ½ tsp salt and a little pepper. Using your hands, squeeze the mixture well to mix thoroughly.

2 Divide into 8 equal pieces and shape each into a cylinder around a soaked wooden skewer, making them about a third of the length of the skewers.

3 Brush with oil and place on the broiler rack. Grill about 2in (5cm) from the heat source for about 8 minutes, turning once until golden and cooked through.

4 Meanwhile, mix the tzatziki ingredients together, season with salt and pepper, and chill until ready to serve.

5 Serve the koftas, garnished with lemon wedges, with the tzatziki, couscous, and mixed greens.

IF ADDING MEAT, use a small eggplant instead of a large one, omit the breadcrumbs, and add the lamb to the bowl with the remaining kebab ingredients at step 1. Continue as above but cook for 10–12 minutes.

INGREDIENTS

1 large eggplant, sliced
2–3 tbsp olive oil, for brushing
1 cup breadcrumbs
2 large garlic cloves, crushed
1 small onion, grated
2 tsp ground cumin
1 tsp ground coriander
1 tsp dried mint
2 tbsp chopped cilantro
½ tsp salt
freshly ground black pepper
1 large egg, beaten
lemon wedges, to garnish
couscous and mixed greens,
   to serve

For the tzatziki
5½oz (150g) Greek-style yogurt
1 garlic clove, crushed
2in (5cm) piece cucumber,
   peeled and grated
2 tsp dried mint

OPTIONAL MEAT
14oz (400g) lean ground lamb

Grilled marinated halloumi on seeded vegetable ribbons

SERVES 4   PREPARATION **20 MINS, PLUS MARINATING**   TO COOK **6 MINS**

Salty halloumi, fragrant with herbs and garlic, marries beautifully with sweet-tasting vegetables here. Take care not to overcook the veg—it should retain some bite.

INGREDIENTS

1 lime
½ cup olive oil
1 tsp dried chile flakes
1 tsp dried oregano
½ tsp dried mint
1 garlic clove, crushed
salt and freshly ground
    black pepper
9oz (250g) block halloumi
    cheese, cut into 8 slices
Mediterranean flatbreads
    (khobez), and a dish each
    of olives and pickled
    chiles, to serve

For the vegetable ribbons

2 thin parsnips, peeled
    but left whole
2 large carrots, peeled
    but left whole
2 zucchini, trimmed
    but left whole
1 tbsp sesame oil
2 tbsp black onion seeds
2 tbsp sesame seeds

OPTIONAL MEAT

4–8 slices pancetta

1 Put 8 wooden skewers in cold water to soak. Finely grate the zest of the lime into a shallow dish. Squeeze the juice into a separate dish. Whisk 6 tbsp olive oil into the zest with half the lime juice, chiles, herbs, garlic, and plenty of pepper. Add the cheese slices, turn to coat completely, and leave to marinate for several hours or overnight, turning once or twice.

2 Peel the vegetables with a potato peeler, holding them firmly at each side and turning at intervals to shave them all around. There will be a central piece you cannot peel, which can be set aside to use for soup.

3 Heat the remaining olive oil in a large frying pan or wok. Add all the vegetables and stir-fry for 2 minutes until beginning to soften. Cover and cook for a further 2 minutes until tender but still with a little crunch. Add the sesame oil, remaining lime juice, onion seeds, and sesame seeds, and toss well. Season lightly with salt and pepper. Remove from the heat.

4 Preheat an oiled, flat grill pan or broiler. Remove the cheese from the marinade and thread a piece on each of the soaked wooden skewers. Grill for 1 minute on each side, pressing down with a metal spatula, until charred brown in places. Place on a plate and drizzle the remaining marinade over.

5 Toss the ribbons over a high heat once more to heat through. Serve the vegetable ribbons with the cheese sticks, Mediterranean flatbreads, olives, and pickled chiles.

IF ADDING MEAT, broil the pancetta and serve with the cheese and vegetable ribbons.

Broiled stuffed red peppers with chile and cheese

SERVES 4   **PREPARATION** **15 MINS**   **TO COOK** **20 MINS**

When available, baby bell peppers stuffed like this make a great starter (use 8 and halve the filling). The large peppers are enough for a light main meal.

INGREDIENTS

4 large red bell peppers
9oz (250g) medium-fat
   soft cheese
6oz (175g) aged Cheddar
   cheese, grated
1 cup fresh breadcrumbs
1–2 green chiles,
   finely chopped
2 tbsp chopped parsley, plus
   extra to garnish
2 tbsp chopped cilantro
salt and freshly ground
   black pepper
olive oil
crusty bread and mixed
   greens, to serve

OPTIONAL FISH

7oz (185g) can tuna, drained
   and flaked

1 Preheat the broiler. Cut the stalk ends off the peppers and discard. Split them down one side and carefully remove any remaining seeds and pith, taking care not to break the peppers.

2 Mix the cheeses with the breadcrumbs, chiles, herbs, and salt and pepper to taste. Divide the cheese mixture among the peppers, spreading it evenly inside them.

3 Place the peppers on oiled foil in the broiler pan. Brush with oil. Broil for 8–10 minutes on each side until the cheese is melting and bubbling and the peppers are soft but not blackened.

4 Carefully transfer to plates (including any lovely gooey bits that have oozed out). Drizzle with a little more oil and sprinkle with a little parsley to garnish. Serve immediately with plenty of crusty bread and mixed greens.

IF ADDING FISH, use only 2oz (60g) grated Cheddar cheese and add the tuna to the mixture at step 2.

Grills and bakes
Grilled avocado with sun-dried tomato dressing

SERVES 4   PREPARATION **10 MINS**   TO COOK **8 MINS**

Cooked avocados are delicious, as long as they are ripe—underripe ones will taste bitter. Ricotta cheese can be substituted for cottage cheese in this recipe.

1 Halve the avocados and remove the pits. Brush the cut surfaces and the skin with olive oil.

2 Whisk the olive oil with 2 tbsp tomato oil, white balsamic vinegar, garlic, and some salt and pepper, then stir in the sun-dried tomatoes and basil. Set aside.

3 Preheat a grill pan. Mix the cheese with the olives and set aside. Place the avocados cut-side down on the grill and cook for 3 minutes until striped brown, pressing down gently with a metal spatula for even cooking of the cut side. Turn the avocados over and cook for a further 2–3 minutes until hot through. It does not matter if the skins burn a little, but take care not to overcook the avocados as they will become unpleasantly mushy.

4 Place the avocado halves on serving plates and spoon the cool cheese into the centers. Spoon the dressing over and serve with walnut or multigrain bread and a watercress and orange salad.

IF ADDING SHELLFISH, halve the amount of the cheese and mix with the shrimp at step 3.

INGREDIENTS

4 large or 8 small
   ripe avocados
2 tbsp olive oil, plus
   extra for brushing
6 sun-dried tomatoes in oil,
   drained and chopped,
   oil reserved
1 tbsp white balsamic vinegar
1 small garlic clove, crushed
salt and freshly ground
   black pepper
2 tbsp chopped basil
9oz (250g) plain cottage
   cheese, or flavored
   with chives
2 tbsp black olives, chopped
walnut or multigrain bread
   and watercress and orange
   salad, to serve

OPTIONAL SHELLFISH
3½oz (100g) small cooked,
   peeled shrimp (thawed
   if frozen)

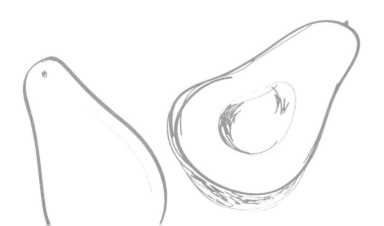

Mixed vegetable cottage pie with rutabaga crust

SERVES 4   PREPARATION **30 MINS**   TO COOK **40 MINS**

This rich, intensely flavored variation on a family favorite will please even the most dedicated meat-eater. Parsnips may be substituted for the rutabaga in the topping.

INGREDIENTS

1 tbsp vegetable oil
1 onion, finely chopped
4oz (115g) white
  mushrooms, sliced
2 carrots, grated
2 turnips, grated
2oz (60g) shelled fresh
  or thawed frozen peas
2 × 14oz (400g) cans pinto
  beans, rinsed and drained
2 cups vegetable stock
1 tbsp soy sauce
1 tbsp mushroom ketchup
  or Worcestershire sauce
1 tsp dried mixed herbs
salt and freshly ground
  black pepper
¼ cup all-purpose flour
1 small rutabaga, cut into
  small chunks
1lb (450g) potatoes, peeled
  and cut into small chunks
knob of butter
¼ cup milk
grated nutmeg
2oz (60g) sharp Cheddar
  cheese, grated
shredded greens, to serve

OPTIONAL MEAT

1lb 2oz (500g) ground beef

1 Heat the oil in a large saucepan. Add the onion and fry, stirring, for 3 minutes until lightly golden. Add the mushrooms, carrots, turnips, peas, and pinto beans. Stir in the stock, soy sauce, mushroom ketchup, herbs, and salt and pepper to taste. Bring to a boil, reduce the heat, cover, and simmer gently for 10 minutes until the vegetables are tender. Blend the flour with ¼ cup water. Stir into the pan and cook, stirring, for 2 minutes to thicken.

2 While the other vegetables are simmering, cook the rutabaga and potato in salted boiling water for 15 minutes or until tender. Drain and return to the pan, cooking over low heat to dry out slightly. Mash with the butter, milk, a generous grating of nutmeg, and a generous grinding of pepper. Beat well with a wooden spoon until smooth.

3 Preheat the oven to 375°F (190°C). Spoon the mixture into a 2 quart ovenproof dish or 4 individual dishes. Top with the rutabaga mash and fluff up with a fork. Sprinkle the cheese over and bake in the oven for about 40 minutes until golden. Serve hot with some shredded greens.

IF ADDING MEAT, omit the beans and brown the ground beef with the onions at step 1. Stir until no longer pink and all the grains of meat are separate, then continue as before.

Baked ricotta with roasted zucchini and tomatoes

SERVES 4   **PREPARATION 5 MINS**   **TO COOK 35 MINS**

Using the ripest tomatoes and the best olive oil, **this dish captures the flavors of the Mediterranean.** Serve with freshly baked bread and a green salad.

INGREDIENTS

¼ cup olive oil, plus extra
   for drizzling and greasing
2 zucchini, sliced
1 garlic clove, finely chopped
salt and freshly ground
   black pepper
2 tsp chopped rosemary
12 cherry tomatoes, halved
9oz (250g) ricotta
   cheese, drained
2 tbsp grated
   Parmesan cheese
ciabatta and crisp green salad,
   to serve

OPTIONAL MEAT

4 thin slices Parma
   ham, shredded

1 Preheat the oven to 425°F (220°C). Lightly oil 2 small baking dishes. Put the zucchini slices in one, toss with 2 tbsp oil, and sprinkle with the garlic, some salt and pepper, and the rosemary. Roast for 10 minutes. Carefully turn over the slices.

2 Arrange the tomatoes in the second baking dish. Drizzle with the remaining oil and season with salt and pepper. Bake with the zucchini for a further 10 minutes until the tomatoes have softened and started to collapse and the zucchini is tender and lightly golden. Remove from the oven.

3 Spoon half the ricotta into a lightly oiled 2 cup gratin dish and roughly spread it out. Arrange the zucchini slices on top, then the tomatoes. Spoon the remaining ricotta on top and roughly spread out —it won't cover the vegetables completely.

4 Sprinkle with Parmesan, drizzle with a little extra oil, and add a good grinding of pepper. Bake for 15 minutes until lightly golden on top. Serve hot with ciabatta and a crisp green salad.

IF ADDING MEAT, scatter the Parma ham over the tomatoes and zucchini at step 3 before topping with the ricotta cheese.

Kohlrabi and potato gratin

SERVES 4–6   **PREPARATION 15–20 MINS**   TO COOK **1 HR 30 MINS**

This dish is **enlivened with the addition of finely sliced kohlrabi**—a brassica that has the taste and crunch of a broccoli stem or cabbage heart and is also good raw.

1 Preheat the oven to 350°F (180°C) and grease an 8in (20cm) ovenproof gratin dish with butter.

2 Slice the potatoes and kohlrabi quarters into even rounds, ⅛in (3mm) thick, using a mandolin or a food processor fitted with a fine slicing blade. Rinse the slices in cold water, drain, and pat dry with kitchen paper or a clean tea towel.

3 Arrange the potatoes and kohlrabi in layers in the prepared dish. Season with salt and pepper.

4 Bring the cream to a boil in a saucepan with the garlic and nutmeg, then pour the cream over the potatoes. Dot the top with a few knobs of butter.

5 Cover with foil and place in the oven for about 1–1½ hours, or until the vegetables are tender. During the last 10 minutes of cooking, remove the foil and increase the heat to get a fine golden crust on the top. Serve hot, straight from the oven.

IF ADDING MEAT, marinate the lamb chops in the mint sauce with garlic, sugar, oil, and some salt and pepper for at least 1 hour. Quickly brown in a frying pan, then transfer to the oven and roast for 10 minutes (or grill for 2–3 minutes on each side).

INGREDIENTS

3 tbsp butter, softened, plus
   extra for greasing
1lb (450g) even-sized red
   potatoes, peeled
1lb (450g) kohlrabi, peeled,
   trimmed, and quartered
sea salt and freshly ground
   black pepper
2 cups heavy cream
1 garlic clove, cut in half
pinch of ground nutmeg

OPTIONAL MEAT

8 lamb chops
2 tbsp bottled mint sauce
1 garlic clove, crushed
pinch of sugar
2 tbsp olive oil

Tomato and zucchini gougère

SERVES 4   PREPARATION **35 MINS**   TO COOK **1 HR**

This gougère is **crisp and golden on the outside and soft, light, and cheesy inside**. For a short cut, use a 14oz (400g) can of chopped tomatoes and omit the tomato paste.

INGREDIENTS

2 tbsp olive oil
1 onion, chopped
1 leek, sliced
2 large zucchini, sliced
1 garlic clove, crushed
2 beefsteak tomatoes,
    peeled and chopped
1 tbsp tomato paste
1 tsp dried basil
generous pinch of
    granulated sugar
salt and freshly ground
    black pepper
2 tbsp grated
    Parmesan cheese
a few torn basil leaves,
    to garnish

For the cheese choux
1 cup all-purpose flour
8 tbsp butter
4 large eggs, beaten
4oz (115g) Cheddar
    cheese, grated

OPTIONAL MEAT
handful of diced cooked ham

1 Heat the oil in a saucepan. Add the onion, leek, zucchini, and garlic and fry, stirring, for 2 minutes to soften slightly. Add the tomatoes, cook for 1 minute, stirring, then reduce the heat, cover, and cook gently for 10 minutes.

2 Remove the lid, stir in the tomato paste, basil, and sugar, and boil rapidly for about 5 minutes, stirring frequently, until the vegetables are bathed in a light tomato sauce. Season with salt and pepper to taste and set aside.

3 Preheat the oven to 400°F (200°C). To make the cheese choux, sift the flour and ¾ tsp salt into a bowl. Put 1¼ cup water in a saucepan and add the butter. Over low heat, stir until the butter melts. Bring to a boil, then reduce the heat, add the flour, and beat with a wooden spoon until the mixture forms a soft ball and leaves the sides of the pan clean.

4 Remove from the heat, leave to cool slightly, then gradually beat in the eggs, a little at a time, until smooth and glossy but the mixture still holds its shape. Beat in the Cheddar cheese.

5 Lightly grease a large, shallow 1 quart ovenproof dish. Spoon the cheese choux all around the edge and the vegetable mixture in the center. Sprinkle the choux with the Parmesan. Bake in the oven for 30 minutes, then cover loosely with foil and bake for a further 30 minutes until the pastry is risen, crisp, and golden brown. Serve hot, garnished with a little torn basil.

IF ADDING MEAT, stir the ham into the tomato and zucchini mixture before spooning into the dish at step 5.

Grills and bakes
Mushroom pot with feta and herb topping

SERVES 4 **PREPARATION** **15 MINS** **TO COOK** **50 MINS**

This is a hearty stew made with **meaty mushrooms for a rich depth of flavor.** Try baking individual portions if you have some mini ovenproof casserole dishes.

1 Heat the oil in a large Dutch oven or lidded ovenproof pan, add the onion, and cook for 2–3 minutes over low heat. Stir in the garlic, oregano, paprika, lemon zest, and some salt and pepper, and cook for a further 1–2 minutes.

2 Add the green peppers and cook over low heat for 5 minutes or until beginning to soften, then add the mushrooms and cook for a further 5 minutes. Increase the heat, add the wine, and simmer for 1 minute. Add the stock and bring to a boil. Partially cover and cook over low-medium heat for 20 minutes; it should begin to thicken slightly. If it is too thin, uncover, increase the heat a little, and cook for a further 3–4 minutes.

3 Preheat the oven to 350°F (180°C). To make the topping, mix together the feta, eggs, half the parsley, and a little salt and pepper; you may not need much salt as feta is already salty. Pour this over the mushroom mixture and bake in the oven for 15–20 minutes until the egg has set and the top is golden. Remove and sprinkle with the remaining parsley to serve.

IF ADDING MEAT, fry the pork with the onion at step 1. Continue as before, but omit the crimini mushrooms.

INGREDIENTS

2 tbsp olive oil
1 red onion, finely chopped
2 garlic cloves, finely chopped
2 tsp dried oregano
1 tsp paprika
grated zest of ½ lemon
salt and freshly ground
  black pepper
2 green bell peppers, halved,
  seeded, and sliced
7oz (200g) crimini
  mushrooms, quartered
7oz (200g) baby
  button mushrooms
½ cup dry white wine
2 cups hot vegetable stock

For the topping
5½oz (150g) feta
  cheese, crumbled
2 large eggs
handful of flat-leaf
  parsley, finely chopped

OPTIONAL MEAT
12oz (350g) pork loin,
  cut into small cubes

Watercress and beet roulade with smooth cheese sauce

SERVES 4   **PREPARATION 30 MINS**   TO COOK **18 MINS**

This light and luscious roulade is also **delicious served cold with dill-flavored mayonnaise**. For an alternative filling, the chunky tomato sauce on p201 is ideal.

INGREDIENTS

1 bunch watercress,
    finely chopped
2 tbsp chopped parsley
2 tbsp grated Parmesan
    cheese, plus extra
    for dusting
4 large eggs, separated

For the cheese sauce

2 tbsp all-purpose flour
1¼ cup milk
1 tbsp butter
½ tsp English mustard
2oz (60g) Cheddar
    cheese, grated
salt and freshly ground
    black pepper

For the filling

3½oz (100g) crème fraîche
1 scallion, finely chopped
2 cooked beets (approx.
    4½oz/125g), finely chopped
1 tbsp chopped dill, plus
    extra to garnish (optional)
squeeze of lemon juice
grated nutmeg

OPTIONAL FISH

7oz (185g) can tuna, drained
    and flaked

1 First, make the sauce. Put the flour in a small saucepan. Whisk in the milk, then add the butter. Bring to a boil and cook for 2 minutes, whisking constantly, until thickened. Stir in the mustard and Cheddar cheese until melted and add salt and pepper to taste. Cover with a circle of damp wax or parchment paper to prevent a skin forming and keep warm.

2 To make the filling, mix the ingredients together in a small saucepan with a generous grating of nutmeg and a little salt and pepper. Heat through, stirring gently. Keep warm.

3 Preheat the oven to 400°F (200°C). Grease a 7 × 11in (18 × 28cm) Swiss roll pan and line with parchment paper.

4 Put the watercress in a bowl, then add the parsley and Parmesan. Beat in the egg yolks and some salt and pepper. Whisk the egg whites until stiff and fold into the watercress mix with a rubber spatula. Transfer to the prepared pan and smooth the surface. Bake in the oven for about 8 minutes until risen and just firm to the touch.

5 Place a clean sheet of parchment paper on a clean tea towel on the work surface. Dust the parchment with a little grated Parmesan. Turn out the roulade onto the prepared paper, then loosen the cooking paper and remove gently.

6 Quickly spread the roulade with the beet filling, leaving a small border all around. Roll up, using the parchment to help. Transfer to a serving plate and garnish with some chopped dill, if using. Cut in slices and serve with the cheese sauce.

IF ADDING FISH, omit the beet and add the tuna to the crème fraîche with the scallion at step 2. Flavor as before.

Butternut squash tagine

SERVES 4   PREPARATION **20 MINS**   TO COOK **1 HR**

Most squashes ripen once the summer draws to a close and autumnal fare takes over. **This spicy tagine uses the best of early-autumn produce.**

INGREDIENTS

¼ cup olive oil

2 red onions, finely chopped

1 large red bell pepper, seeded and diced

4 garlic cloves, chopped

1 thumb-sized piece fresh ginger, finely chopped

1 tsp chile powder

1 tsp ground cinnamon

2 tsp smoked paprika

2 tsp ground coriander

1 tbsp ground cumin

2 × 14oz (400g) cans chopped tomatoes

2 cups vegetable stock

2 tbsp honey

salt and freshly ground black pepper

14oz (400g) butternut squash, peeled, seeded, and diced

2 × 14oz (400g) cans chickpeas, drained and rinsed

3½oz (100g) dried apricots, chopped

bunch of cilantro leaves, chopped

couscous, to serve

OPTIONAL MEAT

1lb 2oz (500g) lean lamb, diced

1 Pour the oil into a large Dutch oven. Add the onions, red pepper, garlic, and ginger, and fry over low heat for 2 minutes until softened, but not brown.

2 Add the chile, cinnamon, paprika, coriander, and cumin. Continue to cook for a further 2 minutes over low heat to release the flavor of the spices. Add the tomatoes, stock, and honey, and season with salt and pepper. Bring the sauce to a boil and turn down the heat. Simmer slowly, uncovered, for 30 minutes.

3 Add the butternut squash, chickpeas, and apricots and continue to cook for 10–15 minutes until the squash is soft, but not falling apart. Add more water if it is beginning to look a little dry. Season again and stir in the chopped cilantro. Serve with couscous.

IF ADDING MEAT, brown the lamb with the onion and vegetables at step 1. Partially cover and simmer gently for 1 hour at step 2. Add the butternut squash and continue as before, but omitting the chickpeas.

Stuffed butternut squash

SERVES 4   **PREPARATION 15 MINS**   **TO COOK 1 HR 15 MINS**

This is a vibrantly colored dish that would work just as well with pumpkin. Use Cheddar, Parmesan, or goat cheese instead of the Gruyère, if preferred.

1 Preheat the oven to 375°F (190°C). Brush 2 baking sheets with oil. With a sharp knife, score a crisscross pattern on the flesh of each butternut squash half and brush with oil. Sit the squash on the greased baking sheets, flesh-side down, and roast for about 1 hour until the flesh begins to soften. Now scoop out most of the flesh, leaving a thin layer still attached to the skins, and reserve the hollowed squash halves.

2 Place the flesh in a bowl and mash with a fork. Add the hazelnuts, cranberries, parsley, chile flakes, and salt and pepper to the mashed squash and mix well. Divide the mixture between the squash halves.

3 Sprinkle the cheese over and return the squash halves to the oven. Bake for a further 10–15 minutes until the cheese is bubbling. Serve the squash with a lightly dressed arugula salad.

IF ADDING MEAT, melt a knob of butter in a saucepan and fry the ground turkey, stirring until no longer pink and all the grains are separate. Add to the squash with the cranberries at step 2, omitting the hazelnuts. Continue as before, but bake for 15–20 minutes until piping hot and cooked through.

INGREDIENTS

1 tbsp olive oil, plus extra
   for greasing
2 butternut squash (approx.
   1½lb/675g each), halved
   lengthways and seeded
3½oz (100g) hazelnuts, toasted
   and roughly chopped
2½oz (75g) dried cranberries,
   roughly chopped
small handful of flat-leaf
   parsley, finely chopped
pinch of dried chile flakes
salt and freshly ground
   black pepper
8oz (225g) Gruyère
   cheese, grated
arugula salad, to serve

OPTIONAL MEAT
knob of butter
4oz (115g) ground turkey

Squash and cider cobbler

SERVES 6   PREPARATION **20 MINS**   TO COOK **1 HR**

Here, autumn vegetables are **simmered in cider and topped with an herby scone**. Try brushing the potatoes with oil and sprinkling with caraway seeds before baking.

INGREDIENTS

1 butternut squash, halved, seeded, peeled, and cut into bite-sized cubes

2 tbsp olive oil

pinch of grated nutmeg

a few sage leaves, roughly chopped

salt and freshly ground black pepper

1 onion, finely chopped

2 garlic cloves, finely chopped

2 leeks, sliced

14oz (400g) can chopped tomatoes

1¼ cups hard cider

1¾ cups vegetable stock

1¾ cups self-rising flour

7 tbsp butter, chilled and diced

a few sprigs of rosemary, finely chopped

5 tbsp buttermilk

7oz (200g) Savoy cabbage, cored and roughly chopped

baked potatoes, to serve (optional)

OPTIONAL FISH

1lb (450g) meaty white fish fillet, such as haddock, skinned and cut in cubes

1 Preheat the oven to 400°F (200°C). Put the squash on a baking sheet, add half the oil, and toss to coat thoroughly. Add the nutmeg and sage, season well with salt and pepper, and toss again. Roast for 15 minutes, then remove and set aside.

2 Heat the remaining oil in a large Dutch oven or lidded ovenproof pan, add the onion, and cook for 2–3 minutes. Season, stir in the garlic and leeks, and cook over low heat for 2 minutes more. Add the tomatoes and cider, then 1¾ cups stock, or enough to cover the vegetables. Bring to a boil, reduce to a simmer, and stir in the squash. Simmer gently for 5–10 minutes.

3 For the cobbler topping, place the flour and a pinch of salt in a bowl. Add the butter and rub it in with the fingertips until it resembles breadcrumbs. Stir in the rosemary and add the buttermilk, a little at a time, until it forms a soft dough. Alternatively, make the topping in a food processor, adding the buttermilk a little at a time and pulsing until the dough forms.

4 Stir the cabbage into the simmering vegetables, then tear off large lumps of the dough, flatten slightly, and place on top of the vegetables. Bake in the oven for 25–30 minutes or until golden and bubbling. Cover loosely with foil if it starts to brown too much. Serve alone or with baked potatoes.

IF ADDING FISH, put the diced fish in with the cabbage at step 4, then continue as before. Use a small butternut squash.

Stuffed mushrooms with spinach, pine nuts, and halloumi

SERVES 4   PREPARATION **10 MINS**   TO COOK **20 MINS**

Portabello mushrooms make great bases for fillings.
Serve one as a starter or two for a main course, and substitute crumbled feta for the halloumi, if you prefer.

1 Shake off excess water from the spinach, then cook in a pan with no extra water, stirring, for 2–3 minutes until wilted. Drain thoroughly in a colander, squeeze out as much moisture as possible, then chop or snip with scissors.

2 Preheat the oven to 375°F (190°C). Remove the stalks from the mushrooms and chop the stalks finely. Place the mushrooms in an oiled baking dish and add 6 tbsp water to the dish.

3 Heat the oil in a large frying pan and fry the onion and mushroom stalks over medium heat for 2–3 minutes, stirring, until softened. Add the garlic, pine nuts, cinnamon, herbs, and spinach. Season with salt and pepper to taste.

4 Spoon the mixture into the mushrooms and top with a slice of halloumi. Drizzle with a little extra oil and bake for about 20 minutes until the mushrooms are tender and the cheese is lightly golden. Place on serving plates with the mushroom juices spooned over and sprigs of parsley as a garnish. Serve with crusty bread and a mixed salad.

IF ADDING MEAT, cook the bacon on a separate baking sheet while baking the mushrooms, or fry them until golden. Crumble the bacon and serve the mushrooms with the crumbled bacon on top.

INGREDIENTS

7oz (200g) spinach, well washed

8 portabello mushrooms, peeled if necessary

2 tbsp olive oil, plus extra for drizzling

1 onion, finely chopped

2 garlic cloves, crushed

2oz (60g) pine nuts

1 tsp ground cinnamon

1 tsp dried oregano

3 tbsp chopped flat-leaf parsley, plus sprigs, to garnish

salt and freshly ground black pepper

8oz (250g) block halloumi, cut into 8 slices

crusty bread and mixed salad, to serve

OPTIONAL MEAT

8 bacon slices

Four ways with
Eggplants

Eggplant and goat cheese crostini ▶

TAKES 30 mins, plus chilling **SERVES** 4

Preheat the oven to 350°F (180°C). Brush 12 slices of **French bread** on both sides with **olive oil**. Toast for 10 minutes. Halve 1 **garlic clove** and rub the cut side over each slice. Preheat the grill. Slice 1 **eggplant** into ¼in (5mm) thick rounds, brush each side with oil, and grill both sides until cooked. Quarter the eggplant slices and place in a bowl. Add 1 tbsp olive oil, 2 tbsp chopped **mint**, and 1 tbsp **balsamic vinegar**. Toss and season with **salt** and freshly ground **black pepper**. Spread the crostini with 2oz (60g) **soft goat cheese**, top with eggplant, and serve.

◀ Steamed eggplant salad

TAKES 35 mins **SERVES** 6

Cut 2 medium peeled **eggplant** into ¾in (2cm) cubes and steam, covered, for 10 minutes. When cool, squeeze gently to extract as much water as possible. In a bowl, combine 2oz (60g) crumbled **soft goat cheese**, 2 ripe **tomatoes**, seeded and diced, 1 small finely diced **red onion**, a handful of finely chopped **flat-leaf parsley**, 2oz (60g) lightly toasted and roughly chopped **walnuts**, and 1 tbsp lightly toasted **sesame seeds**. For the dressing, whisk together 1 crushed **garlic clove**, ¼ cup **walnut oil**, and the juice of 1 **lemon**. Drizzle over the salad, season with **salt** and freshly ground **black pepper**, and toss to mix.

The eggplants most commonly available are the deep purple variety—but you may also find **the prettily mottled Rosa Bianca**, the round Prosperosa, which is ideal for stuffing, or **crispy-textured East Asian varieties**.

Tomato and eggplant confit ▶

TAKES 15 mins, plus standing **SERVES** 6

Heat 2 tbsp **olive oil** and 5 tbsp **vegetable** or **sunflower oil** in a large frying pan over medium-high heat until the oil begins to smoke. Add 10oz (300g) **eggplants**, cut into 3in (7½cm) batons, and fry, stirring often, for 3 minutes, or until golden brown. Drain. Add ¼ cup **garlic-infused oil** to the pan, then add 4½oz (125g) **cherry tomatoes**, halved. Cook for 2 minutes, or until softened. Place the batons in a bowl. Add 10 torn **basil leaves** and the tomatoes and mix gently. Cover and leave to infuse for up to 1 hour in a warm place. Season with **salt** and freshly ground **black pepper**. Serve warm.

◀ Grilled eggplants with pomegranate vinaigrette

TAKES 20 mins **SERVES** 6

To make the vinaigrette, whisk together 6 tbsp **olive oil**, 3 tbsp **pomegranate syrup**, and 3 tbsp chopped **cilantro**, and season with **salt** and freshly ground **black pepper**. Set aside. Preheat the grill pan over high heat. Cut 3 large **eggplants** into ½in (1cm) thick slices. Brush both sides of the eggplant slices with olive oil, season, then grill both sides until tender. Layer the eggplants and 2 very finely sliced **shallots** in a serving dish and pour over the vinaigrette. Scatter with **pomegranate seeds** and serve.

Potatoes Dauphinoise with Emmental

SERVES 4–6   **PREPARATION 25 MINS**   TO COOK **45 MINS**

This fantastically hearty supper dish is a twist on the classic Dauphinoise recipe, with **the Emmental lifting the humble potato to a higher level**.

INGREDIENTS

3lb 3oz (1½kg) potatoes, peeled and thinly sliced
1¼ cups whole milk
1¼ cups heavy cream
5½oz (150g) Emmental cheese, sliced
2 garlic cloves, crushed
salt and freshly ground black pepper
green beans or a salad, to serve

OPTIONAL MEAT
7oz (200g) diced pancetta

1 Preheat the oven to 400°F (200°C). In a large pan, simmer the potatoes in the milk and cream for 10–15 minutes, then remove with a slotted spoon. Reserve the milk and cream mixture.

2 Layer the potatoes and cheese in a large gratin dish, sprinkling the garlic over the cheese and seasoning with salt and pepper. Pour the milk and cream over, cover with foil, and cook in the oven for 45 minutes. Remove the foil for the last 15 minutes of cooking time to brown the top. Serve with green beans or a salad.

IF ADDING MEAT, dry-fry the pancetta in a frying pan and drain on paper towels. Sprinkle between the layers of potato with the garlic and cheese and bake as before.

Gratin of Swiss chard with beans

SERVES 4–6   **PREPARATION 10 MINS, PLUS SOAKING**   TO COOK **1 HR 20 MINS, PLUS RESTING**

This rich, warming dish uses only the dark green leaves of the chard, but cut the stems into lengths, steam them for a few minutes, and serve alongside.

1 Preheat the oven to 400°F (200°C). Drain the soaked beans, put them in a large pan of water, and bring to a boil. Turn down to a strong simmer and skim off any foam that has collected on the surface. Continue to cook for around 40 minutes, or until soft.

2 In a large, deep-sided pan, heat the oil, add the garlic and chard, and cook, stirring, for about 1 minute until the chard has collapsed but is still al dente.

3 Add the cooked beans to the chard. Mix well, stir in the cream, and season with paprika and salt and pepper.

4 Pour everything into a 1 quart gratin dish and top with breadcrumbs made by pulsing the white bread, Parmesan, and basil in a food processor. Cook at the top of the oven for about 30 minutes until golden brown. Leave the gratin to rest for 10 minutes before serving.

IF ADDING MEAT, at step 2, fry the chorizo in the oil until the fat runs and the oil turns red, then stir in the garlic and Swiss chard and continue as before. Use ½ tsp smoked paprika instead of 1 tsp.

INGREDIENTS

14oz (400g) dried navy
  or cannellini beans,
  soaked overnight
2 tbsp olive oil
4 garlic cloves, crushed
14oz (400g) Swiss chard,
  destalked and
  finely shredded
2 cups heavy cream
1 tsp smoked paprika
salt and freshly ground
  black pepper
3½oz (100g) white bread
2oz (60g) Parmesan
  cheese, grated
8 basil leaves

OPTIONAL MEAT

5½oz (150g) dry Spanish
  chorizo, finely diced

Lentil, mushroom, and egg loaf with celery root remoulade

SERVES 8   **PREPARATION 30 MINS**   TO COOK **1 HR**

This loaf is **best made a day in advance** so that it has time to cool properly and firm up. Serve with baby plum tomatoes and baked potatoes.

INGREDIENTS

4 savoy cabbage leaves
2 tbsp olive oil, plus extra
  for greasing
knob of butter
2 shallots, finely chopped
4oz (115g) crimini
  mushrooms, sliced
2 × 14oz (400g) cans green
  lentils, rinsed and drained
2 cups fresh breadcrumbs
2 tbsp chopped thyme
2 tbsp chopped parsley
1 tbsp mushroom ketchup
  or Worcestershire sauce
1 tsp ground coriander
salt and freshly ground
  black pepper
1 large egg, beaten
3 hard-boiled eggs, peeled

For the remoulade
¼ cup mayonnaise
¼ cup crème fraîche
2 tsp grated horseradish or
  hot horseradish relish
2 tsp white balsamic vinegar
1 small celery root

OPTIONAL MEAT
8oz (225g) ground
  raw chicken

1 Cut the thick central stalks out of 4 large outer leaves from the cabbage. Blanch the leaves in boiling water for 2 minutes, then drain, rinse with cold water, and drain again. Dry on paper towels. Oil a 9 x 5in (23 x 13cm) loaf pan. Line with overlapping cabbage leaves, outer sides against the pan and stalk ends upward, allowing enough to hang over the top edge all around to form a wrap for the loaf.

2 Heat the oil and butter in a large pan. Add the shallots and fry, stirring, for 2 minutes. Add the mushrooms and fry for 2 minutes, stirring. Remove from the heat. Add the lentils, breadcrumbs, herbs, ketchup, coriander, and salt and pepper. Mix with the beaten egg.

3 Preheat the oven to 375°F (190°C). Spoon half the lentil mixture into the pan and press down. Lay the boiled eggs down the center, end-to-end, and press gently into the mixture. Top with the remaining mixture, pressing gently. Fold the overhanging leaves over.

4 Cover the pan with oiled foil, twisting it under the rim to secure. Bake in the oven for 1 hour until just firm. Remove from the oven and leave to cool, then weigh down with cans of food and chill to firm.

5 An hour before serving, make the remoulade. Blend the mayonnaise, crème fraîche, horseradish, and balsamic vinegar in a bowl. Peel the celery root, slice thinly, and cut into thin matchsticks, or shred in a food processor. Place immediately in the dressing and toss well. Season with salt and pepper. Cover the bowl with plastic wrap and chill.

6 Turn the loaf out onto a serving dish. Serve sliced with the remoulade. Any leftovers are delicious with pickles and crusty bread for another meal.

IF ADDING MEAT, use half the quantity of lentils and add the ground chicken to the mixture at step 2.

Zucchini and carrot pavé

SERVES 4 **PREPARATION 15 MINS** TO COOK **40 MINS**

This baked slab, or pavé, of lightly spiced vegetables is delicious hot or cold. It can also be served in little squares as bite-sized snacks or canapés.

1 Preheat the oven to 375°F (190°C). Mix all the ingredients except the sesame seeds in a bowl until thoroughly blended.

2 Transfer to an oiled 7 × 11in (18 × 28cm) shallow baking dish. Sprinkle liberally with the sesame seeds. Bake in the oven for 40 minutes until golden and firm to the touch.

3 Cool for 5 minutes, then cut into quarters. Place each pavé on a serving plate. Garnish with sprigs of parsley and drizzle the plates with a splash of sesame oil. Serve with new potatoes and a mixed salad.

IF ADDING FISH, mix in the salmon with the remaining ingredients in step 1 and use just 1 carrot.

INGREDIENTS

1 large onion, finely chopped
2 large zucchini, grated
2 large carrots, grated
4oz (115g) Cheddar
  cheese, grated
¾ cup all-purpose flour
1 tsp ground cumin
1 tsp dried mixed herbs
1 tsp dried chile flakes
salt and freshly ground
  black pepper
6 tbsp sunflower or vegetable oil
5 large eggs, beaten
2 tbsp sesame oil, plus
  extra for drizzling
3–4 tbsp sesame seeds
a few sprigs of parsley,
  to garnish
new potatoes and mixed
  salad, to serve

OPTIONAL FISH

7oz (200g) can pink salmon,
  drained, skin removed,
  and flaked

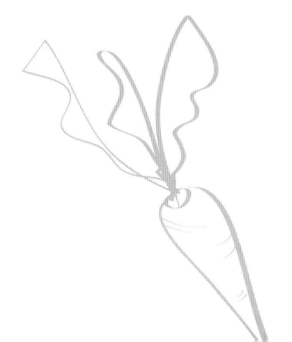

Potato and mixed nut moussaka

SERVES 4–6   **PREPARATION 45 MINS**   **TO COOK 45 MINS**

A simple, rustic dish, this is delicious served with a Greek salad, topped with cubes of feta cheese and drizzled with olive oil and red wine vinegar.

INGREDIENTS

1½lb (675g) potatoes, scrubbed and cut into ¼in (5mm) slices

2 tbsp olive oil, plus extra for greasing

1 large onion, chopped

2 garlic cloves, crushed

2 zucchini, sliced

1 green bell pepper, seeded and chopped

14oz (400g) can chopped tomatoes

14oz (400g) can cannellini beans, rinsed and drained

4oz (115g) chopped unsalted mixed nuts

2 tbsp tomato paste

2 tsp dried oregano

1 tsp ground cinnamon

3 tbsp sliced black kalamata olives

salt and freshly ground black pepper

14oz (400g) crème fraîche

2 large eggs

1¾oz (50g) Parmesan cheese, grated

OPTIONAL MEAT

12oz (350g) ground lamb

1 Cook the potatoes in boiling water for about 5 minutes, or until tender but still holding their shape. Drain, rinse with cold water, and drain again.

2 Heat the oil in a large saucepan and add the onion, garlic, zucchini, and green pepper. Fry, stirring, for 5 minutes, turning the vegetables over as they soften slightly. Add the tomatoes, beans, nuts, tomato paste, 1 tsp oregano, cinnamon, olives, and plenty of pepper. Bring to a boil, reduce the heat, and simmer for about 15 minutes until the vegetables are tender and the sauce is thick, stirring occasionally.

3 Preheat the oven to 350°F (180°C). Put half the vegetable mixture into a lightly oiled 2 quart rectangular ovenproof dish and spread it out. Top with a layer of half the potatoes. Repeat the layers with the remaining vegetable mixture and potatoes.

4 Beat the crème fraîche with the eggs, remaining oregano, Parmesan, and some salt and pepper. Spread over the top of the potatoes. Bake in the oven for about 45 minutes until the top is golden and set. Leave to cool for a while to intensify the flavors, and serve warm.

IF ADDING MEAT, dry-fry the ground lamb in the pan at the beginning of step 2, stirring until no longer pink and all the grains are separate. Remove it before adding the oil and frying the vegetables, omitting the beans and nuts. Stir in the browned lamb with the tomatoes and remaining ingredients.

Curried leek, celery root, and edamame loaf

SERVES 8 **PREPARATION** 25 MINS **TO COOK** 1 HR 30 MINS

Dried breadcrumbs are available at the grocery store, or bake stale bread in a low oven until straw-colored and crisp, then crush and store in an airtight container.

INGREDIENTS

2 tbsp sunflower or vegetable oil, plus extra for greasing
3 tbsp dried breadcrumbs
knob of butter
2 leeks, thinly sliced
1 small celery root (approx. 12oz/350g), peeled and grated
1 potato, grated
2 tbsp Madras curry paste
3 cups cooked, shelled edamame beans, thawed if frozen
1 cup breadcrumbs
2 tbsp mango chutney
2 large eggs, beaten
salt and freshly ground black pepper
baby potatoes roasted in their skins and mixed salad, to serve

For the curried mayonnaise
½ cup mayonnaise
1 tbsp curry paste
1 tbsp smooth mango chutney
squeeze of lemon juice

OPTIONAL MEAT
8oz (225g) lean ground lamb

1 Preheat the oven to 375°F (190°C). Grease a 9 x 5in (23 x 13cm) loaf pan and coat completely with dried breadcrumbs.

2 Heat the oil and butter in a large saucepan and fry the leeks, stirring, for 2 minutes to soften. Stir in the celery root and potato and cook for 1 minute, stirring—add a splash of water if the potato starts to stick. Cover the pan, reduce the heat, and cook gently for 10 minutes until soft but not brown, stirring occasionally.

3 Add the curry paste and cook, stirring, for 30 seconds. Remove from the heat. Mash the edamame and add with the remaining ingredients, seasoning well with salt and pepper.

4 Press the mixture into the prepared pan. Cover with oiled foil, twisting and folding under the rim to secure, then bake in the oven for 1½ hours until firm to the touch. Remove from the oven and leave to rest for 10 minutes.

5 Meanwhile, mix the ingredients for the mayonnaise together, seasoning with salt and pepper to taste.

6 Turn the loaf out onto a serving plate and serve sliced warm or cold with the curried mayonnaise, baby potatoes roasted in their skins, and a mixed salad.

IF ADDING MEAT, use only 1½ cups of beans and work the lamb into the mixture at step 3, then cook as before.

Red lentil and mixed root crumble with sour cream and chives

SERVES 4   **PREPARATION** **45 MINS**   **TO COOK** **45 MINS**

To make full use of the oven, **thread small potatoes on metal skewers** to bake with the crumble—the metal skewers will speed up the cooking time of the potatoes.

1 Heat the oil and butter in a shallow Dutch oven and fry the grated vegetables, stirring, for 2 minutes. Add the lentils and stock and bring to a boil. Reduce the heat, cover, and simmer gently for 25 minutes until the lentils and vegetables are cooked and most of the liquid has been absorbed. Add the vinegar, tarragon, parsley, and salt and pepper to taste and simmer for a further 5 minutes, stirring occasionally.

2 Meanwhile, preheat the oven to 375°F (190°C). To make the crumble, mix the oats and flour together in a bowl with a generous pinch of salt. Rub in the butter until the mixture resembles breadcrumbs. Stir in the cheeses and the caraway seeds.

3 Sprinkle the crumble over the vegetables and press down gently. Bake in the oven for about 45 minutes until the top is golden-brown.

4 Meanwhile, blend the sour cream with the chives in a small bowl, season with salt and pepper, and chill until ready to serve. When the crumble is cooked, serve hot with the chilled sour cream and chives, baked potatoes, and a green salad.

IF ADDING MEAT, use turkey instead of lentils. Fry in the butter and oil at step 1 until the grains are separate and no longer pink before adding the vegetables. Reduce the stock to about 2 cups.

INGREDIENTS

2 tbsp sunflower or vegetable oil
knob of butter
1 red onion, grated
2 large beets, grated
2 large carrots, grated
1 turnip, grated
4oz (115g) red lentils
2½ cups vegetable stock
1 tbsp red wine vinegar
1 tbsp chopped tarragon
1 tbsp chopped parsley
salt and freshly ground
   black pepper
5½oz (150g) sour cream
2 tbsp snipped chives
baked potatoes and green
   salad, to serve

For the crumble
1½ cups rolled oats
⅓ cup flour
6 tbsp butter, cut into
   small pieces
3oz (85g) Cheddar
   cheese, grated
1oz (30g) Parmesan
   cheese, grated
1 tbsp caraway seeds

OPTIONAL MEAT
8oz (225g) ground turkey

Carrot, onion, and Stilton hot dogs

MAKES 12   PREPARATION **20 MINS, PLUS CHILLING**   TO COOK **5 MINS**

These hot dogs can be made in advance and kept in the refrigerator for several days before cooking. They are equally good with Cheddar cheese instead of Stilton.

INGREDIENTS

knob of butter
1 onion, finely chopped
4 carrots, grated
3¾ cup rolled oats
¾ cup all-purpose flour,
    plus extra for dusting
6oz (175g) crumbled
    Stilton cheese (or similar
    crumbly blue cheese)
2 tbsp tomato paste
1 tbsp soy sauce
2 tbsp mushroom ketchup
    or Worcestershire sauce
1 tsp dried mixed herbs
2 tbsp chopped parsley
2 large eggs, beaten
salt and freshly ground
    black pepper
vegetable oil, for frying
hot dog buns, yellow mustard,
    and a salad, to serve

For the garnish
knob of butter
4 large onions, halved
    and thinly sliced
4 ripe tomatoes, seeded
    and chopped

OPTIONAL MEAT
1lb (450g) pork sausage meat

1 Heat the butter in a saucepan. Add the onion and carrots and fry gently for 2 minutes, stirring. Remove from the heat and transfer to a food processor. Add the remaining ingredients and plenty of salt and pepper, then blend well. Chill the mixture for about 30 minutes, if necessary, to firm before shaping.

2 With floured hands, shape the mixture into 12 long sausages (like slightly fat hot dogs). Chill for at least 30 minutes to firm.

3 Meanwhile, make the garnish. Melt the butter in the same saucepan, add the onions, and fry, stirring, for 2 minutes. Reduce the heat, cover, and cook gently for 10 minutes until soft and lightly golden, stirring occasionally. Stir in the tomatoes and cook for 1 minute. Season to taste.

4 Shallow-fry the sausages in a little hot oil for about 5 minutes, turning occasionally, until golden brown. Drain on paper towels.

5 Place the sausages in the buns and add the onion and tomato garnish and a squeeze of yellow mustard. Serve with a salad on the side.

IF ADDING MEAT, omit the oats, tomato paste, soy sauce, mushroom ketchup, parsley, and eggs. At step 1, soften the onion and carrots and allow to cool slightly, then work in the sausage meat, 1¾oz (50g) flour, 4oz (115g) Stilton cheese, and 1 tsp dried mixed herbs. Shape into sausages and cook as before.

Mixed vegetable satay

SERVES 4   **PREPARATION 25 MINS**   **TO COOK 10 MINS**

This recipe is **also good with cooked new potatoes**, mixed with pieces of blanched zucchini and shiitake mushrooms. Soak 12 wooden skewers beforehand.

INGREDIENTS

3 large carrots, cut into
   bite-sized chunks
2 parsnips, cut into
   bite-sized chunks
1 small rutabaga, cut into
   bite-sized chunks
1 large turnip, cut into
   bite-sized chunks
salt
5 tbsp butter
2 tbsp honey
½ tsp chile powder
squeeze of lemon juice
lime wedges, to garnish
plain boiled rice and green
   salad, to serve

For the sauce
2 scallions, finely chopped
8 tbsp crunchy peanut butter
1 tbsp honey
2 tbsp soy sauce
2 tsp dried chile flakes

OPTIONAL MEAT
12oz (350g) steak tenderloin or
   boneless, skinless chicken
   breasts, cut into cubes

1 Cook the vegetables in lightly salted boiling water for about 5 minutes until just tender but still with a little texture. Drain, rinse with cold water, and drain again. Thread the vegetables onto 12 soaked wooden skewers, alternating them. Lay on the broiler rack.

2 Preheat the broiler. Melt the butter and honey together and mix with the chile powder, lemon juice, and a generous pinch of salt. Brush over the kebabs. Broil, turning once, for 8–10 minutes until lightly golden, brushing with the remaining butter and honey mixture during cooking.

3 Put all the sauce ingredients with ¾ cup water in a small saucepan and heat, stirring, until the peanut butter has melted. Bring to a boil and simmer for 1 minute until the mixture forms a thick sauce. Spoon into individual small bowls for dipping (or trickle over for serving).

4 Lay the kebabs on a bed of boiled rice and garnish with lime wedges. Serve with a green salad and with the sauce alongside or spooned over.

IF ADDING MEAT, replace half the quantity of vegetables with the diced steak tenderloin or chicken.

Cajun stuffed potatoes with crushed avocado

SERVES 4   **PREPARATION 15 MINS**   **TO COOK 2 HRS 15 MINS**

For a substantial meal, **use very large baking potatoes**. To reduce baking time by about half, microwave the potatoes first for 15 minutes, until almost tender.

1 Preheat the oven to 400°F (200°C). Prick the potatoes all over with a fork, coat in oil, then cover all over in the spice blend and place on a baking sheet. Bake in the oven for 2 hours until the skins are really crisp and the potatoes feel soft when squeezed.

2 Meanwhile, if using corn cobs, remove the kernels (see p321). Melt half the butter in a saucepan, add the scallions, chile, and red pepper, and cook, stirring, for 2 minutes. Add the corn, cumin, and oregano. Reduce the heat, cover, and cook gently for 5 minutes. Set aside.

3 Put the avocado flesh into a bowl. Crush well with the chile flakes and lime juice, leaving some texture, and season with salt and pepper to taste. Chill until ready to serve.

4 When the potatoes are cooked, remove them from the oven. Once they are cool enough to handle, cut in half and scoop out most of the soft potato into a large bowl, leaving a small wall of potato to keep the shells firm. Pop the shells back into the oven to dry out a little while finishing the filling.

5 Mash the potato with the remaining butter, then work in the corn filling, cilantro, and cheese. Season with salt and pepper to taste. Pile into the potato skins and return to the oven for 10–15 minutes until hot through and browning on top. Serve with a dollop of the crushed avocado on top and a green salad.

IF ADDING MEAT, use half the quantity of corn kernels and stir in the ham at the end of step 2 after cooking the vegetables.

INGREDIENTS

4 large baking
    potatoes, scrubbed
2 tbsp olive oil
2 tbsp Cajun spice blend
2 corn cobs (or 8–10oz/
    225–300g corn kernels)
4 tbsp butter
2 scallions, chopped
1 fat green chile, seeded
    and chopped
1 red bell pepper, seeded,
    cut into thin strips, and
    chopped
1 tsp ground cumin
1 tsp dried oregano
2 tbsp chopped cilantro
2 large handfuls of grated
    aged Cheddar cheese
green salad, to serve

For the crushed avocado

2 ripe avocados, pitted and
    peeled (see pp324–5)
1 tsp dried chile flakes
1 tbsp lime juice
salt and freshly ground
    black pepper

OPTIONAL MEAT

large handful of
    ham, chopped

Pestos, pickles, salsas, and dips

Classic basil pesto

MAKES 1 SMALL JAR (approx. 6oz/175g)   **PREPARATION 10 MINS**

Toss spoonfuls of this classic green pesto with freshly cooked spaghetti, or **mix it with extra virgin olive oil and a splash of vinegar or lemon juice for dressing salads.**

INGREDIENTS

1oz (30g) basil

2 garlic cloves, lightly crushed

1oz (30g) pine nuts

salt and freshly ground
  black pepper

1oz (30g) Parmesan
  cheese, grated

5 tbsp extra virgin olive oil

1 Pick the leaves off the thicker stalks in the basil and discard the stalks. Place the leaves in a food processor with the garlic, pine nuts, salt and pepper, cheese, and 1 tbsp oil. Purée until the pesto is well-blended, stopping and scraping down the sides as necessary. With the machine running, trickle in 3 tbsp of the remaining oil until you have a glistening paste.

2 Alternatively, pound the herbs and garlic in a mortar with a pestle. Gradually add the nuts, crushing them to a paste with the herbs. Add salt and pepper, then work in a little of the cheese and a little of the oil. Continue until both are used up, except for 1 tbsp oil, and the paste is glistening.

3 Spoon into a clean, sterilized jar and top with the remaining oil to prevent air getting in. Screw the lid on and store in the refrigerator. Use within 2 weeks.

Pea, mint, and pistachio pesto

MAKES 1 JAR (approx. 12oz/350g)   **PREPARATION 25 MINS**

This pesto is great with pasta but is also delicious spread on crostini or endive spears as an appetizer, or beaten with some crème fraîche as a dip.

1 Put the pistachios in a bowl, cover with boiling water, and leave to stand for 5 minutes. Drain, then rub off the skins with a new disposable kitchen cloth.

2 Meanwhile, boil the peas in a little salted water for 5 minutes until tender. Drain, rinse with cold water, and drain again.

3 Place the mint leaves in a food processor with the pistachios, peas, scallions, garlic, nutmeg, pepper, Parmesan, and 2 tbsp oil. Purée until well-blended, stopping and scraping down the sides as necessary. With the machine running, trickle in 3 tbsp oil until you have a glistening paste. Taste and adjust the seasoning, if needed.

4 Alternatively, pound the herbs, scallions, and garlic in a mortar with a pestle. Gradually add the peas and nuts, crushing them to a paste with the herbs. Add the seasoning, then work in a little of the cheese and a little of the oil. Continue until both are used up, except for 1 tbsp oil, and the paste is glistening.

5 Spoon into a clean, sterilized jar and top with the remaining oil to prevent air getting in. Screw the lid on and store in the refrigerator. Use within 2 weeks.

INGREDIENTS

1oz (30g) shelled
   pistachio nuts
4oz (115g) shelled fresh
   or frozen peas
salt and freshly ground
   black pepper
¾oz (20g) mint, leaves picked
2 scallions, chopped
1 garlic clove, crushed
generous pinch of
   grated nutmeg
1oz (30g) Parmesan
   cheese, grated
6 tbsp extra virgin olive oil

Roasted red pepper, almond, and chile pesto

MAKES 1 SMALL JAR (approx. 6oz/175g)   **PREPARATION 10 MINS**

As well as stirring it through pasta, **try spreading this zingy pesto on bruschetta** and topping it with tomatoes and basil. It also works well on pizza bases.

INGREDIENTS

1 red bell pepper, roasted
  (see p326), seeded,
  and roughly chopped
4 sun-dried tomatoes
  in oil, drained
1–2 fat red chiles, seeded and
  roughly chopped
2 garlic cloves, lightly crushed
1oz (30g) ground almonds
1oz (30g) grated
  Parmesan cheese
2 tbsp tomato oil from the jar
salt and freshly ground
  black pepper
¼ cup extra virgin olive oil

1 Place the red pepper in a food processor with the sun-dried tomatoes, chiles, garlic, almonds, cheese, tomato oil, and a generous sprinkling of salt and pepper. Run the machine until well blended, stopping and scraping down the sides as necessary. With the machine running, trickle in 2 tbsp olive oil until you have a glistening paste.

2 Alternatively, put the red pepper, tomatoes, chiles, and garlic in a mortar and pound with a pestle. Gradually add the almonds and salt and pepper. Work in a little of the cheese, then add a little each of the tomato oil and olive oil. Continue until the cheese, tomato oil, and 2 tbsp olive oil are used up and you have a glistening paste.

3 Spoon into a clean, sterilized jar, top with the remaining olive oil to prevent air getting in, screw the lid on, and store in the refrigerator. Use within 2 weeks.

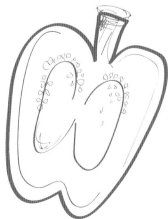

Lemon, carrot, and leek marmalade

MAKES 1 JAR (approx. 10oz/300g)   **PREPARATION 10 MINS**   **TO COOK 20 MINS**

The sharp fruitiness of the lemon combined with the sweetness of the carrots and the mild onion tang of the leeks makes this **a great relish to serve with cheese.**

INGREDIENTS

1 lemon, scrubbed

1 star anise

1 leek, white part only, thinly sliced

1 carrot, grated

2 sweet apples

5 tbsp granulated sugar

1 tbsp cider or white wine vinegar

1 Quarter the lemon lengthways and remove the seeds. Place the quarter, rind-side up, on a cutting board and cut crossways into thin slices. Put in a medium pan with ⅔ cup water and the star anise. Bring to a boil, cover, reduce the heat, and simmer for about 15 minutes, or until the lemon is really soft (once you add the sugar it won't soften any more).

2 Add the leek and carrot, stir well, then cover and simmer for a further 5 minutes. There should be about 2 tbsp liquid left. If more, boil rapidly to reduce; if less, add a little more water.

3 Meanwhile, peel, core, and quarter the apples. Chop the flesh and add to the lemon mixture with the sugar and cider or vinegar. Stir gently until the sugar dissolves, then boil for 2 minutes, stirring, until everything is tender, but still with a little texture.

4 Leave to cool, then spoon the mixture into a clean, sterilized jar with a non-metallic vinegar-proof lid. For added flavor, leave the star anise in the marmalade, or remove it before screwing the lid on, if preferred. This is not a relish with pantry longevity, but it can be kept in the refrigerator for a few weeks.

Kimchi

MAKES 1 LARGE JAR (approx. 1lb 2oz/500g)   **PREPARATION 10 MINS, PLUS MARINATING**

This fermented pickle is delicious served with cheese or hard-boiled eggs, or simply with fresh crusty bread. It will improve in the refrigerator—keep for up to a week.

1 Separate the Napa cabbage chunks into individual leaves and place in a large colander in the sink. Add the salt, toss well, and leave to stand for 2 hours. Rinse thoroughly under cold water, tossing to remove the salt. Drain and dry on paper towels. Place in a large plastic container with a sealable lid.

2 Meanwhile, toast the seeds in a dry frying pan, stirring until fragrant and lightly golden. Pour immediately out of the pan into a bowl to prevent further cooking. When cold, add to the Napa cabbage. Add the sliced shallot and herbs.

3 Blend the remaining ingredients together and add to the vegetable mixture. Toss well. Cover and leave to marinate in the refrigerator for at least 24 hours before serving.

INGREDIENTS

small head Napa cabbage, cut
  into small chunks
1 tbsp salt
1 tbsp black onion seeds
1 tbsp sesame seeds
1 tbsp cumin seeds
1 shallot, halved and
  thinly sliced
2 tbsp chopped cilantro
1 tbsp chopped parsley
2 tbsp sambal oelek
4 tbsp rice vinegar
1 tbsp lime juice
1 tbsp toasted sesame oil

Four ways with
Onions

Onion confit ▶

TAKES 50 mins **MAKES** 1lb 10oz (750g)

Melt 2 tbsp **butter** in a heavy-based saucepan.
Peel and finely slice 2lb (900g) **onions** and add
to the melted butter. Stir and cook for about
5 minutes, or until soft and translucent. Now
add ½ cup **brown sugar**, 3 tbsp **sherry
vinegar**, 1½ tbsp **crème de cassis** (optional),
and 2 tsp **salt**. Stir the ingredients well and
simmer uncovered for 30–40 minutes, stirring
occasionally so that the confit does not stick to
the pan or burn. To serve, try the confit spread on
bruschetta with grilled **goat cheese**, or in wraps
with grated **Cheddar cheese** and some greens.

◀ Onion bhajis

TAKES 30 mins **SERVES** 4

Mix together 8oz (225g) chopped **onions**, 4oz
(115g) **besan** (gram flour), 2 tsp **cumin seeds**,
½ tsp **turmeric**, 1 tsp ground **coriander**, and
1 **green** or **red chile**, seeded and very finely
chopped. Add about ½ cup cold water to bind
the mixture to a thick batter. Heat **vegetable oil**
in a deep-fat fryer to 375°F (190°C). When hot,
place spoonfuls of the mixture, roughly the size
of golf balls, into the oil. Fry, turning occasionally,
until golden all over. Remove the bhajis using a
slotted spoon and drain. Return them to the pan
and quickly fry a second time until crisp and
golden brown all over. Drain and serve hot.

Most main-course dishes include onions, but **here they are the star ingredient**. Choose scallions for salads and stir-fries, brown or white onions for general use, red ones for a sweeter flavor, and **shallots for a milder taste**.

Onion and almond soup ▶

TAKES 1 hr 10 mins **SERVES** 4

Add 3½oz (100g) **almonds** to boiling water, cover, and soak for 15 minutes. Slip off the skins. Purée in a blender with ½ cup hot **vegetable stock**. Fry ¼ tsp **nigella seeds** in 4 tbsp **butter** for 1 minute. Add 4 diced **onions** and 1 chopped **red chile**, cover, and cook for 25 minutes. Uncover and when the onions are golden, add 1 tsp **brown sugar**. Cook until it catches on the bottom. Add 2 tbsp **balsamic vinegar** and cook until sticky. Add 2 cups stock and the almond paste; simmer for 20 minutes. Purée in a blender. Return to the pan, add ½ cup **half-and-half**, and season. Reheat, garnish with fried sliced onion, and serve.

◀ Onion tart

TAKES 1 hr 10 mins **SERVES** 6

Preheat the oven to 400°F (200°C). Heat 1 tbsp **olive oil** in a non-stick frying pan, add 4 sliced **onions**, sweat gently for 15 minutes, remove from the heat, and stir in 1 tbsp **all-purpose flour**. Add a little of 1¼ cups **milk** and stir. Return the pan to the heat and slowly stir in the milk. Add 1 tsp mild **paprika** and season with **salt** and freshly ground **black pepper**. Remove from the heat. Roll out 10oz (300g) **pie dough** and use to line a tart pan. Trim excess dough and bake blind (see p338). Reduce the oven to 350°F (180°C). Spoon the onion mixture into the shell and top with 1 tsp **paprika**. Bake for 15–20 minutes. Serve.

Indian-spiced vegetable chutney

MAKES 3 JARS (approx. 12oz/350g each)   **PREPARATION 30 MINS**   TO COOK **2 HR 15 MINS**

A selection of vegetables simmered in Indian spices and vinegar give this colorful chutney its flavor. Add 1–2 finely chopped green chiles for heat.

INGREDIENTS

2lb (900g) butternut squash, seeds removed, peeled, and cut into bite-sized chunks

2 onions, finely chopped

8oz (225g) apples, peeled, cored, and chopped

3 zucchini, halved lengthways and chopped

1¾oz (50g) ready-to-eat pitted dates, chopped

2 cups cider vinegar

2 tbsp medium or hot curry powder

1 tsp ground cumin

1in (2½cm) piece fresh ginger, grated or finely chopped

2 cups granulated or light brown sugar

1 Put the squash, onions, apples, zucchini, and dates in a preserving pan or a large, heavy-based, stainless steel saucepan. Pour in the vinegar, add the spices and ginger, and mix well.

2 Bring the mixture to a boil, then reduce the heat and simmer for 40–45 minutes, or until the vegetables are soft, stirring occasionally.

3 Add the sugar, stir until it has dissolved, then continue to cook at a gentle simmer for 1–1½ hours, or until the chutney is thick and the liquid has been absorbed. Stir continuously near the end of the cooking time so that the chutney doesn't catch on the base of the pan.

4 Ladle into warm, sterilized jars leaving ¼in (5mm) headspace. Cover, seal with non-metallic vinegar-proof lids, and heat process for 5 minutes, then label.

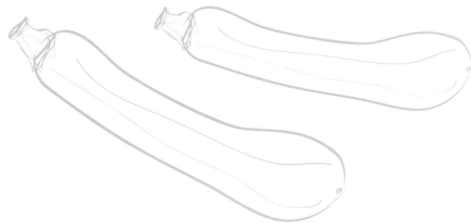

Corn relish

MAKES 2 LARGE JARS (approx. 1lb 2oz/500g each)   **PREPARATION 25 MINS**   **TO COOK 20 MINS**

Made from diced fruit or vegetables, relish is part-pickle, part-chutney, but cooked for a shorter time than the latter. **It packs a tangy punch of flavor.**

1 Strip the kernels from the cobs using a sharp knife (see p321). Blanch them in a saucepan of boiling water for 2 minutes, then drain well.

2 Put the corn and the other ingredients in a saucepan, bring to a boil, and stir. Simmer gently, stirring, for 15–20 minutes.

3 Check the seasoning, then spoon into warmed sterilized jars, leaving ¼in (5mm) headspace. The relish should be a spoonable consistency and wetter than a chutney.

4 Cover, seal with non-metallic or vinegar-proof lids, and heat process for 5 minutes, then label. Once opened, store the jars in the refrigerator.

INGREDIENTS

4 corn cobs
2 bell peppers, green or red, seeded and diced
2 celery sticks, finely sliced
1 red chile, seeded and sliced
1 onion, peeled and sliced
2 cups white wine vinegar
1 cup granulated sugar
2 tsp sea salt
2 tsp mustard powder
½ tsp ground turmeric

Beet relish

MAKES 2 LARGE JARS (approx. 1lb 2oz/500g each)　**TO COOK 2 HRS 15 MINS**

Sweet with a hint of spice, this relish is delicious served with cheese or cold cuts. To save time making the relish, you can cook the beets the night before.

INGREDIENTS

3lb (1.35kg) beets
1 tsp granulated sugar
1lb (450g) shallots,
　finely chopped
2 cups cider vinegar
　or white wine vinegar
1 tbsp pickling spices, placed
　in a muslin spice bag
2 cups granulated sugar

1 Put the beets in a preserving pan or a large, heavy-based, stainless steel saucepan. Pour over enough water to cover them and add the 1 tsp granulated sugar. Bring to a boil and simmer for 1 hour, or until the beets are soft and cooked. Drain and leave to cool. When cool enough to handle, peel and dice into small, neat pieces.

2 Put the shallots and vinegar in the rinsed preserving pan or saucepan and cook for 10 minutes over low heat. Add the chopped beets and the muslin bag of pickling spices. Stir, add the 2 cups sugar, and cook gently until the sugar has dissolved. Bring to a boil and cook at a rolling boil for 5 minutes, then reduce the heat to a simmer and cook for about 40 minutes, or until the mixture thickens.

3 Ladle into warm, sterilized jars leaving ¼in (5mm) headspace. Cover, seal with non-metallic vinegar-proof lids, and heat process for 5 minutes, then label. Allow the flavors to mature for 1 month, and refrigerate after opening.

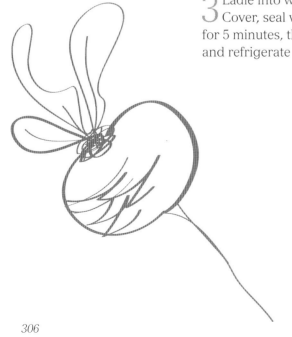

Red onion marmalade

MAKES 2 JARS (approx. 12oz/350g each)   **PREPARATION 20 MINS**   TO COOK **1 HR 10 MINS**

This delicious marmalade—made with sweet, sticky onions—has become a modern classic. It is **perfect served with cheese**.

1 Heat the oil in a preserving pan or a large, heavy-based, stainless steel saucepan. Add the onions and a pinch of salt and pepper. Cook over low-medium heat for about 30 minutes until the onions soften and turn translucent, stirring occasionally so they don't catch and burn. Slow cooking is essential at this point, as this is where the delicious caramel taste is developed.

2 Increase the heat a little, add the wine and vinegars, and stir to combine. Bring to a boil, then reduce the heat. Stir in the sugar and cook over low heat, stirring occasionally, for 30–40 minutes until most of the liquid has evaporated.

3 Remove the pan from the heat. Taste and adjust the seasoning if necessary (although the flavors will mature with time). Spoon into warmed, sterilized jars with non-metallic vinegar-proof lids, making sure there are no air gaps. Cover with waxed paper discs, seal, label, and store in the refrigerator for 1 month to allow the flavors to mature. Keep refrigerated after opening.

INGREDIENTS

2 tbsp olive oil
2¼lb (1kg) red onions, peeled, halved, and sliced
salt and freshly ground black pepper
⅔ cup red wine
3 tbsp balsamic vinegar
3 tbsp white wine vinegar
6 tbsp light brown sugar

Tapenade

MAKES 1 SMALL JAR (approx. 7oz/200g)   **PREPARATION 15 MINS**

This full-flavored olive spread is popular in the Mediterranean. It is great with crudités, spread on crostini, tossed with pasta, or in dressings.

INGREDIENTS

2 large garlic cloves
9oz (250g) Mediterranean
  black olives, pitted
1½ tbsp capers, drained
  and rinsed
1 tsp thyme leaves
1 tsp chopped rosemary
2 tbsp lemon juice
2 tbsp extra virgin olive oil
1 tsp Dijon mustard
freshly ground black pepper

1 Place the garlic, olives, capers, thyme, and rosemary in a food processor or blender and purée until smooth. Add the lemon juice, oil, mustard, and pepper to taste, then blend until the paste is thick.

2 Transfer to a bowl and chill until ready to use. Alternatively, spoon into a clean, sterilized jar and store in the refrigerator—it will keep for several weeks.

Avocado salsa

SERVES 4–6   **PREPARATION** **15 MINS**

A delicious salsa that **goes brilliantly with spicy foods,** this is also wonderful served with grilled halloumi or an omelet—you could even use it as a filling for the latter.

1 Cut the avocado flesh into small cubes and place in a bowl. Add all the remaining ingredients except the crushed chiles and toss gently until well combined, taking care not to crush the avocados.

2 Pile into a serving dish, sprinkle with the crushed chiles, and chill until ready to serve. It is best used within 2 hours or the avocado may discolor.

INGREDIENTS

2 large, just-ripe avocados, halved, pitted, and peeled (see pp324–5)
4 scallions, chopped
1 red bell pepper, halved, seeded, and diced
2 tomatoes, seeded and diced
1 fat red chile, seeded and thinly sliced
¼ cucumber, diced
6 radishes, sliced
2 tbsp lime juice
2 tbsp olive oil
salt and freshly ground black pepper
2 tbsp roughly chopped cilantro
1 tsp dried chile flakes, to garnish

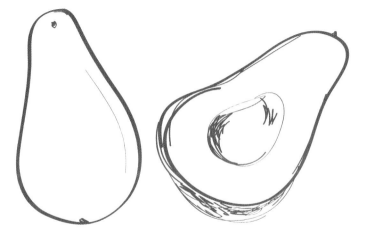

Pico de Gallo

SERVES 4   **PREPARATION** **10 MINS, PLUS CHILLING**

This simple salsa is delicious with fajitas, tacos, and plain quesadillas, or just with corn tortilla chips as a nibble before a meal.

INGREDIENTS

1 large red onion,
   finely chopped
2–3 large tomatoes,
   finely chopped
1 large green chile, such as
   jalapeño, seeded and
   finely chopped
large handful of
   cilantro, chopped
juice of 1 lime
salt and freshly ground
   black pepper

1 Mix all the vegetables with the cilantro in a bowl. Add the lime juice and season with salt and pepper.

2 Cover with plastic wrap and chill for at least 30 minutes to allow the flavors to develop before serving.

Yogurt, eggplant, and pine nut dip

SERVES 8–10   **PREPARATION 15 MINS**   TO COOK **40 MINS**

This dip is also delicious with a pinch of cinnamon added as well as (or instead of) the cumin. **It is great served with olives, and pickled chiles, too.**

INGREDIENTS

1 large eggplant
1 tbsp olive oil
2–3 tbsp tahini
2 garlic cloves, finely chopped
  or crushed
juice of 1 lemon, plus extra
  if needed
pinch of ground cumin
salt and freshly ground
  black pepper
pita bread, to serve

1 Preheat the oven to 400°F (200°C). Pierce the eggplant a few times all over with a knife. Next, using your hands, rub the eggplant with oil. Roast in the oven for 30–40 minutes until it begins to char and the flesh is tender.

2 When the eggplant is cool enough to handle, peel off the skin and put the roasted flesh in a blender or food processor. Add the tahini, garlic, lemon juice, and cumin, and blend to a purée.

3 Taste and season with salt and pepper, adding more lemon juice if needed. Blend again briefly. Spoon into a bowl or serving dish and serve with pita bread.

Hummus

SERVES 8–10   **PREPARATION 10 MINS**

Try this nutritious dip spread on spears of endive, celery sticks, hollowed-out chunks of cucumber, or, for a colorful effect, wedges of red pepper.

1 Put all the ingredients except the oil in a blender or food processor. Blend to a smooth purée.

2 With the motor running, gradually add the oil, a little at a time, until the hummus reaches the preferred consistency. Taste and season with salt, adding some more lemon juice if you like. Blend again. Serve as a dip with some warm pita bread.

INGREDIENTS

14oz (400g) can chickpeas, drained and rinsed
2 garlic cloves, crushed
juice of 1 lemon, plus extra if needed
2–3 tbsp tahini
pinch of sweet paprika
salt
2–3 tbsp olive oil
pita bread, to serve

Techniques

Slice, dice, seed, peel, pummel, and knead your way to culinary perfection with these essential step-by-step techniques. Find out how to prepare and cook your favorite vegetables, herbs, and spices—as well as base recipes such as risotto rice and pie crust.

Techniques
Dicing onions
Slice thickly for large dice and thinly for fine dice.

1 Using a sharp chef's knife, hold the onion firmly in one hand, then cut it in half lengthways. Peel off the skin, but leave the root intact so that the layers are held together.

2 Lay one half on a cutting board, cut-side down. Make a few slices into the onion horizontally, making sure that you cut up to, but not through, the root.

3 Hold the onion firmly, then, with the tip of the knife, slice down vertically, cutting close to the root. Repeat, slicing at regular intervals.

4 Cut across the slices for even dice. Use the root to hold the onion steady; discard this part when the rest of the onion has been diced.

Washing and slicing leeks

Leeks are related to onions but have a much milder flavor.

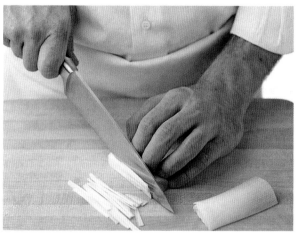

1 Trim off the root and some of the dark leaf top. Cut in half lengthways. Spread the layers apart and rinse well to remove any soil, then pat dry.

2 Lay the halved leek, flat-side down, on the cutting board and slice it into thick or thin strips, according to the recipe.

Peeling and chopping or crushing garlic

Garlic needs to be chopped or crushed to release all of its flavor.

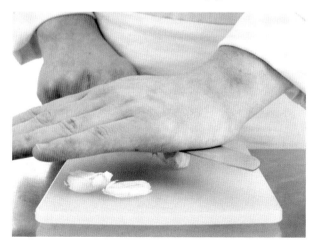

1 Place the garlic clove on a cutting board. Push down with the flat side of a large knife; this makes it easier to peel. Cut off the ends.

2 Slice lengthways, then cut across into tiny chunks. Collect them into a pile and finely chop again or crush with the flat of the knife.

Peeling and seeding tomatoes

Choose firm tomatoes; vine-ripened ones have the best flavor.

1 Hold the tomato steady and use a sharp knife to score an "X" through the skin at the base. Immerse completely in boiling water for about 20 seconds, or until the skin splits.

2 Using a slotted spoon, carefully remove the tomato from the boiling water and immediately plunge it into a bowl of iced water to cool it.

3 When the tomato is cool enough to handle, use a paring knife to peel off the skin, starting at the base where the "X" was made.

4 Slice the tomato in half, then gently squeeze the seeds out and discard. Place the seedless tomato on a board, hold firmly, and slice into strips.

Peeling raw beets and cutting into batonettes

Raw beets can also be very thinly sliced or grated.

1 Hold the beet firmly in one hand and peel the skin thinly, using a vegetable peeler or small paring knife. If you wish, wear latex gloves to keep your hands from getting stained.

2 Place the beet on a clean cutting board and hold it steady. Use a chef's knife to trim the sides, doing this as evenly as possible in order to form a square shape.

3 Hold the trimmed block gently but firmly. Cut into equal slices— ⅛in (3mm) thick for julienne and ¼in (5mm) thick for batonettes.

4 Stack the slices a few at a time to prevent them from sliding. Cut each batch into square-edged strips as thick as the slices.

Making zucchini batonettes

Young zucchini with glossy skins will not need peeling.

1 Place the zucchini on a board and cut off both ends. Cut it in half lengthways, then hold it on its side and cut into slices ¼in (5mm) thick.

2 Put each slice on the board and cut across with a sharp chef's knife to make equal-sized batonettes, about ¼in (5mm) wide.

Making carrot batonettes

For the best flavor, scrape young carrots; older ones need peeling.

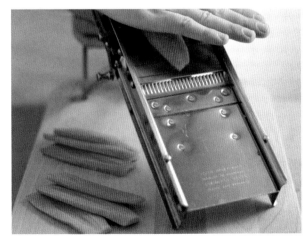

1 Set the mandolin blade to a thickness of ¼in (5mm) and hold the mandolin steady. Slide the carrot up and down to make uniform slices.

2 Stack the carrot slices and cut in half crossways. Trim off the rounded sides then cut the slices lengthways into equal strips.

Preparing asparagus

Look for fresh, sprightly spears with tightly closed tips.

1 Lay the spears on a board with the ends in line. Cut off about 1–1¾in (2½–4cm) of woody stem. If very fresh, the stems can be snapped off.

2 To ensure tender spears, hold the tip very carefully, then use a vegetable peeler to peel off a thin layer of skin from all sides of the stalk.

Preparing corn

Corn tastes best when used fresh rather than canned or frozen.

1 Remove the husks and all the silk thread from the corn-on-the-cob. Rinse the husked corn under cold running water.

2 Place the blunt end on a cutting board. Using a sharp chef's knife, slice straight down the cob. Rotate the cob and repeat.

Techniques
Preparing whole artichokes
Look for artichokes with tightly closed leaves and firm stalks.

1 Put the artichoke on a cutting board and hold firmly by the stalk. Then, with a pair of strong kitchen scissors, snip off the tough tips of the outer leaves.

2 Next, using a sharp chef's knife, cut through the stalk at the base of the artichoke head. Alternatively, if it is very fresh, twist off the stalks and the connective strings will come away, too.

3 Pull out any tough, darker green leaves and discard. Cut through the pointed tip. The artichoke is now ready to cook.

Eating whole artichokes

Steam in a vegetable steamer for 30 minutes. Dip the fleshy leaves in melted **butter** or **French dressing** and draw between your teeth to scrape off the flesh. When the outer leaves are eaten, pull away the cone of pale inner leaves, scoop out the choke underneath, and eat the succulent heart.

To **roast**, scoop out the cone and choke. Stuff with **breadcrumbs**, **Parmesan cheese**, and **olive oil**, and roast.

Preparing artichoke hearts

Make sure you remove the hairy choke as it is inedible.

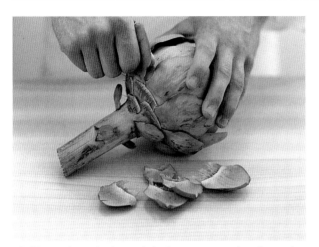

1 Place the whole artichoke on a cutting board. Carefully cut or pull away all of the leaves from the artichoke first, then cut the stalk from the base and discard.

2 Hold the artichoke firmly on the board and, using a sharp knife, cut off the soft middle cone of leaves, which can be found just above the hairy choke.

3 Trim away the bottom leaves with a paring knife. Scoop out the hairy choke if you plan to cut the heart into pieces for cooking.

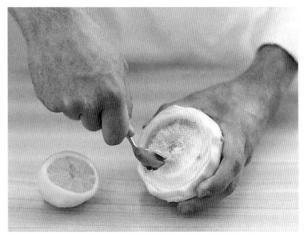

4 Using a spoon, scoop out the choke fibers. Rub the exposed flesh with lemon juice to keep it from browning.

Preparing avocados

Once ripe enough to eat, avocados are easy to peel and pit.

1 Hold the avocado firmly in one hand then, with a chef's knife, slice straight into the flesh, making sure that you cut all the way around the pit.

2 Once the avocado has been cut all the way around, gently twist the two halves in opposite directions and carefully pull them apart to separate them.

3 Strike the cutting edge of your knife into the pit and lift the knife (wiggling it if need be) to remove the pit from the avocado.

4 To release the pit from the knife, use a wooden spoon to carefully pry it away, then discard it.

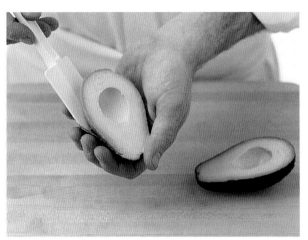

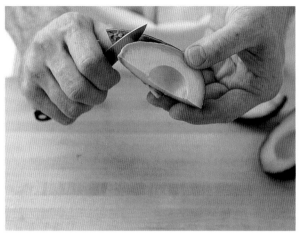

5 Use a spatula to remove the flesh from the skin, keeping it whole if possible. Then place the avocado on a cutting board and cut into slices or wedges.

6 Alternatively, quarter the avocado and hold it very gently to avoid damaging the flesh. Then use a small paring knife to peel away the skin.

7 To dice the avocado, cut it into neat slices lengthways, then repeat the cuts crossways to the desired size.

Storing avocado

Store the fruit in a **cool, dark place** but do not chill. Once cut and exposed to oxygen, an avocado will discolor quickly. The easiest way to slow this process is by rubbing the exposed flesh with the cut side of a **lemon or lime wedge**. Lay a sheet of **plastic wrap** over the top, pressing down as close to the flesh as possible, and store in a refrigerator until needed.

Preparing bell peppers

Red, green, orange, and yellow bell peppers add color to a dish.

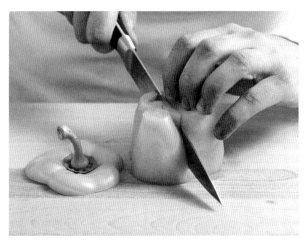

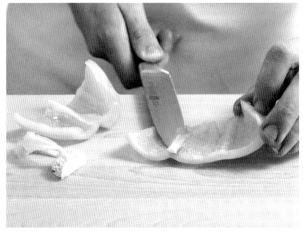

1 Place the pepper on its side. Cut off the top and bottom, then stand it on one of the cut ends and slice in half. Remove the core and seeds.

2 Lay each section flat. Remove the pale, fleshy ribs. Cut into smaller sections, following the divisions of the pepper, and chop as required.

Roasting and peeling peppers

Charring the skin makes peeling easier and lends a smoky flavor.

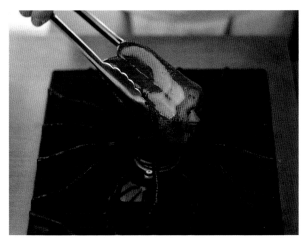

1 Use a pair of tongs to hold the pepper over a flame or place it under a hot broiler to char the skin, turning occasionally. Cool in a plastic bag.

2 When it has cooled, peel away the skin. Pull off the stalk, with the core attached. Discard the seeds and dice the flesh or cut it into strips.

Preparing chiles

Removing the seeds and veins from chiles will reduce their heat.

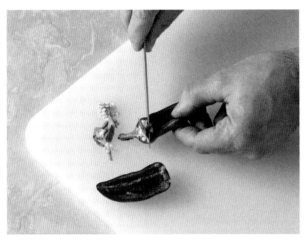

1 Cut the chile in half lengthways. Using the tip of your knife, scrape out the seeds and remove the membrane and stem.

2 Place the chile half flesh-side down and flatten. Turn over and slice lengthways into strips. For dice, slice the strips crossways into equal pieces.

Roasting and grinding chiles

Remove the stems and seeds before dry-roasting the chiles.

1 To impart a smoky flavor to chiles, dry-roast in a heavy-based frying pan over high heat. Remove when they begin to darken.

2 Use a mortar and pestle to grind dry-roasted chiles to a powder. Alternatively, they can be soaked, sieved, and ground to a paste.

Techniques
Roasting potatoes
Scoring the potatoes before roasting gives them a good crust.

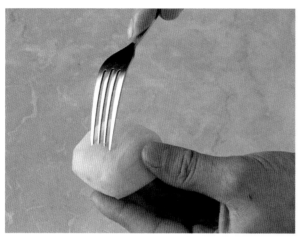

1 Peel and cut into equal-sized pieces. Boil in lightly salted water for 10 minutes. Drain and set aside until cool, then score with a fork.

2 Heat a pan with a layer of vegetable oil in the oven at 400°F (200°C). Coat the potatoes in the hot oil and roast for 1 hour, or until crisp.

Mashing potatoes
Use floury varieties, which have a soft, fluffy texture when cooked.

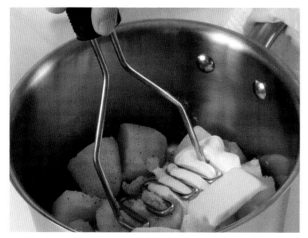

1 Boil until tender, drain, then return to the pan. Add butter, cream or milk, salt and freshly ground black pepper, and nutmeg to taste.

2 Cover and leave for 5 minutes. Mash with a potato masher until smooth and fluffy. Add extra butter and cream or milk if needed.

Pan-frying potatoes

Choose firm potatoes that have unbroken skins and no bruises.

1 Clean unpeeled potatoes by washing in water and scrubbing to remove any dirt. Heat a thin layer of vegetable oil in a frying pan until hot.

2 Over medium heat, fry a single layer of slices for 10 minutes. Turn over and fry until golden and tender. Drain on paper towels and season.

Making fries

Double-frying fries ensures that they will be really crisp.

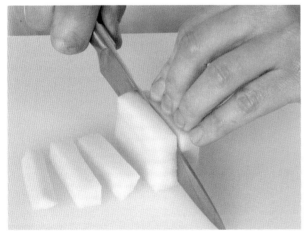

1 Cut large, floury potatoes into fry shapes. Heat oil for deep-frying to 325°F (160°C). Fry for 5–6 minutes until soft, but not brown. Drain.

2 Reheat the oil to 350°F (180°C) and fry all the fries again for 2–3 minutes until crisp and golden. Drain on paper towels.

Boiling green vegetables

Texture and color are best preserved if the cooking is brief.

1 Bring a pan of salted water to a boil. Add the prepared vegetables. Bring to a rapid boil and cook until they are tender.

2 Drain through a colander and serve, or, to set the green color and stop the vegetables cooking, rinse under cold running water.

Stir-frying vegetables

Speed is the key to successful stir-frying; toss and stir continuously.

1 When the wok (or pan) is hot, add sunflower, canola, or peanut oil, tilting the pan to spread the oil. Then toss in garlic or ginger.

2 Add the desired vegetables and toss them continuously. Add a couple of tablespoons of water, cover, and cook briefly until tender.

Steaming vegetables

As the vegetables are not immersed, nutrients are better preserved.

1 Bring 1in (2½cm) of water to a boil in the bottom pan of a steamer. Place the prepared vegetables in the upper basket and position on top.

2 When the steam rises, cover the pan with a fitted lid and cook until the vegetables are just tender when pierced with a knife.

Sautéing firm vegetables

Use this quick method of cooking for batonettes or dice.

1 Set a sauté pan over high heat. When hot, add a thin layer of oil. Once the oil is hot, add the vegetables and keep turning them to cook evenly.

2 Keep tossing the vegetables in the pan. Once they take on a light golden-brown color and become tender, remove from the heat and serve.

Preparing herbs
Fresh herbs can be used whole, chopped, or pounded.

To strip the leaves off woody herbs, hold the top end and run the thumb and forefinger of the other hand along the stalk.

For a bouquet garni, tie a sprig of thyme and parsley with a bay leaf. Rosemary or sage could also be used. Discard before serving.

Chopping tender herbs
Herbs with easily bruised leaves should be chopped bunched together.

1 To chop herbs with tender leaves, such as basil, without bruising them, stack the leaves together and roll them into a tight bunch.

2 Holding the bunch steady and using the knife in a rocking motion, chop finely, turning the leaves 90 degrees halfway through.

Preparing spices
Bruising, cutting, and grinding help to release the aroma of spices.

To prepare whole fresh spices such as lemongrass, bruise them by pressing down with the flat side of a heavy knife. This will help to release their volatile oils.

To prepare spice roots such as ginger, turmeric, and horseradish, grate them or finely chop them by hand, using a knife. Peel off the skin beforehand.

When spices are fried until lightly colored, the oil takes on their flavor. It can then be used along with the spices.

To dry-roast spices, place them in an oven preheated to 325°F (160°C), or toast them in a dry pan until lightly browned.

Techniques
Cooking rice by absorption
Always soak and rinse the rice before cooking; use stock for flavor.

1 Put the rice and 1½ times as much water in a saucepan. Bring to a boil, stir, simmer uncovered until the water is absorbed, then take off the heat.

2 Cover with a tea towel and lid, steam for 20 minutes, then remove the towel and replace the lid. Leave for 5 minutes. Fluff with a fork and serve.

Rehydrating instant couscous
Couscous is normally enriched with oil or butter before serving.

1 Pour twice its volume of boiling water or stock over the couscous. Cover with plastic wrap and leave for 5 minutes. Fluff with a fork.

2 Add 1 tbsp olive oil, a knob of butter or other flavorings, and seasoning. Fluff up the grains again until they are separate, then serve.

Making risotto

Short to medium grains that swell but maintain their shape are ideal.

1 Heat 3 cups stock in a saucepan to a simmer.
In another pan, heat 1 tbsp olive oil and 5 tbsp butter. Stir in 10oz (280g) risotto rice, coating the grains in the butter and oil.

2 Add ⅓ cup white wine and boil, stirring until absorbed. Add a ladle of the hot stock and stir until absorbed. Continue adding the stock, one ladle at a time, and stirring constantly.

3 When all the stock is added and the rice is tender but with a bite (about 20 minutes), add some butter, season, and remove from the heat.

4 The risotto should have a creamy texture. It is best served immediately or it will continue to cook and become too soft.

Making pie dough by hand

Pie dough can be used for both sweet and savory baking.

1 Sift 1 cup all-purpose flour and a pinch of salt into a bowl (or use whole wheat flour without sifting). Add 6 tbsp cold diced butter, margarine, or other fat. Lightly stir.

2 Using your fingertips, rub together the flour and butter until the mixture forms the consistency of coarse crumbs. Sprinkle 2 tbsp iced water over the mixture.

3 Use your fingers to gather the dough together and roll around to form a ball. Wrap in plastic wrap and chill for 30 minutes before using.

The art of good pie dough

Butter gives the best flavor, but half butter and half lard or vegetable shortening gives a shorter crust.

Keep the ingredients cold and handle them as little as possible.

Do not over-mix the dough or it will be tough.

Leave to chill and rest before rolling. Always roll away from you and turn the dough, not the rolling pin.

Making pie dough in a food processor

Be careful not to over-process the dough; pulse on a low speed.

1 Fit the metal blade into a food processor. Add the butter, salt, egg yolk, sugar, and milk and purée until smooth. Gradually add the sifted flour.

2 Pulse the mixture until it starts to come together to form a ball. Wrap in plastic wrap and refrigerate for at least 2 hours.

Lining a pie dish with dough

Remove excess dough and decorate the edges for a finished look.

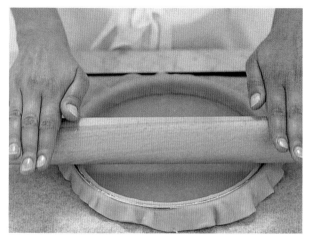

1 Roll the dough out and press gently into the bottom of the pan and against the sides. Roll a rolling pin over the top to trim off excess dough.

2 For a fluted edge, push an index finger against the outer rim and pinch the dough with the other index finger and thumb to form a ruffle.

Baking dough blind

Pre-cook dough if its filling will be baked only briefly, or not at all.

1 After lining a pie dish with dough, carefully prick the bottom all over with a fork. This will allow trapped air to escape during baking and prevent puffing.

2 Cut out a circle of parchment paper, slightly larger than the dish. Fold it in half 3 times to make a triangle. Snip the edges at regular intervals with scissors.

3 Place the parchment circle into the dish. Fill it with an even layer of ceramic baking beans. Bake at 350°F (180°C) for 15–20 minutes.

4 Leave to cool, then remove the beans and parchment. For a fully baked crust, bake for a further 5–8 minutes, or until golden.

Making a classic omelet

Always check eggs are free from any cracks; discard broken ones.

1 Beat and season the eggs. Melt a knob of butter in a non-stick frying pan over medium heat. When frothy, add the eggs, tilting the pan so that they can spread across it.

2 Stir with a fork to distribute the eggs evenly. Stop stirring as soon as they are set. Fold the side of the omelet nearest to you halfway across the circle.

3 To form a neatly rolled omelet, sharply tap the handle to encourage the omelet to curl over and slide to the edge.

4 When the omelet is cooked to your taste, tilt the pan over a serving plate until the omelet slides onto it, seam-side down. Serve at once.

Index

Page numbers in *italics* indicate descriptions of ingredients. Page numbers in **bold** indicate illustrated preparation techniques. Variations on main recipes are indicated by (*V*).

A

almonds *32*
　Cauliflower, broccoli, & tomato braise with cheese crumble 177
　Cinnamon, almond, & raisin brown rice pilaf with grilled eggplant 101
　Onion & almond soup 303
　Roasted red pepper, almond, & chile pesto 298–9

anchovies (optional)
　Baked stuffed tomatoes 200
　French bean, garlic, & tomato omelet 216
　Pasta primavera 88
　Tomato & onion tart 251
　Vegetable-stuffed pizzas 184

apples
　Celery & apple salad with blue cheese dressing 65
　Creamy butternut squash & butter bean stew 175
　Fennel & goat cheese salad 76
　Indian-spiced vegetable chutney 304
　Lemon, carrot, & leek marmalade 300
　Potato pancakes with applesauce & chive yogurt 138
　Thai vegetable salad with cabbage & peanuts 70

artichokes & artichoke hearts *16*, **322–3**
　Antipasti salad 64
　Artichoke, black olive, tomato, & feta tart 249
　Jerusalem *see* Jerusalem artichokes

arugula *19*
　Arugula, pear, blue cheese, & walnut quesadillas 208
　Celery & apple salad with blue cheese dressing 65
　Fennel & goat cheese salad 76
　Squash with cranberries & chestnuts 71

asparagus *17*, **321**
　Asparagus & cream cheese quiche 236
　Asparagus frittata on crostini 97
　Asparagus, mushroom, & garlic sauce pizzas 186–7

Asparagus with mustard sauce 96
Asparagus & scallion soufflé omelet 224
Cheese & asparagus turnovers 244
Crêpes with asparagus 96
Grilled asparagus & Gorgonzola 97
Lemon & asparagus pasta 81
Pasta with asparagus & zucchini 80
Pasta primavera 88
Thai-style beansprout & shredded vegetable fritters 116–17
Warm pea pancakes with grilled asparagus 131

avocados *26*, **324–5**
　Avocado, baby spinach, & chile wraps 190
　Avocado, cucumber, & sorrel soup 59
　Avocado mousse with lime 163
　Avocado with roasted cherry tomatoes & paprika dressing 162
　Avocado salsa 120, 309
　Avocado, tomato, & mozzarella salad 163
　Cajun stuffed potatoes with crushed avocado 293
　Farfalle with spinach, avocado, baby plum tomatoes, & pumpkin seeds 82–3
　Grilled avocado with sun-dried tomato dressing 267
　Guacamole & Cheddar quesadillas 206–7
　Maki sushi wraps 196–7
　Quesadilla with avocado, scallion, & chile 162

B

bacon & pancetta (optional)
　Artichoke, black olive, tomato, & feta tart 249
　Arugula, pear, blue cheese, & walnut quesadillas 208
　Asparagus, mushroom, & garlic sauce pizzas 186–7
　Celery root & pecan soufflé pie 253
　Celery & celery root soup 56
　Creamy spinach & rosemary soup 53
　Crêpes with mushrooms, garlic, & cheese 126
　Grilled marinated halloumi on seeded vegetable ribbons 264–5
　Mixed mushroom & garlic omelets 221
　Mushroom burgers with chips & dip 121
　Parsnip & walnut pancakes with maple butter 132
　Potatoes Dauphinoise with Emmental 282

Stuffed mushrooms with spinach, pine nuts, & halloumi 279
Veggie burgers with melting cheese 124–5
Warm pea pancakes with grilled asparagus 131
Wild mushroom & Taleggio tart 242
see also lardons

bamboo shoots
　Vegetable ramen noodle bowl 102–3
　Vietnamese vegetable & tofu curry 164

barley *see* pearl barley

basil *35*
　Basil oil 54
　Classic basil pesto 296

batters
　beer 114
　blini 134
　galette 133
　pancake 126
　tempura 141

beans, canned/dried *30–1*
　Bean patties 120
　Black-eyed peas with spinach & tomato curry 152
　Chile bean fajitas 191
　Creamy butternut squash & butter bean stew 175
　Creamy bean ragout with shredded kale 170
　Curried leek, celery root, & soy bean loaf 288
　Eggplant, zucchini, & flageolet salad with mozzarella & red pesto dressing 68–9
　Mushroom & black-eyed pea stroganoff 174
　Potato & mixed nut moussaka 286–7
　Red bean & chestnut bourguignon 168–9
　Vegetable chow mein with black beans 91
　Veggie burgers with melting cheese 124–5
　see also pinto beans; haricot beans

beans, fresh/frozen *25*
　see also specific types (eg fava beans)

beansprouts
　Shiitake mushrooms & water chestnut teriyaki 262
　Thai-style beansprout & shredded vegetable fritters 116–17
　Vegetable egg foo yung 225
　Vegetable spring rolls 140
　Vietnamese vegetable & beansprout summer rolls 202

beef (optional)
　Aromatic curry of pumpkin 161
　Bean patties 120

Celery & apple salad with blue cheese dressing 65
Chile bean fajitas 191
Chile bean & vegetable braise with fried eggs 172–3
Endive salad with spinach & pears 67
Fiery peanut & pepper noodles 104
Mixed vegetable cottage pie with rutabaga crust 268–9
Mixed vegetable satay 292
Mushroom & black-eyed pea stroganoff 174
Red bean & chestnut bourguignon 168–9
Spiced crushed carrot, pine nut, & cottage cheese frittata 228
Spicy lentil & pepper pizzas 188
Turnip noodle soup with pimento & chilli 57

beets *23*, **319**
Beet & caraway blinis with sour cream 134–5
Beet relish 306
Beet risotto 108
Beet, zucchini, & goat cheese pizzas 182–3
Borscht 47
Red lentil & mixed root crumble with sour cream & chives 289
Swiss chard, beet, & goat cheese frittata 229
Watercress & beet roulade with smooth cheese sauce 274–5

bhajis, Onion 302
Bhatura 156–7
biryani, Vegetable 111
black pudding (optional), Butternut squash, spinach, & goat cheese frittata 226–7
blinis, Beet & caraway 134–5
blue cheeses
Arugula, pear, blue cheese, & walnut quesadillas 208
Blue cheese croûtes 52
Blue cheese dressing 65
Carrot, onion, & Stilton hot dogs 290–1
Endive salad with spinach & pears 67
Grilled asparagus & Gorgonzola 97
Creamy broccoli & blue cheese puffs 248
Pumpkin, spinach, & Gorgonzola lasagne 86–7
Red pepper & chile tart (*V*) 239
Roasted squash & Gorgonzola tart 233
Spinach, fresh tomato, & blue cheese pizza 181

bockwurst (optional), Vegetable choucroute garni 176

boiling 330
bok choy *15*
Butternut squash, spinach, & goat cheese frittata (*V*) 226–7
Mixed mushroom & bok choy stir-fry with soba noodles 92–3
Spicy mixed greens & pea stir-fry with hoisin sauce & toasted sesame seeds 98
Thai noodle stir-fry 94
Vegetable egg foo yung 225
Vegetable ramen noodle bowl 102–3

Borscht 47
bourguignon, Red bean & chestnut 168–9
bread (as ingredient)
Blue cheese croûtes 52
Endive gazpacho 43
Gazpacho 42
Gruyère croûtes 44–5
Wild mushroom & hollandaise tartlets 250
see also bruschetta & crostini

breads
Bhatura 156–7
Pizza bases 180

broccoli *16*
Broccoli rabe, ricotta, & rosemary calzones 185
Cauliflower, broccoli, & tomato braise with cheese crumble 177
Creamy broccoli & blue cheese puffs 248
Potato soup with broccoli, shallot, & mascarpone cheese 52
Spicy spaghetti with broccoli 89
Vegetable chow mein with black beans 91

bruschetta & crostini
Asparagus frittata 97
Eggplant & goat cheese 280
Mushroom 63
Onion confit 302
Roasted mixed pepper 247
Roasted red pepper, almond, & chile pesto 298–9

Brussels sprouts *14*
Spicy mixed greens & pea stir-fry with hoisin sauce & toasted sesame seeds 98

Buckwheat galettes with cheese & caramelized onions 133
bulgur wheat
Bulgur wheat with okra 74
Tabbouleh lettuce wraps 198

burgers & patties 120–5, 129–30
butter, Maple 132
butternut squash *see* squashes & pumpkins

C
cabbages *14*
Asparagus, mushroom, & garlic sauce pizzas 186–7
Chickpea & vegetable goulash (*V*) 167
Chile bean fajitas 191
Creamy butternut squash & butter bean stew (*V*) 175
Lentil, mushroom, & egg loaf with celery root remoulade 284
Squash & cider cobbler 278
Thai vegetable salad with cabbage & peanuts 70
Vegetable spring rolls 140

calzones 184–5
carrots *23*, **320**
Aromatic curry of pumpkin (*V*) 161
Baked vegetable & chickpea pilau 100
Bean patties (*V*) 120
Carrot, onion, & Stilton hot dogs 290–1
Carrot & orange soup 58
Carrot raita 118
Cashew nut paella 106–7
Cauliflower pakoras with carrot raita 118
Creamy bean ragout with shredded kale (*V*) 170
Grilled marinated halloumi on seeded vegetable ribbons 264–5
Jerusalem artichoke soup with saffron & thyme 60
Leek, barley, & root vegetable broth with basil oil 54–5
Lemon, carrot, & leek marmalade 300
Lentil & carrot rissoles 123
Maki sushi wraps 196–7
Mixed root tempura with dipping sauce 141
Mixed vegetable cottage pie with rutabaga crust 268–9
Mixed vegetable curry 148
Mixed vegetable satay 292
Pizza primavera 189
Red bean & chestnut bourguignon 168–9
Red lentil & mixed root crumble with sour cream & chives 289
Root vegetable & fennel pasties with seed pastry 257
Seasonal vegetables in spinach & garlic sauce 145
Seeded vegetable ribbons 264–5
Spiced crushed carrot, pine nut, & cottage cheese frittata 228
Split pea, noodle, & vegetable pot 95
Spring vegetable stew with fresh herb dumplings 166

Stir-fried ribbon vegetables with coconut noodles 99
Sweet potato, roasted pepper, & white bean hotpot 171
Thai vegetable salad with cabbage & peanuts 70
Vegetable biryani 111
Vegetable choucroute garni 176
Vegetable chow mein with black beans 91
Vegetable dahl with tandoori paneer 150–1
Vegetable egg foo yung 225
Vegetable spring rolls 140
Vegetables with lentils 155
Veggie burgers with melting cheese 124–5
Vietnamese vegetable & beansprout summer rolls 202
Zucchini, carrot, & Gruyère pancakes 127
Zucchini & carrot pavé 285

cashew nuts *32*
Cashew nut paella 106–7
Snow pea, sweet potato, & cashew nut red curry 146–7
Spicy mixed greens & pea stir-fry with hoisin sauce & toasted sesame seeds 98
Stir-fried ribbon vegetables with coconut noodles 99

cauliflowers *16*
Cauliflower, broccoli, & tomato braise with cheese crumble 177
Cauliflower pakoras with carrot raita 118
Mixed vegetable curry 148
Pizza primavera 189
Seasonal vegetables in spinach & garlic sauce 145
Vegetable chow mein with black beans (*V*) 91
Vegetable samosas 258

cavolo nero *14*
Creamy butternut squash & butter bean stew 175

celery *17*
Celery & apple salad with blue cheese dressing 65
Celery & celery root soup 56
Corn relish 305
Mixed mushroom & bok choy stir-fry with soba noodles 92–3
Potato, celery, & walnut cakes with mushrooms 130

celery root *23*
Celery & celery root soup 56
Celery root & pecan soufflé pie 253

Creamy bean ragout with shredded kale 170
Curried leek, celery root, & soy bean loaf 288
Lentil & carrot rissoles (*V*) 123
Lentil, mushroom, & egg loaf with celery root remoulade 284
Mixed root tempura with dipping sauce 141
Zucchini, carrot, & Gruyère pancakes (*V*) 127

chapatti wraps, Spicy potato & mango chutney 199

chard *see* Swiss chard

Cheddar cheese
Asparagus & cream cheese quiche 236
Asparagus, mushroom, & garlic sauce pizzas 186–7
Cajun stuffed potatoes with crushed avocado 293
Carrot, onion, & Stilton hot dogs (*V*) 290–1
Cauliflower, broccoli, & tomato braise with cheese crumble 177
Celery root & pecan soufflé pie 253
Cheese & asparagus turnovers 244
Cheese choux pastry 272
Cheese, red pepper, & corn chowder 48–9
Cheese soufflé omelet with corn & pepper 222–3
Chile bean fajitas 191
Corn, Cheddar cheese, & chile sauce quesadillas 205
Corn & jalapeño tart 243
Creamy broccoli & blue cheese puffs (*V*) 248
Grilled stuffed romano peppers with chile & cheese 266
Guacamole & Cheddar quesadillas 206–7
Mixed vegetable cottage pie with rutabaga crust 268–9
Onion confit wraps 302
Quesadilla with avocado, scallion, & chile 162
Sage & onion quesadilla 203
Smooth cheese sauce 274–5
Stuffed butternut squash (*V*) 277
Stuffed crêpes with spinach, ricotta, & pine nuts 136
Tomato & zucchini gougère 272
Watercress & beet roulade with smooth cheese sauce 274–5
Whole wheat shortcrust dough 253
Zucchini & carrot pavé 285

cheese
Corn & jalapeño tart 243

Crêpes with mushrooms, garlic, & cheese 126
Red lentil & mixed root crumble with sour cream & chives 289
Red pepper & chile tart 239
Wild mushroom & Taleggio tart 242
see also blue cheeses; specific cheeses (e.g. goat cheese)

chestnuts *32*
Red bean & chestnut bourguignon 168–9
Squash with cranberries & chestnuts 71
Stuffed portobello mushrooms en croûte 234–5

chicken (optional)
Avocado, baby spinach, & chile wraps 190
Baked vegetable & chickpea pilau 100
Corn, Cheddar cheese, & chile sauce quesadillas 205
Corn fritters with tomato salsa 115
Corn & jalapeño tart 243
Cheese & asparagus turnovers 244
Cheese, red pepper, & corn chowder 48–9
Cheese soufflé omelet with corn & pepper 222–3
Creamy butternut squash & butter bean stew 175
Fennel & Gruyère tart 238
Jerusalem artichoke soup with saffron & thyme 60
Lentil & carrot rissoles 123
Lentil, mushroom, & egg loaf with celery root remoulade 284
Mixed vegetable curry 148
Mixed vegetable satay 292
Potato & green bean stew 154
Rainbow pepper Mexican tacos 195
Seasonal vegetables in spinach & garlic sauce 145
Shiitake mushrooms & water chestnut teriyaki 262
Spicy potato & mango chutney chapatti wraps 199
Spring vegetable stew with fresh herb dumplings 166
Thai noodle stir-fry 94
Vegetable biryani 111
Vegetable choucroute garni 176
Vegetable chow mein with black beans 91
Vegetable dahl with tandoori paneer 150–1
Vegetable egg foo yung 225
Vegetable ramen noodle bowl 102–3
Vietnamese vegetable & tofu curry 164

chicken livers (optional)
Pasta with asparagus & zucchini 80
Warm pasta, kale, & duck egg salad
with truffle oil 72–3
chickpeas *31*
Baked vegetable & chickpea pilau 100
Butternut squash tagine 276
Chickpea & spinach masala with
bhatura 156–7
Chickpea & vegetable goulash 167
Falafel with dill & cucumber dip 122
Hummus 313
chiles *27*, **327**
Chinese leaves *18*
Kimchi 301
Spicy mixed greens & pea stir-fry
with hoisin sauce & toasted sesame
seeds 98
chips & wedges 121, 129, **329**
chorizo (optional)
Chickpea & vegetable goulash 167
Gratin of Swiss chard with beans 283
Guacamole & Cheddar quesadillas
206–7
Red pepper & chile tart 239
Spanish tortilla 212
Sweet potato & leek tortillas with
fresh tomato sauce 214–15
choucroute garni, Vegetable 176
choux pastry, Cheese 272
chow mein, Vegetable, with black
beans 91
chutneys *see* pickles & relishes
cobbler, Squash & cider 278
coconut *32*
coconut (desiccated), Spice paste 155
coconut milk & cream
Aromatic curry of pumpkin 161
Heart of palm green curry 160
Mixed vegetable curry 148
Potato & green bean stew 154
Red curry of oyster mushrooms &
tofu 159
Snow pea, sweet potato, & cashew
nut red curry 146–7
Split pea, noodle, & vegetable pot 95
Stir-fried ribbon vegetables with
coconut noodles 99
Thai-style baby eggplant curry 165
Vietnamese vegetable & tofu curry 164
confits 281, 302
corn *26*, **321**
Bulgur wheat with okra 74
Cajun stuffed potatoes with crushed
avocado 293
Cheese, red pepper, & corn chowder
48–9
Cheese soufflé omelet with corn &
pepper 222–3

Corn, Cheddar cheese, & chile sauce
quesadillas 205
Corn fritters with tomato salsa 115
Corn & jalapeño tart 243
Corn & pepper empanadas 259
Corn relish 305
Heart of palm green curry 160
Potato salad niçoise 77
Rainbow pepper Mexican tacos 195
Seasonal vegetables in spinach &
garlic sauce 145
Vegetable chow mein with black
beans 91
Vegetable-stuffed pizzas 184
Vegetables with lentils (*V*) 155
cottage cheese
Butternut squash, spinach, & goat
cheese frittata (*V*) 226–7
Grilled avocado with sun-dried
tomato dressing 267
Spiced crushed carrot, pine nut, &
cottage cheese frittata 228
cottage pie, Mixed vegetable, with
rutabaga crust 268–9
couscous **334**
Moroccan couscous salad 218
cranberries
Squash with cranberries & chestnuts
71
Stuffed butternut squash 277
cream cheese
Asparagus & cream cheese quiche 236
Avocado mousse with lime 163
Cream cheese & roasted pepper
quesadillas 209
Grilled stuffed romano peppers with
chile & cheese 266
Root vegetable & fennel pasties with
seed pastry 257
crostini *see* bruschetta & crostini
croûtes 44–5, 52
crumbles 177, 289
cucumbers *24*
Avocado, cucumber, & sorrel soup 59
Avocado salsa 309
Dill & cucumber dip 122
Gazpacho 42
Guacamole & Cheddar quesadillas
206–7
Maki sushi wraps 196–7
Potato salad niçoise 77
Tabbouleh lettuce wraps 198
Vegetable chow mein with black
beans (*V*) 91
Vegetable egg foo yung 225
Vietnamese vegetable & beansprout
summer rolls 202
curry leaves *37*
Curry leaf oil 50

D
daikon *22*
Stir-fried ribbon vegetables with
coconut noodles 99
Vegetable choucroute garni 176
Dauphinoises 128, 282
dips
Aioli 139
Dill & cucumber 122
Hummus 313
Red pepper & walnut 247
Tahini 121
Tzatziki 219, 263
Yogurt, eggplant, & pine nut 312
dressings
Balsamic vinegar 64
Blue cheese 65
Curried mayonnaise 288
Niçoise 77
Paprika 162
Pomegranate vinaigrette 281
Red pesto 68
Remoulade 284
Sun-dried tomato 267
Thai salad 70
Vinaigrette 67
Walnut oil 66, 280
duck (optional)
Carrot & orange soup 58
Mint, new potato, pea, & lettuce
tortilla 220
Snow pea, sweet potato, & cashew
nut red curry 146–7
Spicy mixed greens & pea stir-fry
with hoisin sauce & toasted sesame
seeds 98
Thai-style baby eggplant curry 165
duck eggs, Warm pasta, kale, & duck
egg salad with truffle oil 72–3
dumplings, Fresh herb 166

E
eggplants *26*
Eggplant, zucchini, & flageolet salad
with mozzarella & red pesto
dressing 68–9
Eggplant & goat cheese crostini 280
Eggplant koftas with tzatziki 263
Eggplant & potato tortillas 213
Eggplant salad 66
Asparagus, mushroom, & garlic
sauce pizzas (*V*) 186–7
Chickpea & vegetable goulash 167
Cinnamon, almond, & raisin brown
rice pilaf with grilled eggplant 101
Grilled zucchini & sun-dried tomato
wraps (*V*) 192–3
Grilled eggplants with pomegranate
vinaigrette 281

Mediterranean vegetable & feta filo pie 254–5

Mediterranean vegetable fritters with aioli 139

Okra & eggplant spicy masala 153

Ratatouille in tomato crêpes 137

Roasted eggplant, feta, & tomato quesadillas 204

Steamed eggplant salad 280

Thai-style baby eggplant curry 165

Tomato & eggplant confit 281

Vegetable choucroute garni 176

Vietnamese vegetable & tofu curry 164

Yogurt, eggplant, & pine nut dip 312

eggs

Carrot, onion, & Stilton hot dogs 290–1

Chile bean & vegetable braise with fried eggs 172–3

Corn & pepper empanadas 259

Egg & fennel potato salad 128

Lentil, mushroom, & egg loaf with celery root remoulade 284

Mushroom pot with feta & herb topping 272

pasta dough 85

Piperade 217

Potato salad niçoise 77

Spinach, fresh tomato, & blue cheese pizza (V) 181

Warm pasta, kale, & duck egg salad with truffle oil 72–3

Warm pea pancakes with grilled asparagus 131

Zucchini & carrot pavé 285

see also dishes normally made with eggs (e.g. omelets)

Emmental cheese

Arugula, pear, blue cheese, & walnut quesadillas 208

Buckwheat galettes with cheese & caramelized onions 133

Potatoes Dauphinoise with Emmental 282

Veggie burgers with melting cheese 124–5

empanadas, Corn & pepper 259

enchiladas, Chile bean fajitas (V) 191

endive *18*

Endive gazpacho 43

Endive salad with spinach & pears 67

English muffins, Wild mushroom & hollandaise tartlets 250

escarole *15*

Asparagus, mushroom, & garlic sauce pizzas 186–7

Spring vegetable stew with fresh herb dumplings 166

F

Falafel with dill & cucumber dip 122

fava beans *25*

Bulgur wheat with okra 74

Zucchini, fava bean, & fresh pea quiches 252

Linguine with baby fava beans, cherry tomatoes, & scallions 90

Potato salad niçoise (V) 77

Quinoa, fava bean, & dill salad 75

Vegetables with lentils (V) 155

fajitas, Chile bean 191

fennel *17*

Egg & fennel potato salad 128

Fennel & goat cheese salad 76

Fennel & Gruyère tart 238

Fennel soup with Parmesan thins 46

Root vegetable & fennel pasties with seed pastry 257

feta cheese

Artichoke, black olive, tomato, & feta tart 249

Cinnamon, almond, & raisin brown rice pilaf with grilled eggplant 101

Crêpes with asparagus 96

Mediterranean vegetable & feta filo pie 254–5

Mushroom pot with feta & herb topping 272

Potato cakes 129

Red pepper & chile tart (V) 239

Roasted eggplant, feta, & tomato quesadillas 204

Spanakopita 245

Swiss chard & cheese tart 237

Zucchini stuffed with golden raisins, red onion, & pine nuts 218

filo dough dishes 245, 254–5

fish (optional)

Borscht 47

Crushed pea fritters in beer batter with a tomato tartare sauce 119

Grilled zucchini & sun-dried tomato wraps 192–3

Mediterranean vegetable fritters with aioli 139

Potato salad niçoise 77

Red curry of oyster mushrooms & tofu 159

smoked *see* smoked fish; smoked salmon

Spinach & yogurt curry 149

Split pea, noodle, & vegetable pot 95

Squash & cider cobbler 278

Vegetables with lentils 155

see also anchovies; salmon; tuna

foo yung, Vegetable egg 225

French beans

Antipasti salad 64

French bean, garlic, & tomato omelet 216

frittatas 97, 226–9

see also omelets; tortillas (eggs)

fritters 114–19, 139, 219

G

galettes, Buckwheat 133

garlic *21*, **317**

garlic sausage (optional), Swiss chard & cheese tart 237

Gazpacho 42, 43

goat cheese

Beet, zucchini, & goat cheese pizzas 182–3

Beet risotto 108

Butternut squash, spinach, & goat cheese frittata 226–7

Creamy broccoli & blue cheese puffs (V) 248

Eggplant & goat cheese crostini 280

Eggplant salad 66

Fennel & goat cheese salad 76

Grated zucchini with goat cheese omelet 219

Onion confit bruschetta 302

Steamed eggplant salad 280

Stuffed butternut squash (V) 277

Swiss chard, beet, & goat cheese frittata 229

Traffic-light risotto 109

gougère, Tomato & zucchini 272

goulash, Chickpea & vegetable 167

gravlax (optional), Beet & caraway blinis with sour cream 134–5

green beans *25*

Mixed vegetable curry 148

Pasta primavera 88

Potato & green bean stew 154

Potato salad niçoise 77

Seasonal vegetables in spinach & garlic sauce 145

Vegetable dahl with tandoori paneer 150–1

Vegetables with lentils 155

see also French beans

greens *18–19*

see also specific types (e.g. lettuces)

Gruyère cheese

Cheese soufflé omelet with corn & pepper 222–3

Fennel & Gruyère tart 238

French red onion soup with brandy & Gruyère croûtes 44–5

Stuffed butternut squash 277

Swiss chard & cheese tart 237

Veggie burgers with melting cheese 124–5

Zucchini, carrot, & Gruyère pancakes 127

guacamole
Guacamole & Cheddar quesadillas 206–7

Rainbow pepper Mexican tacos (V) 195

H

halloumi
Grilled marinated halloumi on seeded vegetable ribbons 264–5

Stuffed mushrooms with spinach, pine nuts, & halloumi 279

Vegetable choucroute garni 176

ham (optional)
Buckwheat galettes with cheese & caramelized onions 133

Cajun stuffed potatoes with crushed avocado 293

Cauliflower, broccoli, & tomato braise with cheese crumble 177

Cream cheese & roasted pepper quesadillas 209

Creamy broccoli & blue cheese puffs 248

French red onion soup with brandy & Gruyère croûtes 44–5

Leek, sage, walnut, & tomato tartlets 240–1

Lentil soup 61

Lettuce soup with peas 51

Roasted eggplant, feta, & tomato quesadillas 204

Tomato & zucchini gougère 272

Zucchini, carrot, & Gruyère pancakes 127

Zucchini & pea mini wraps 194

see also Parma ham

haricot beans *31*
Gratin of Swiss chard with beans 283

Leek, barley, & root vegetable broth with basil oil (V) 54

Spring vegetable stew with fresh herb dumplings 166

Sweet potato, roasted pepper, & white bean hotpot 171

hazelnuts *32*
Stuffed butternut squash 277

Wild mushroom & Taleggio tart 242

Heart of palm green curry 160

herbs *34–5*, **332**
Fresh herb dumplings 166

Herby scones 278

Hollandaise sauce 250

hot dogs, Carrot, onion, & Stilton 290–1

hotpot, Sweet potato, roasted pepper, & white bean 171

Hummus 313
Grilled zucchini & sun-dried tomato wraps 192–3

J

Jerusalem artichokes *23*
Jerusalem artichoke soup with saffron & thyme 60

K

Kadhai paneer with peppers 144

kale *15*
Creamy bean ragout with shredded kale 170

Warm pasta, kale, & duck egg salad with truffle oil 72–3

Kimchi 301

koftas, Eggplant, with tzatziki 263

kohlrabi *17*
Kohlrabi & potato gratin 271

L

lamb (optional)
Butternut squash tagine 276

Cauliflower pakoras with carrot raita 118

Cinnamon, almond, & raisin brown rice pilaf with grilled eggplant 101

Curried leek, celery root, & soy bean loaf 288

Eggplant koftas with tzatziki 263

Eggplant & potato tortillas 213

Eggplant salad 66

Falafel with dill & cucumber dip 122

Green peas pilau 110

Kadhai paneer with peppers 144

Kohlrabi & potato gratin 271

Leek, barley, & root vegetable broth with basil oil 54–5

Mediterranean vegetable & feta filo pie 254–5

Okra & eggplant spicy masala 153

Potato & mixed nut moussaka 286–7

Quinoa, fava bean, & dill salad 75

Root vegetable & fennel pasties with seed pastry 257

Spanakopita 245

Sweet potato, roasted pepper, & white bean hotpot 171

Tabbouleh lettuce wraps 198

Vegetable samosas 258

lamb's lettuce *18*
Fennel & goat cheese salad 76

lardons (optional)
Beet, zucchini, & goat cheese pizzas 182–3

Caramelized shallot tart 232

Linguine with baby fava beans, cherry tomatoes, & scallions 90

Mushroom orzotto 105

Zucchini, fava bean, & fresh pea quiches 252

lasagne, Pumpkin, spinach, & Gorgonzola 86–7

leeks *21*, **317**
Carrot & orange soup 58

Curried leek, celery root, & soy bean loaf 288

Leek, barley, & root vegetable broth with basil oil 54–5

Leek, sage, walnut, & tomato tartlets 240–1

Lemon, carrot, & leek marmalade 300

Mixed root tempura with dipping sauce 141

Spring vegetable stew with fresh herb dumplings 166

Squash & cider cobbler 278

Sweet potato & leek tortillas with fresh tomato sauce 214–15

legumes *30–1*
see also specific types (e.g. lentils)

lemons
Lemon & asparagus pasta 81

Lemon, carrot, & leek marmalade 300

Moroccan couscous salad 218

lentils *30, 31*
Lentil & carrot rissoles 123

Lentil, mushroom, & egg loaf with celery root remoulade 284

Lentil soup 61

Red lentil & mixed root crumble with sour cream & chives 289

Spicy lentil & pepper pizzas 188

Spinach & yogurt curry 149

Vegetable dahl with tandoori paneer 150–1

Vegetables with lentils 155

lettuces *18–19*
Antipasti salad 64

Endive gazpacho (V) 43

Lettuce soup with peas 51

Mint, new potato, pea, & lettuce tortilla 220

Potato salad niçoise 77

Tabbouleh lettuce wraps 198

Vietnamese vegetable & beansprout summer rolls 202

limes
Avocado mousse with lime 163

Guacamole & Cheddar quesadillas 206–7

Rainbow pepper Mexican tacos 195

Red curry of oyster mushrooms & tofu 159

M

Maki sushi wraps 196–7
Maple butter 132
marmalades *see* pickles & relishes
mascarpone cheese
  Baked stuffed tomatoes 200
  Potato soup with broccoli, shallot, &
    mascarpone cheese 52
  Wild mushroom & hollandaise
    tartlets 250
meat *see* specific types (e.g. chicken)
moussaka, Potato & mixed nut 286–7
mousse, Avocado, with lime 163
mozzarella cheese
  Antipasti salad 64
  Asparagus, mushroom, & garlic
    sauce pizzas 186–7
  Avocado, tomato, & mozzarella salad
    163
  Broccoli rabe, ricotta, & rosemary
    calzones 185
  Cheese, tomato, & mushroom pizza
    180
  Eggplant, zucchini, & flageolet salad
    with mozzarella & red pesto
    dressing 68–9
  Pizza primavera 189
  Spicy lentil & pepper pizzas 188
  Spinach, fresh tomato, & blue cheese
    pizza 181
  Tomato, red onion, & mozzarella
    salad 201
  Vegetable-stuffed pizzas 184
muffins (English), Wild mushroom &
    hollandaise tartlets 250
mushrooms *28–9*
  Asparagus, mushroom, & garlic
    sauce pizzas 186–7
  Cashew nut paella 106–7
  Cheese, tomato, & mushroom pizza
    180
  Cinnamon, almond, & raisin brown
    rice pilaf with grilled eggplant
    101
  Creamy bean ragout with shredded
    kale 170
  Crêpes with mushrooms, garlic, &
    cheese 126
  Lentil, mushroom, & egg loaf with
    celery root remoulade 284
  Mixed mushroom & garlic omelets
    221
  Mixed mushroom & bok choy stir-fry
    with soba noodles 92–3
  Mixed vegetable cottage pie with
    rutabaga crust 268–9
  Mixed vegetable satay (*V*) 292
  Mushroom & black-eyed pea
    stroganoff 174

Mushroom bruschetta 63
Mushroom burgers with chips & dip
    121
Mushroom & cider sauce 234–5
Mushroom orzotto 105
Mushroom pot with feta & herb
    topping 272
Mushroom soup 62
Mushrooms in garlic sauce 63
Pizza primavera 189
Potato, celery, & walnut cakes with
    mushrooms 130
Red bean & chestnut bourguignon
    168–9
Red curry of oyster mushrooms &
    tofu 159
Seasonal vegetables in spinach &
    garlic sauce 145
Shiitake mushrooms & water
    chestnut teriyaki 262
Spicy mixed greens & pea stir-fry
    with hoisin sauce & toasted sesame
    seeds 98
Stuffed mushrooms with spinach,
    pine nuts, & halloumi 279
Stuffed portobello mushrooms en
    croûte 234–5
Sweet potato, roasted pepper, &
    white bean hotpot 171
Thai noodle stir-fry 94
Tofu & mushroom stroganoff 62
Vegetable egg foo yung 225
Vegetable ramen noodle bowl 102–3
Vegetable spring rolls 140
Vegetable-stuffed pizzas 184
Warm pasta, kale, & duck egg salad
    with truffle oil 72–3
Wild mushroom & hollandaise
    tartlets 250
Wild mushroom & Taleggio tart 242

N

noodle dishes 57, 91–5, 98–9, 102–4,
    165, 202, 262
nori, Maki sushi wraps 196–7
nuts *32*
  Potato & mixed nut moussaka 286–7
  see also specific types (e.g. chestnuts)

O

oats
  Carrot, onion, & Stilton hot dogs 290–
    1
  Red lentil & mixed root crumble with
    sour cream & chives 289
oils *33*, 50, 54
okra
  Bulgur wheat with okra 74
  Okra & eggplant spicy masala 153

Olive tapenade 308
omelets 216, 219, 221–5, **339**
  see also frittatas; tortillas (eggs)
onions *20*, **316**
  Buckwheat galettes with cheese &
    caramelized onions 133
  Carrot, onion, & Stilton hot dogs 290–1
  Chickpea & spinach masala with
    bhatura 156–7
  Indian-spiced vegetable chutney 304
  Kadhai sauce 144
  Limoges potato & onion pie 256
  Mixed vegetable curry 148
  Onion & almond soup 303
  Onion bhajis 302
  Onion confit 302
  Onion tart 303
  Piperade 217
  Sage & onion quesadilla 203
  Spanish tortilla 212
  Tomato & onion tart 251
  Vegetable biryani 111
  Vegetables with lentils 155
  see also red onions; shallots; scallions
orzotto, Mushroom 105

P

paella, Cashew nut 106–7
pakoras, Cauliflower, with carrot raita
    118
palm hearts, Heart of palm green
    curry 160
pancake dishes 96, 126–7, 131–8
pancetta (optional) *see* bacon &
    pancetta
paneer
  Kadhai paneer with peppers 144
  Vegetable dahl with tandoori paneer
    150–1
Parma ham (optional)
  Antipasti salad 64
  Baked ricotta with roasted zucchini &
    tomatoes 270
  Spinach, fresh tomato, & blue cheese
    pizza 181
Parmesan cheese
  Beet risotto 108
  Cauliflower, broccoli, & tomato braise
    with cheese crumble 177
  Fennel soup with Parmesan thins 46
  Gratin of Swiss chard with beans 283
  Pasta with butternut squash, chile, &
    Parmesan cheese 84
  pestos 296–9
  Ricotta & squash ravioli 85
  Stuffed butternut squash (*V*) 277
  Vegetable-stuffed pizzas 184
  Warm pea pancakes with grilled
    asparagus 131

parsnips *23*
Celery root & pecan soufflé pie (*V*) 253
Creamy bean ragout with shredded kale (*V*) 170
Grilled marinated halloumi on seeded vegetable ribbons 264–5
Lentil & carrot rissoles (*V*) 123
Mixed root tempura with dipping sauce 141
Mixed vegetable cottage pie with rutabaga crust (*V*) 268–9
Mixed vegetable satay 292
Parsnip & walnut pancakes with maple butter 132
Seeded vegetable ribbons 264–5
pasta dishes 72–3, 80–90, 246, 298
pasta dough 85
pastes, Spice 148, 155
pasties, Root vegetable & fennel 257
pastry
Cheese choux 272
Dough 232, 236, 252, 259, **336–8**
Samosa 258
Whole wheat dough 251, 253, 257
pastry dishes 232–3, 236–9, 242–3, 249, 251–3, 257, 259, 303, **337–8** *see also* gougère; pies; tarts, tartlets, turnovers, & quiches
patties & burgers 120–5, 129–30
pavé, Zucchini & carrot 285
pea shoots *19*
Zucchini & pea mini wraps 194
peanut butter
fiery peanut & pepper noodles 104
Mixed vegetable satay 292
Tofu & mushroom stroganoff 62
peanuts *32*
Spicy mixed greens & pea stir-fry with hoisin sauce & toasted sesame seeds 98
Thai vegetable salad with cabbage & peanuts 70
pearl barley
Leek, barley, & root vegetable broth with basil oil 54–5
Mushroom orzotto 105
pears
Arugula, pear, blue cheese, & walnut quesadillas 208
Endive salad with spinach & pears 67
Spicy watercress soup 50
peas & snow peas *25*
Baked vegetable & chickpea pilau 100
Cashew nut paella 106–7
Crushed pea fritters in beer batter with a tomato tartare sauce 119
dried *see* split peas
Green peas pilau 110

Lettuce soup with peas 51
Mint, new potato, pea, & lettuce tortilla 220
Mixed vegetable cottage pie with rutabaga crust 268–9
Pea, mint, & pistachio pesto 297
Seasonal vegetables in spinach & garlic sauce 145
Snow pea, sweet potato, & cashew nut red curry 146–7
Spicy mixed greens & pea stir-fry with hoisin sauce & toasted sesame seeds 98
Thai noodle stir-fry 94
Vegetable biryani 111
Vegetable chow mein with black beans 91
Vegetable egg foo yung 225
Vegetable samosas 258
Warm pea pancakes with grilled asparagus 131
Zucchini, fava bean, & fresh pea quiches 252
Zucchini & pea mini wraps 194
pecan nuts *32*
Celery root & pecan soufflé pie 253
pepperoni (optional), Cheese, tomato, & mushroom pizza 180
peppers *26, 27,* **326**
Avocado, baby spinach, & chile wraps 190
Avocado salsa 309
Baked vegetable & chickpea pilau 100
Beet, zucchini, & goat cheese pizzas (*V*) 182–3
Butternut squash tagine 276
Cajun stuffed potatoes with crushed avocado 293
Cashew nut paella 106–7
Cheese, red pepper, & corn chowder 48–9
Cheese soufflé omelet with corn & pepper 222–3
Chickpea & vegetable goulash 167
Chile bean fajitas 191
Chile bean & vegetable braise with fried eggs 172–3
Corn & jalapeño tart 243
Corn & pepper empanadas 259
Corn relish 305
Cream cheese & roasted pepper quesadillas 209
fiery peanut & pepper noodles 104
Gazpacho 42
Grilled stuffed romano peppers with chile & cheese 266
Kadhai paneer with peppers 144

Maki sushi wraps (*V*) 196–7
Mediterranean vegetable & feta filo pie 254–5
Mediterranean vegetable fritters with aioli 139
Mushroom pot with feta & herb topping 272
Pasta with roasted peppers 246
Piperade 217
Potato & mixed nut moussaka 286–7
Rainbow pepper Mexican tacos 195
Ratatouille in tomato crêpes 137
Red pepper & chile tart 239
Red pepper salad 246
Red pepper & walnut dip 247
Roasted mixed pepper bruschetta 247
Roasted red pepper, almond, & chile pesto 298–9
Spicy lentil & pepper pizzas 188
Sweet potato, roasted pepper, & white bean hotpot 171
Thai noodle stir-fry 94
Thai-style beansprout & shredded vegetable fritters 116–17
Tofu & mushroom stroganoff 62
Traffic-light risotto 109
Turnip noodle soup with pimento & chile 57
Vegetable choucroute garni 176
Vegetable chow mein with black beans 91
Vegetable ramen noodle bowl 102–3
pestos 296–9
Red pesto dressing 68
pickles & relishes 300–1, 304–8
pie dough 232, 236, 252, 259, **336–8**
whole wheat 251, 253, 257
pies 234–5, 245, 248, 253–6, 268–9
pigeon (optional), Fennel & goat cheese salad 76
pilaus & pilafs 100–1, 110
pine nuts *32*
Classic basil pesto 296
Spiced crushed carrot, pine nut, & cottage cheese frittata 228
Stuffed mushrooms with spinach, pine nuts, & halloumi 279
Stuffed crêpes with spinach, ricotta, & pine nuts 136
Yogurt, eggplant, & pine nut dip 312
Zucchini stuffed with golden raisins, red onion, & pine nuts 218
pinto beans *30*
Bean patties 120
Chile bean & vegetable braise with fried eggs 172–3
Mixed vegetable cottage pie with rutabaga crust 268–9

Spring vegetable stew with fresh herb dumplings 166

Piperade 217

pistachio nuts, Pea, mint, & pistachio pesto 297

pizzas 180–9, 298
pizza dough 180

Pomegranate vinaigrette 281

pork (optional)
Chickpea & spinach masala with bhatura 156–7
Chickpea & vegetable goulash 167
Mixed mushroom & bok choy stir-fry with soba noodles 92–3
Mushroom pot with feta & herb topping 272
Potato pancakes with applesauce & chive yogurt 138
Potato & tomato curry 158
Pumpkin, spinach, & Gorgonzola lasagne 86–7
Ricotta & squash ravioli 85
Sage & onion quesadilla 203
Vegetable choucroute garni 176
Vegetable spring rolls 140
see also bacon & pancetta: sausages

potatoes *22*, **328–9**
Aromatic curry of pumpkin 161
Cajun stuffed potatoes with crushed avocado 293
Cajun-spiced potato wedges 129
Carrot & orange soup 58
Cheese, red pepper, & corn chowder 48–9
Chickpea & spinach masala with bhatura 156–7
Creamy butternut squash & butter bean stew 175
Creamy spinach & rosemary soup 53
Crushed pea fritters in beer batter with a tomato tartare sauce 119
Curried leek, celery root, & soy bean loaf 288
Dauphinoise potatoes 128
Egg & fennel potato salad 128
Eggplant & potato tortillas 213
Kohlrabi & potato gratin 271
Leek, barley, & root vegetable broth with basil oil 54–5
Limoges potato & onion pie 256
Mint, new potato, pea, & lettuce tortilla 220
Mixed vegetable cottage pie with rutabaga crust 268–9
Mixed vegetable curry 148
Mixed vegetable satay (*V*) 292
Mushroom soup 62
Potato cakes 129

Potato, celery, & walnut cakes with mushrooms 130
Potato & green bean stew 154
Potato & mixed nut moussaka 286–7
Potato pancakes with applesauce & chive yogurt 138
Potato salad niçoise 77
Potato soup with broccoli, shallot, & mascarpone cheese 52
Potato & tomato curry 158
Potatoes Dauphinoise with Emmental 282
Root vegetable & fennel pasties with seed pastry 257
Spanish tortilla 212
Spicy potato & mango chutney chapatti wraps 199
Spicy watercress soup 50
Spring vegetable stew with fresh herb dumplings 166
Vegetable biryani 111
Vegetable dahl with tandoori paneer 150–1
Vegetable samosas 258
Vegetables with lentils 155

poultry *see* specific types (e.g. chicken)

puff pastry dishes 234–5, 240–1, 244, 248, 256

puffs, Creamy broccoli & blue cheese 248

pumpkins *see* squashes & pumpkins

Q

quail eggs, Spinach, fresh tomato, & blue cheese pizza (*V*) 181

quesadillas 162, 203–9

quiches *see* tarts, tartlets & quiches

Quinoa, fava bean, & dill salad 75

R

radishes *23*
Avocado salsa 309
Vegetable ramen noodle bowl 102–3
Vietnamese vegetable & beansprout summer rolls 202

ragout, Creamy bean, with shredded kale 170

raita, Carrot 118

Ratatouille in tomato crêpes 137

ravioli, Ricotta & squash 85

red onions *20*
Beet, zucchini, & goat cheese pizzas 182–3
Butternut squash tagine 276
Cajun-spiced potato wedges 129
Eggplant, zucchini, & flageolet salad with mozzarella & red pesto dressing 68–9

Eggplant salad 66
French red onion soup with brandy & Gruyère croûtes 44–5
Green peas pilau 110
Mediterranean vegetable & feta filo pie 254–5
Pico de gallo 310–11
Pizza primavera 189
Potato salad niçoise 77
Rainbow pepper Mexican tacos 195
Red bean & chestnut bourguignon 168–9
Red lentil & mixed root crumble with sour cream & chives 289
Red onion marmalade 307
Red pepper & chile tart 239
Shiitake mushrooms & water chestnut teriyaki 262
Steamed eggplant salad 280
Tomato, red onion, & mozzarella salad 201
Zucchini stuffed with golden raisins, red onion, & pine nuts 218

relishes & pickles 300–1, 304–8

remoulade, Celery root 284

rice dishes 100–1, 106–11, 196–7, **334**, **335**

ricotta cheese
Baked ricotta with roasted zucchini & tomatoes 270
Baked stuffed tomatoes 200
Broccoli rabe, ricotta, & rosemary calzones 185
Grilled avocado with sun-dried tomato dressing (*V*) 267
Ricotta & squash ravioli 85
Spiced crushed carrot, pine nut, & cottage cheese frittata (*V*) 228
Stuffed crêpes with spinach, ricotta, & pine nuts 136
Zucchini fritters with dill tzatziki 219

risotti 108–9, **335**

rissoles, Lentil & carrot 123

roulade, Watercress & beet, with smooth cheese sauce 274–5

rutabagas *23*
Leek, barley, & root vegetable broth with basil oil 54–5
Mixed root tempura with dipping sauce 141
Mixed vegetable cottage pie with rutabaga crust 268–9
Mixed vegetable satay 292

S

salads 64–77, 128, 163, 201, 218, 246, 280

salami (optional)
Ratatouille in tomato crêpes 137

Roasted squash & Gorgonzola tart 233

salmon (optional)
Beet & caraway blinis with sour cream 134–5
Farfalle with spinach, avocado, baby plum tomatoes, & pumpkin seeds 82–3
Spicy watercress soup 50
Traffic-light risotto 109
Zucchini & carrot pavé 285
see also smoked salmon

salsas 115, 120, 309–11
samosas, Vegetable 258
satay, Mixed vegetable 292
sauces
Aioli 139
Apple 138
Bechamel (white sauce) 86
Cheese & corn 222–3
Chile 140
Chunky tomato 201
Dipping 141
Fresh tomato 214–15
Garlic & cheese 186
Hollandaise 250
Kadhai 144
Mushroom & cider 234–5
Mustard 96
Pestos 296–9
Smooth cheese 274–5
Tomato tartare 119

sauerkraut, Vegetable choucroute garni 176
sausages & sausagemeat (optional)
Carrot, onion, & Stilton hot dogs 290–1
Creamy bean ragout with shredded kale 170
Pasta with butternut squash, chile, & Parmesan cheese 84
Potato soup with broccoli, shallot, & mascarpone cheese 52
Stuffed portobello mushrooms en croûte 234–5
see also specific types (e.g. chorizo)

sautéing 331
scones, Herby 278
seafood *see* shellfish & seafood
seeds *33*
shallots *20*
Beet relish 306
Caramelized shallot tart 232
Endive salad with spinach & pears 67
Potato soup with broccoli, shallot, & mascarpone cheese 52

shellfish & seafood (optional)
Cashew nut paella 106–7
Endive gazpacho 43

Fennel soup with Parmesan thins 46
Heart of palm green curry 160
Lemon & asparagus pasta 81
Mediterranean vegetable fritters with aioli 139
see also shrimp

shrimp (optional)
Avocado, cucumber, & sorrel soup 59
Black-eyed peas with spinach & tomato curry 152
Bulgur wheat with okra 74
Chinese pumpkin fritters 114
Gazpacho 42
Grilled avocado with sun-dried tomato dressing 267
Maki sushi wraps 196–7
Mixed root tempura with dipping sauce 141
Pizza primavera 189
Stir-fried ribbon vegetables with coconut noodles 99
Thai vegetable salad with cabbage & peanuts 70
Thai-style beansprout & shredded vegetable fritters 116–17
Vegetable egg foo yung 225
Vietnamese vegetable & beansprout summer rolls 202

smoked fish (optional)
Beet risotto 108
Piperade 217
Potato salad niçoise 77

smoked salmon (optional)
Asparagus & cream cheese quiche 236
Asparagus & scallion soufflé omelet 224
Broccoli rabe, ricotta, & rosemary calzones 185
Maki sushi wraps 196–7
Spicy spaghetti with broccoli 89
Wild mushroom & hollandaise tartlets 250

snow peas *see* peas & snow peas
sorrel *14*
Avocado, cucumber, & sorrel soup 59
soufflé omelets 222–4
soups 42–61, 62, 200, 303
soy beans *31*
Curried leek, celery root, & soy bean loaf 288
Mixed mushroom & bok choy stir-fry with soba noodles 92–3

Spanakopita 245
spices *36–7*, **333**
Spice pastes 148, 155
spinach *15*
Avocado, baby spinach, & chile wraps 190

Black-eyed peas with spinach & tomato curry 152
Butternut squash, spinach, & goat cheese frittata 226–7
Chickpea & spinach masala with bhatura 156–7
Creamy spinach & rosemary soup 53
Endive salad with spinach & pears 67
Farfalle with spinach, avocado, baby plum tomatoes, & pumpkin seeds 82–3
Fennel & goat cheese salad 76
Pumpkin, spinach, & Gorgonzola lasagne 86–7
Red curry of oyster mushrooms & tofu 159
Roasted squash & Gorgonzola tart 233
Seasonal vegetables in spinach & garlic sauce 145
Spanakopita 245
Spinach, fresh tomato, & blue cheese pizza 181
Spinach & yogurt curry 149
Stuffed mushrooms with spinach, pine nuts, & halloumi 279
Stuffed crêpes with spinach, ricotta, & pine nuts 136
Swiss chard, beet, & goat cheese frittata (*V*) 229
Swiss chard & cheese tart (*V*) 237
Traffic-light risotto 109
Zucchini & pea mini wraps 194

Split pea, noodle, & vegetable pot 95

scallions *21*
Asparagus & scallion soufflé omelet 224
Avocado salsa 309
Corn & jalapeño tart 243
Fiery peanut & pepper noodles 104
Gazpacho 42
Guacamole & Cheddar quesadillas 206–7
Linguine with baby fava beans, cherry tomatoes, & scallions 90
Maki sushi wraps 196–7
Mint, new potato, pea, & lettuce tortilla 220
Mixed mushroom & bok choy stir-fry with soba noodles 92–3
Pea, mint, & pistachio pesto 297
Quesadilla with avocado, scallion, & chile 162
Snow pea, sweet potato, & cashew nut red curry 146–7
Spicy spaghetti with broccoli 89
Spring vegetable stew with fresh herb dumplings 166

Thai-style beansprout & shredded vegetable fritters 116–17
Vegetable chow mein with black beans 91
Vegetable ramen noodle bowl 102–3
Vegetable spring rolls 140
Vietnamese vegetable & beansprout summer rolls 202
spring rolls 140, 202
squashes & pumpkins *24*
Aromatic curry of pumpkin 161
Butternut squash, spinach, & goat cheese frittata 226–7
Butternut squash tagine 276
Chile bean & vegetable braise with fried eggs 172–3
Chinese pumpkin fritters 114
Creamy butternut squash & butter bean stew 175
Indian-spiced vegetable chutney 304
Pasta with butternut squash, chile, & Parmesan cheese 84
Pumpkin, spinach, & Gorgonzola lasagne 86–7
Ricotta & squash ravioli 85
Roasted squash & Gorgonzola tart 233
Squash & cider cobbler 278
Squash with cranberries & chestnuts 71
Stuffed butternut squash 277
Traffic-light risotto 109
steak (optional) *see* beef
steaming 331
stir-frying 330
stroganoffs 62, 174
sugarsnap peas *see* peas & snow peas
summer rolls 202
sushi wraps, Maki 196–7
sweet potatoes *22*
Aromatic curry of pumpkin (*V*) 161
Celery root & pecan soufflé pie (*V*) 253
Chickpea & vegetable goulash (*V*) 167
Creamy butternut squash & butter bean stew (*V*) 175
Miso chips 121
Pumpkin, spinach, & Gorgonzola lasagne (*V*) 86–7
Snow peas, sweet potato, & cashew nut red curry 146–7
Sweet potato & leek tortillas with fresh tomato sauce 214–15
Sweet potato, roasted pepper, & white bean hotpot 171
Swiss chard *15*
Butternut squash, spinach, & goat cheese frittata (*V*) 226–7
Gratin of Swiss chard with beans 283

Swiss chard, beet, & goat cheese frittata 229
Swiss chard & cheese tart 237

T
tacos, Rainbow pepper Mexican 195
tagine, Butternut squash 276
tahini
Hummus 313
Yogurt, eggplant, & pine nut dip 312
Tapenade 308
taramasalata (optional), Grilled zucchini & sun-dried tomato wraps 192–3
tarts, tartlets & quiches 232–3, 236–43, 249–53, 303, **337–8**
tempura, Mixed root, with dipping sauce 141
tofu
Red curry of oyster mushrooms & tofu 159
Tofu & mushroom stroganoff 62
Vegetable ramen noodle bowl 102–3
Vietnamese vegetable & tofu curry 164
tomatoes *27*, **318**
Antipasti salad 64
Artichoke, black olive, tomato, & feta tart 249
Avocado with roasted cherry tomatoes & paprika dressing 162
Avocado salsa 309
Avocado, tomato, & mozzarella salad 163
Baked ricotta with roasted zucchini & tomatoes 270
Baked stuffed tomatoes 200
Beetroot, zucchini, & goat cheese pizzas 182–3
Black-eyed peas with spinach & tomato curry 152
Borscht 47
Broccoli rabe, ricotta, & rosemary calzones 185
Butternut squash tagine 276
Carrot, onion, & Stilton hot dogs 290–1
Cashew nut paella 106–7
Cauliflower, broccoli, & tomato braise with cheese crumble 177
Cheese, tomato, & mushroom pizza 180
Chickpea & spinach masala with bhatura 156–7
Chickpea & vegetable goulash 167
Chile bean fajitas 191
Chile bean & vegetable braise with fried eggs 172–3
Chunky tomato sauce 201
Corn fritters with tomato salsa 115

Corn & pepper empanadas 259
Crêpes with mushrooms, garlic, & cheese (*V*) 126
Crushed pea fritters in beer batter with a tomato tartare sauce 119
Eggplant, zucchini, & flageolet salad with mozzarella & red pesto dressing 68–9
Eggplant salad 66
Endive gazpacho 43
Farfalle with spinach, avocado, baby plum tomatoes, & pumpkin seeds 82–3
French bean, garlic, & tomato omelet 216
Fresh tomato sauce 214–15
Gazpacho 42
Grilled zucchini & sun-dried tomato wraps 192–3
Grilled avocado with sun-dried tomato dressing 267
Guacamole & Cheddar quesadillas 206–7
Kadhai sauce 144
Leek, sage, walnut, & tomato tartlets 240–1
Linguine with baby fava beans, cherry tomatoes, & scallions 90
Maki sushi wraps 196–7
Snow pea, sweet potato, & cashew nut red curry 146–7
Mediterranean vegetable & feta filo pie 254–5
Mixed vegetable curry 148
Okra & eggplant spicy masala 153
Pasta primavera 88
Pico de gallo 310–11
Piperade 217
Pizza primavera 189
Potato & green bean stew 154
Potato & mixed nut moussaka 286–7
Potato salad niçoise 77
Potato & tomato curry 158
Ratatouille in tomato crêpes 137
Red pepper salad 246
Roasted eggplant, feta, & tomato quesadillas 204
Roasted red pepper, almond, & chile pesto 298–9
Sun-dried tomato dressing 267
Spice paste 148
Spicy lentil & pepper pizzas 188
Spicy potato & mango chutney chapatti wraps 199
Spinach, fresh tomato, & blue cheese pizza 181
Spinach & yogurt curry 149
Squash & cider cobbler 278
Steamed eggplant salad 280

Stuffed crêpes with spinach, ricotta, & pine nuts 136
Sweet potato & leek tortillas with fresh tomato sauce 214–15
Sweet potato, roasted pepper, & white bean hotpot 171
Tabbouleh lettuce wraps 198
Tomato & eggplant confit 281
Tomato & zucchini gougère 272
Tomato & onion tart 251
Tomato, red onion, & mozzarella salad 201
Tomato salsa 115
Tomato soup 200
Tomato tartare sauce 119
Traffic-light risotto 109
Vegetable biryani 111
Vegetable dahl with tandoori paneer 150–1
Vegetable-stuffed pizzas 184
Vegetables with lentils 155
tortillas (eggs) 212–15, 220
see also frittatas; omelets
tortillas (flour or corn) *see* quesadillas; wraps
tuna (optional)
Corn & pepper empanadas 259
Eggplant, zucchini & flageolet salad with mozzarella & red pesto dressing 68–9
Grilled stuffed romano peppers with chile & cheese 266
Limoges potato & onion pie 256
Potato, celery, & walnut cakes with mushrooms 130
Swiss chard, beet, & goat cheese frittata 229
Watercress & beet roulade with smooth cheese sauce 274–5
turkey (optional)
Red lentil & mixed root crumble with sour cream & chives 289
Squash with cranberries & chestnuts 71
Stuffed butternut squash 277
turnips *22*
Creamy butternut squash & butter bean stew 175
Creamy bean ragout with shredded kale (*V*) 170
Leek, barley, & root vegetable broth with basil oil 54–5
Mixed vegetable cottage pie with rutabaga crust 268–9
Mixed vegetable satay 292
Red bean & chestnut bourguignon 168–9
Red lentil & mixed root crumble with sour cream & chives 289

Root vegetable & fennel pasties with seed pastry 257
Spring vegetable stew with fresh herb dumplings 166
Stir-fried ribbon vegetables with coconut noodles 99
Turnip noodle soup with pimento & chile 57
Vegetable choucroute garni 176
turnovers 234–5, 244, 248, 257–9
turnovers, Cheese & asparagus 244
Tzatziki 263
Dill 219

W

wakame, Vegetable ramen noodle bowl 102–3
walnuts *32*
Arugula, pear, blue cheese, & walnut quesadillas 208
Leek, sage, walnut, & tomato tartlets 240–1
Parsnip & walnut pancakes with maple butter 132
Potato, celery, & walnut cakes with mushrooms 130
Red pepper & walnut dip 247
Steamed eggplant salad 280
water chestnut teriyaki, Shiitake mushrooms & 262
watercress *18*
Celery & apple salad with blue cheese dressing 65
Endive gazpacho (*V*) 43
Fennel & goat cheese salad 76
Spicy watercress soup 50
Squash with cranberries & chestnuts 71
Watercress & beet roulade with smooth cheese sauce 274–5
wedges & chips 121, 129, **329**
wraps 190–9, 302

Z

zucchini *24*, **320**
Baked ricotta with roasted eggplant & tomatoes 270
Baked vegetable & chickpea pilau 100
Beet, zucchini, & goat cheese pizzas 182–3
Chickpea & vegetable goulash 167
Chile bean fajitas 191
Eggplant, zucchini, & flageolet salad with mozzarella & red pesto dressing 68–9
Fiery peanut & pepper noodles 104
Grated zucchini with goat cheese omelet 219

Grilled zucchini & sun-dried tomato wraps 192–3
Grilled marinated halloumi on seeded vegetable ribbons 264–5
Indian-spiced vegetable chutney 304
Maki sushi wraps (*V*) 196–7
Mediterranean vegetable & feta filo pie 254–5
Mediterranean vegetable fritters with aioli 139
Mixed vegetable satay (*V*) 292
Moroccan couscous salad 218
Pasta with asparagus & zucchini 80
Pasta primavera 88
Pizza primavera 189
Potato & mixed nut moussaka 286–7
Quinoa, fava bean, & dill salad 75
Ratatouille in tomato crêpes 137
Seeded vegetable ribbons 264–5
Snow pwa, sweet potato, & cashew nut red curry 146–7
Split pea, noodle, & vegetable pot 95
Stir-fried ribbon vegetables with coconut noodles 99
Tomato & zucchini gougère 272
Vegetable biryani 111
Vegetable chow mein with black beans 91
Vegetable ramen noodle bowl 102–3
Zucchini, fava bean, & fresh pea quiches 252
Zucchini, carrot, & Gruyère pancakes 127
Zucchini & carrot pavé 285
Zucchini fritters with dill tzatziki 219
Zucchini & pea mini wraps 194
Zucchini stuffed with golden raisins, red onion, & pine nuts 218

Acknowledgments

The author would like to thank: Dorling Kindersley for giving me the opportunity to write this book. As the years have gone by I have become more and more vegetarian orientated and this book has been the perfect opportunity to encourage more people to eat more veg and to celebrate vegetables for what they are—nutritious and delicious. I would like to give special thanks to Diana Vowles, my editor, who has been a pleasure to work with (as always) and Bob Bridle who has managed things so efficiently at DK. I would also like to thank my family (and now my children's partners, too) who are used to eating a diverse range of foods at most meals when I am experimenting and testing new creations. They have always been incredibly encouraging and supportive—but are also my greatest critics!

Dorling Kindersley would like to thank: William Reavell for photography; Stuart West for additional recipe photography; Katherine Raj and Nicky Collings for photography art direction; Penny Stephens for food styling; Liz Hippisley for prop styling; Jade Wheaton for the illustrations; Chris Mooney for editorial assistance; Anna Burges-Lumsden, Jan Fullwood, Katy Greenwood, Anne Harnan, and Ann Reynolds for recipe testing; Claire Cross for proofreading; and Susan Bosanko for the index.

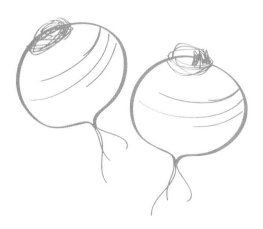